Linux
Weekend Crash Course

Naba Barkakati

Hungry Minds™

Hungry Minds, Inc.
New York, NY • Cleveland, OH • Indianapolis, IN

Linux® Weekend Crash Course™
Published by:
Hungry Minds, Inc.
909 Third Avenue
New York, NY 10022
www.hungryminds.com

Library of Congress Control Number: 2001016712
ISBN: 0-7645-3593-5
Printed in the United States of America
10 9 8 7 6 5 4 3 2 1
1B/RX/QU/QR/IN
Distributed in the United States by Hungry Minds, Inc.
Distributed by CDG Books Canada Inc. for Canada; by Transworld Publishers Limited in the United Kingdom; by IDG Norge Books for Norway; by IDG Sweden Books for Sweden; by IDG Books Australia Publishing Corporation Pty. Ltd. for Australia and New Zealand; by TransQuest Publishers Pte Ltd. for Singapore, Malaysia, Thailand, Indonesia, and Hong Kong; by Gotop Information Inc. for Taiwan; by ICG Muse, Inc. for Japan; by Intersoft for South Africa; by Eyrolles for France; by International Thomson Publishing for Germany, Austria, and Switzerland; by Distribuidora Cuspide for Argentina; by LR International for Brazil; by Galileo Libros for Chile; by Ediciones ZETA S.C.R. Ltda. for Peru; by WS Computer Publishing Corporation, Inc., for the Philippines; by Contemporanea de Ediciones for Venezuela; by Express Computer Distributors for the Caribbean and West Indies; by Micronesia Media Distributor, Inc. for Micronesia; by Chips Computadoras S.A. de C.V. for Mexico; by Editorial Norma de Panama S.A. for Panama; by American Bookshops for Finland.

For general information on Hungry Minds' products and services please contact our Customer Care department; within the U.S. at 800-762-2974, outside the U.S. at 317-572-3993 or fax 317-572-4002.

For sales inquiries and resellers information, including discounts, premium and bulk quantity sales and foreign language translations please contact our Customer Care department at 800-434-3422, fax 317-572-4002 or write to Hungry Minds, Inc., Attn: Customer Care department, 10475 Crosspoint Boulevard, Indianapolis, IN 46256.

For information on licensing foreign or domestic rights, please contact our Sub-Rights Customer Care department at 212-884-5000.

For information on using Hungry Minds' products and services in the classroom or for ordering examination copies, please contact our Educational Sales department at 800-434-2086 or fax 317-572-4005.

For press review copies, author interviews, or other publicity information, please contact our Public Relations department at 317-572-3168 or fax 317-572-4168.

For authorization to photocopy items for corporate, personal, or educational use, please contact Copyright Clearance Center, 222 Rosewood Drive, Danvers, MA 01923, or fax 978-750-4470.

Hungry Minds™ is a trademark of Hungry Minds, Inc.

About the Author

Naba Barkakati is an expert programmer and a successful computer-book author who has experience in a wide variety of systems ranging from MS-DOS and Windows to UNIX and the X Window System. He bought his first personal computer — an IBM PC-AT — in 1984 after graduating with a Ph.D. in electrical engineering from the University of Maryland. While pursuing a full-time career in engineering, Naba dreamed of writing software for the emerging PC software market. As luck would have it, instead of building a software empire like Microsoft, he ended up writing successful computer books.

Over the past 12 years, Naba has produced 25 computer books on topics ranging from C++ programming to Linux. He has written several best-selling titles, such as *The Waite Group's Turbo C++ Bible, Object-Oriented Programming in C++, X Window System Programming, Visual C++ Developer's Guide*, and *Borland C++ 4 Developer's Guide*. His books have been translated into many languages: Spanish, French, German, Polish, Greek, Italian, Chinese, Japanese, and Korean. Naba's most recent books are the best-selling *Red Hat Linux Secrets, Third Edition* and *Red Hat Linux 7 Weekend Crash Course*, also published by Hungry Minds, Inc.

Naba lives in North Potomac, Maryland, with his wife, Leha, and their children, Ivy, Emily, and Ashley.

Credits

Acquisitions Editor
Terri Varveris

Project Editor
Terrence O'Donnell

Contributing Writer
Terry Collings

Technical Editor
Matthew Hayden

Copy Editor
C.M. Jones

Project Coordinator
Regina Synder

Graphics and Production Specialists
Joe Bucki, Adam Mancilla,
Kathie Schutte, Janet Seib,
Kendra Span, Laurie Stevens,
Michael Sullivan, Erin Zeltner

Quality Control Technicians
Valery Bourke, Susan Moritz,
Angel Perez, Dwight Ramsey,
Marianne Santy, Charles Spencer,
Rob Springer

Media Development Manager
Laura Carpenter

Media Development Supervisor
Rich Graves

Permissions Editor
Laura Moss

Media Development Specialist
Greg Stephens

Media Development Coordinator
Marisa Pearman

Proofreading and Indexing
York Production Services

Cover Design
Clark Creative Group

*This book is dedicated
to my wife, Leha, and daughters,
Ivy, Emily, and Ashley.*

Preface

Because of Linux's increasing popularity, many computer users want to learn it quickly. If you work for an organization interested in Linux, you need to get up to speed on how to install, configure, use, and manage Linux systems. The best way to do so is to install Linux and to learn its commands and applications interactively. What potential Linux aficionados — beginners to advanced alike — need is a well-organized set of sessions that teaches them Linux over a weekend.

Linux® Weekend Crash Course™ is such a teaching guide. It provides 30 easy-to-use sessions, each a period of one half hour, that gradually build up your Linux skills. Part of the Hungry Minds' "Weekend Crash Course" series, these sessions — starting with Red Hat Linux installation on Friday evening and ending with several system administration topics on Sunday afternoon — are designed for you to complete over a weekend.

The crash course's pace is fast. Each session starts with a "Session Checklist" — a short list of topics that you learn within the session through hands-on exercises. Each session ends with a "Quiz Yourself" section that enables you to test your new skills by answering questions. For each major part, which corresponds with a time during the weekend, the book also includes Part Review Questions, which cover what is taught in the sessions within that part. You can try answering the Part Review Questions, and you can check your answers in Appendix A.

This book includes CD-ROMs that contain the latest version of Red Hat Linux, which you can install by following the instructions in Sessions 1 through 3. You can use either this version of Red Hat Linux or one of the other widely used Linux distributions you may have installed on your system as you progress through the rest of the sessions in this book.

What You Need to Get Started

To start the sessions, you need a PC on which you can install Red Hat Linux. The minimum system requirements for the PC are Intel 486- or Pentium-compatible processor, 32 MB RAM, 1 GB of disk space, 3.5-inch floppy drive, and a CD-ROM drive. You need to have a 3.5-inch floppy disk to create a boot disk during installation. For some of the other sessions, you need an Ethernet networking card, a modem, and Internet access. You also need a free weekend to go through all the sessions.

Organization of the Book

Linux Weekend Crash Course has 30 sessions organized into six parts. It also has two appendixes.

Part I: Friday Evening guides you through the steps needed to install Red Hat Linux from this book's companion CD-ROMs. Assuming the installation program recognizes most of the hardware, you should be able to finish the installation in an hour or so.

Part II: Saturday Morning focuses on trying out Red Hat Linux quickly, exploring files and directories, learning some Linux commands and text editors, and performing some basic system administration tasks.

Part III: Saturday Afternoon shows you how to set up networking (assuming the PC has an Ethernet card) and how to connect the Linux PC to the Internet (dial-up PPP, but DSL and cable modem are briefly discussed as well). Some of the lessons show you how to use the Linux system in a networked environment as an Internet server (Web, e-mail) or as a Windows file server that uses Samba.

Part IV: Saturday Evening teaches you how to use the GNOME and KDE desktops as well as some of the applications that come bundled with Red Hat Linux.

Part V: Sunday Morning introduces you to various system-administration tasks: configuring X; learning the Linux boot sequence; installing new software packages from RPM and tar files; building a new kernel; scheduling jobs to run at specific times; and performing system backups.

Part VI: Sunday Afternoon focuses on skills that a Linux system administrator should have. The afternoon starts with a lesson on using programming tools to compile and build a new software package. Then it covers system performance monitoring, security, and obtaining further help.

Appendix A: Answers to Part Reviews provides answers to the Part Review Questions that appear after each of the six parts.

Appendix B: What's on the CD-ROMs? describes the contents of the accompanying CD-ROMs.

If you are a new user, you should start with Part I, which covers the installation of Red Hat Linux from the CD-ROMs. Then you can continue sequentially through the sessions. If you have already installed Linux, skip to Part II on Saturday morning.

Conventions Used in This Book

Linux Weekend Crash Course uses a simple, notational style. All listings, filenames, function names, variable names, keywords, and Web addresses are typeset in `monospace font` for ease of reading. The first occurrences of new terms and concepts are in *italic*. Text I direct you to type is in **boldface** and `monospace` type combined.

Following the design of the Hungry Minds' "Weekend Crash Course" series, I use icons to help you pinpoint useful information quickly. Following is what I have in mind for the icons:

 The Note icon marks a general, interesting fact — something I thought you'd like to know.

 The Tip icon marks shortcuts or methods you can follow to make your job easier.

 The Never icon highlights potential pitfalls. With this icon, I'm telling you: "Watch out! This could hurt your system!"

 The Cross-Reference icon points to other sessions in the book that discuss a specific topic — or to specific programs available on the CD-ROMs.

Sidebars

Occasionally, I use sidebars to highlight interesting (but not critical) information. Sidebars explain concepts you may not have encountered before or give a little insight into a related topic. If you're in a hurry, you can safely skip the sidebars. On the other hand, if you find yourself flipping through the book looking for interesting information, I encourage you to read the sidebars.

Each session also contains four time-oriented icons that let you know how you are progressing:

30 Min.
To Go

20 Min.
To Go

10 Min.
To Go

Done!

Reach Out

The publisher and I would like your feedback. Feel free to contact me directly at:

naba@ieee.org

Acknowledgments

I am grateful to Terri Varveris for giving me the opportunity to write *Linux Weekend Crash Course* — a guide that teaches Linux over a weekend. Thanks to Terry Collings for revising the text to accommodate recent changes to the Linux operating system and applications. As the project editor, Terry O'Donnell guided the book through to its successful completion. Terry Collings and I appreciate the guidance and support that Terry O'Donnell provided during this project.

I would like to thank Matthew Hayden for reviewing the manuscript for technical accuracy.

Thanks to everyone at Hungry Minds, Inc., for transforming the raw manuscript into this well-edited and beautifully packaged book.

Of course, there would be no reason for this book if it were not for Linux. For this, I have Linus Torvalds and the legions of Linux developers around the world to thank. Thanks also to Red Hat for providing a copy of Red Hat Linux for this book.

Finally, and as always, my greatest thanks go to my wife, Leha, and our daughters, Ivy, Emily, and Ashley — it is their love and support that keep me going. Thanks for being there!

Contents at a Glance

Contents

☑ **Friday**

☐ Saturday

☐ Sunday

Part I—Friday Evening

PART

I

*Friday
Evening*

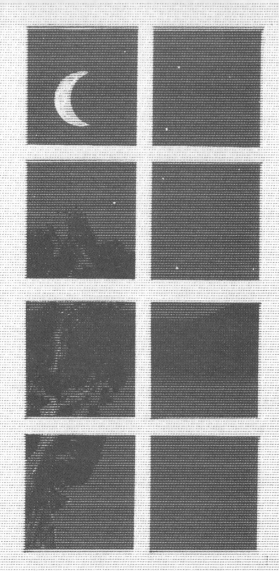

Getting Ready to Install Linux

Session Checklist

✔ Taking stock of your PC's components

✔ Creating a Red Hat boot disk

**30 Min.
To Go**

I n this session, you install Red Hat Linux on your PC. I choose this distribution of Linux because it is the most widely used. However, many of the steps described in this session also apply to installing other Linux distributions.

After installing Red Hat Linux on a PC, the best way to learn it is interactively, using the Linux commands and applications. To that end, this evening's sessions guide you through the steps needed to install Red Hat Linux from this book's companion CD-ROMs. Assuming that the installation program recognizes most of the hardware installed in your PC, you should finish the installation in an hour or so. By the time you get to the third session of this evening, you should have Red Hat Linux installed on your PC. In this session, I guide you through the basic steps of gathering information about your PC's hardware and preparing the Red Hat boot disk needed to start the installation in Session 2.

Taking Stock of Your PC's Components

You have to gather information about your PC's hardware before you install Linux. Like many other operating systems, Linux supports various types of hardware through software components called device drivers. For each type of peripheral device, such as a networking card or a sound card, Linux needs a separate driver. Because Linux is available free (or relatively inexpensively), and because many programmers scattered throughout the world cooperate to develop Linux, you cannot demand support for a specific kind of hardware. Your best bet is to hope that someone who can write a Linux driver has the same hardware you do. In all likelihood, that person will write a driver that eventually will find its way into a version of Linux; then you can use that hardware under Linux. It may take a while for Linux to support new hardware.

You can install and run Linux even if no Linux drivers are available for certain peripherals. At minimum, however, you must have a Linux-compatible processor, bus type, hard disk, video card, monitor, keyboard, mouse, and CD-ROM drive to install Red Hat Linux from the companion CD-ROMs. If you want to run the X Window System and graphical desktops such as GNOME or KDE, you also must ensure that XFree86 (the X Window System for Linux) supports the mouse, the video card, and the monitor.

If your particular video card isn't supported, very likely one of the generic drivers such as Tseng Labs or ATI will work; or you can use a standard VGA mode, which, though not ideal, will enable you to get the X Window System working.

Checking if Linux supports your PC hardware

Before you begin to install Linux on your PC, you need to know if the distribution you are installing supports your hardware. To check if Red Hat Linux supports the hardware in your PC, perform the following steps:

1. Gather the make, model, and other technical details of all hardware installed in your PC. This is your hardware inventory. You can consult the PC's manuals (if you have them). You can also use the current operating system to find information about the hardware. For example, under Windows 95/98, double-click the System icon in the Control Panel to gather some of this information. (Click the Device Manager tab in the System Properties window to view information about specific devices in your system.)

2. With your hardware inventory in hand, visit Red Hat's Web site at
   `http://www.redhat.com/hardware`. This Web site contains a list of
   hardware that the latest version of Red Hat Linux supports. Check your
   PC's hardware against that list, and make sure Red Hat Linux supports
   the key hardware components. If you are installing another distribution,
   you can check that distribution's Web site for compatibility.

Exploring PC hardware

The following sections provide an overview of the PC hardware that Red Hat Linux
supports. Even though Red Hat is specifically referenced here, this information is
also applicable to other Linux distributions. Gather as much information as you
can about the hardware before you proceed to install Red Hat Linux on your PC.

Processor

The *processor* is the *central processing unit (CPU)* — the integrated circuit chip that
performs all the processing in the PC. At minimum, you need an Intel 80386
processor to run Red Hat Linux. Any Intel 80386-, 80486-, Celeron-, or Pentium-
compatible processor can run the Linux operating system. Among the compatibles,
Red Hat Linux can run on AMD K5, K6, and Cyrix processors. Linux also has a sym-
metric multiprocessing kernel (SMP) that supports multiple processors on one
motherboard.

Bus

The *bus* is the standard electrical connection between the processor and its periph-
erals. Several types of PC buses exist. The most popular bus is the *Industry
Standard Architecture (ISA)* bus, formerly called the AT bus because IBM introduced
it in the IBM PC-AT computer in 1984. Other buses include Extended Industry
Standard Architecture (EISA); VESA local bus (VL-bus); Micro Channel Architecture
(MCA); and, most recently, Peripheral Component Interconnect (PCI). Currently,
Red Hat Linux supports all of these buses.

Memory

Commonly referred to as *random-access memory* or *RAM*, memory is not a factor in
compatibility. You do, however, need at least 32MB of RAM to get good performance. Although you may be able to install and run Red Hat Linux on a PC that

has 16MB of RAM, you cannot run the X Window System on that PC. The X Window System manages the graphical interface through an *X server*, which is a large program that needs a lot of memory to run efficiently.

If you are buying a new PC, it probably will come with at least 32MB of RAM — if not 64MB or more. If you have an old PC with less than 8MB of RAM, you may want to add some memory to bring up the total to 16MB (at least). The more physical memory a system has, the more efficiently it runs multiple programs because the programs can all fit in memory. Although Linux can use a part of the hard disk as virtual memory, such disk-based memory is much slower than physical memory. The required amount of physical memory depends on the size of the Linux operating system and the other software that you have to run all the time, such as the X Window System.

Video Card and Monitor

Linux works fine with all video cards in text mode. But when it comes to *XFree86* — the Linux version of the X Window System — the story is quite different. If XFree86 does not support your video card explicitly, you may have to work hard to get XFree86 configured for your video card.

The kind of monitor you use is not particularly critical, but it must be capable of displaying the screen resolutions the video card uses. These resolutions are expressed in terms of the number of picture elements, or *pixels*, horizontally and vertically (such as 1024×768).

Generally, XFree86's support for a video card depends on the *video chipset* — the integrated circuit that controls the monitor and causes the monitor to display output. You can find the name of the video chipset used in a video card from the card's documentation.

Do not be alarmed if you do not see your video card's name in the list that appears at http://www.redhat.com/support/hardware/. Most popular video cards use one of the video chipsets listed at Red Hat's site. In fact, the same chipset can function in many different video cards. For example, the NVidia RIVA TNT chipset is used in many video cards such as Diamond Viper V550, Hercules TNT, STB Velocity 4400, and ELSA ERAZOR II. As you install Red Hat Linux, the Red Hat Linux installation program attempts to detect the video chipset automatically as it sets up the X Window System.

Hard Drive

**20 Min.
To Go**

Linux supports any hard drive that your PC's *basic input/output system (BIOS)* supports. In many older 386 and 486 PCs, you have to use a separate driver to access large hard drives — the system BIOS cannot handle these drives. You can't install Linux on such systems. In short, Linux supports your hard drive only if the system's BIOS supports the hard drive without any additional drivers — with one significant restriction.

> **To be able to boot Linux from a large hard drive (any drive with more than 1,024 cylinders), the Linux Loader (LILO), the Linux kernel, and the LILO configuration files must be located in the first 1,024 cylinders of the drive. This is because the Linux Loader uses BIOS to load the kernel and the BIOS cannot access cylinders beyond the first 1,024.**

For hard drives connected to your PC through a *Small Computer System Interface (SCSI)* controller card, Linux must have a driver that enables the SCSI controller to access and use the hard drive.

> **The only remaining decision about the hard drive is its capacity. If you have an old PC, you may have a relatively low-capacity hard drive — perhaps as low as 500MB. Although you can install Linux and the X Window System within 500MB, doing so does not leave much room for Windows 95/98/2000. (You need at least 2GB of disk space to run both Linux and Windows 95/98/2000.) Therefore, if your old PC has an IDE interface and one small hard disk (500MB or less), you may want to add a second hard drive because most IDE controllers can support two. Adding a second hard drive prevents you from messing up your first hard drive. If you have a SCSI card, you can connect up to seven SCSI devices to it.**

If you are buying a new PC, keep in mind that a complete Red Hat Linux installation (with all the Red Hat packages) takes over 1GB of disk space. On top of that, you need some disk space for your work. Luckily, most new PCs come with hard drive sizes ranging anywhere from 2GB to 20GB. Any hard drive within this range is large enough, so you can keep Windows on one of the partitions and then opt to boot either Windows or Red Hat Linux.

Floppy Disk Drive

As they do for the hard drive, Linux drivers use the PC BIOS to access the floppy disk drive. Therefore, your floppy disk drive is compatible with Linux. You do, however, have to boot Linux from a floppy disk drive during the installation. For this purpose, you need a high-density 3.5" (1.44MB-capacity) floppy disk drive. You can avoid booting from a floppy, provided that you can boot your PC under MS-DOS (not an MS-DOS window under Windows 95/98/2000) and can access the CD-ROM from the DOS command prompt.

Keyboard and Mouse

Red Hat and other Linux distributions support any keyboard that already works with your PC. The mouse, however, needs explicit support in Red Hat Linux. You need a mouse if you want to configure and run XFree86, the X Window System for Linux. Red Hat Linux supports most popular mice, including the commonly found PS/2-style mouse. Red Hat Linux also supports touchpad devices, such as Alps Glidepoint, as long as they are compatible with one of the supported mice.

SCSI Controller

The Small Computer System Interface, commonly called SCSI (and pronounced *scuzzy*), is a standard way of connecting many types of peripheral devices to a computer. SCSI is used in many kinds of computers, from high-end UNIX work-stations to PCs. Typically, you connect hard drives and CD-ROM drives through a SCSI controller. To use a SCSI device on your PC, you need a SCSI controller card that plugs into one of the connector slots on your PC's bus.

A single SCSI controller supports device addresses 0 through 7, with 7 usually assigned to the controller itself. This means you can connect up to seven SCSI devices to your PC. If you want to access and use a SCSI device under Linux, you have to make sure that Red Hat Linux supports your SCSI controller card. The Red Hat Linux release on the companion CD-ROMs supports many popular SCSI controllers.

CD-ROM Drive

CD-ROM (compact disc read-only memory) drives are popular because each CD-ROM can hold up to 650MB of data. This is a relatively large amount of storage compared with a floppy disk. CD-ROMs are reliable and inexpensive to manufacture.

Vendors can use a CD-ROM to distribute a large amount of information at a reasonable cost. This book provides Red Hat Linux on CD-ROMs, so you need a CD-ROM drive to install the software.

Sound Card

With Linux, you also can play sounds on a sound card to enjoy multimedia programs and games. If you have a sound card, you can play audio CDs.

The version of Red Hat Linux on the companion CD-ROMs supports a wide variety of sound cards. Check your sound card against the list posted at Red Hat's Web site (http://www. redhat.com/support/hardware/**).**

Network Card

A network card is necessary only if you connect your Linux PC to a local area network (LAN), which is usually an Ethernet network. Red Hat Linux supports a variety of Ethernet network cards, but using a recognized name brand card, such as 3Com or Intel, will make configuration easier because Linux provides more support for name brand cards. Linux also supports Arcnet and IBM's token-ring network. You can determine the name of the network card by viewing the System Properties window in the Windows 95/98 Control Panel.

If you have a network card and your Linux PC is part of a local area network, you should also gather the following information needed to configure the network:

- The PC's host name
- The Domain name of the network
- The Internet Protocol (IP) address of the PC (or, if the DHCP server provides the IP address, the server's address)
- The Gateway address
- The IP addresses of name servers

If you plan to use Linux on a stand-alone PC at home, you can use Point-to-Point Protocol (PPP) to connect to the Internet over a dial-up connection through an Internet Service Provider (ISP).

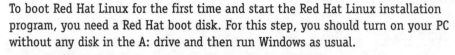

Creating the Red Hat Boot Disk

**10 Min.
To Go**

To boot Red Hat Linux for the first time and start the Red Hat Linux installation program, you need a Red Hat boot disk. For this step, you should turn on your PC without any disk in the A: drive and then run Windows as usual.

You do not need a boot disk if you can start your PC under MS-DOS — not an MS-DOS window in Windows 95 — and access the CD-ROM from the DOS command prompt. If you run Windows 95/98, restart the PC in MS-DOS mode. However, you may not be able to access the CD-ROM in MS-DOS mode because the startup files — AUTOEXEC.BAT **and** CONFIG.SYS **— may not be configured correctly. To access the CD-ROM from DOS, you typically must add a CD-ROM driver in** CONFIG.SYS **and add a line in** AUTOEXEC.BAT **that runs the MSCDEX program. Try restarting your PC in MS-DOS mode and see if the CD-ROM can be accessed. You also may not need a boot disk if your PC is capable of booting from the CD-ROM drive. To check if this is possible, go to your system BIOS and look in the section where you can choose the boot drives. If you can choose CD-ROM, you can select this option and boot directly from the installation CD-ROM. If you succeed, skip this section and proceed to Session 2.**

Like the MS-DOS boot disk, the Red Hat boot disk loads essential operating system files on your PC and starts the Red Hat Linux installation program. Once you install Red Hat Linux, you no longer need the Red Hat boot disk (except when you want to reinstall Red Hat Linux from the CD-ROMs).

The Red Hat boot disk contains an initial version of Red Hat Linux that you use to start Red Hat Linux, prepare the hard disk, and load the rest of Red Hat Linux. Creating the Red Hat boot disk involves using a utility program called RAWRITE.EXE to copy a special file called the Red Hat Linux *boot image* to a disk.

To create the Red Hat boot disk under Windows, follow these steps:

1. Open an MS-DOS window (select Start ➪ Programs ➪ MS-DOS Prompt).

2. In the MS-DOS window, enter the following commands at the MS-DOS prompt. (My comments are in parentheses, and your input is in boldface):

   ```
   d:   (use the drive letter for the CD-ROM drive)
   cd \dosutils
   rawrite
   ```

```
Enter disk image source file name: \images\boot.img
Enter target diskette drive: a
Please insert a formatted diskette into drive A: and press -
ENTER- :
```

3. As instructed, you should put a formatted disk into your PC's A: drive and then press Enter. The RAWRITE.EXE program copies the boot-image file to the disk.

After you see the DOS prompt again, you can take the Red Hat boot disk out of the A: drive and (if you haven't done so already) label it appropriately.

Done!

REVIEW

This session started with an overview of the Red Hat Linux installation process. Then you learned about the hardware installed on your PC and how Red Hat Linux needs to support this hardware. Finally, you prepared a boot disk needed for when you want to start the Red Hat Linux installation.

QUIZ YOURSELF

1. Why do you have to gather information about your PC's hardware before installing Red Hat Linux? (See "Taking Stock of Your PC's Components.")

2. Where can you find a list of hardware that Red Hat Linux supports? (See "Taking Stock of Your PC's Components.")

3. What is the maximum amount of data a CD-ROM stores? (See "CD-ROM Drive.")

4. If your PC has a network card, what parameters do you need to configure the network? (See "Network Card.")

5. What do you do with the Red Hat boot disk? (See "Creating the Red Hat Boot Disk.")

Partitioning the Hard Drive

Session Checklist

✔ Repartitioning your hard drive with FIPS

✔ Starting the Red Hat Linux installation

✔ Partitioning the hard disk for Red Hat Linux

**30 Min.
To Go**

I n the previous session, you gathered information about your PC's hardware and prepared a Red Hat boot disk. This session shows you how to do one more preparatory task — setting aside disk space. It also demonstrates the next step: using the Red Hat boot disk to begin the Red Hat Linux installation and then *partitioning* (dividing) the disk again — this time under Linux — to create the necessary Linux partitions. Then you move on to the next session, which shows you how to finish installing Red Hat Linux.

If you plan to install Red Hat Linux on a second hard disk or you want to completely wipe out your current disk and install Red Hat Linux on it, you do not have to go through the process of repartitioning your hard disk under MS-DOS to create room for Red Hat Linux. Skip the next section and proceed to the "Starting the Red Hat Linux Installation" section.

Repartitioning Your Hard Drive with FIPS

If your PC has a single hard disk drive, chances are that you have Microsoft Windows 95/98 installed on that drive. If your hard drive is at least 1GB, I recommend that you keep Windows installed on your system even if you want to work mostly in Linux. After all, you have to perform some of the Red Hat Linux installation steps under MS-DOS or Windows. Also, you can access the Windows files from all distributions of Linux. Essentially, you get the best of both worlds by keeping MS-DOS and Windows around when you install Red Hat Linux.

If your new PC has one large hard disk (typically larger than 2GB) but two drives — C: and D: — that means the disk already has two partitions. In this case, you may simply want to use the extended partition (drive D:) for Linux. Skip this step and proceed to the "Starting the Red Hat Linux Installation" section.

Typically, your PC's hard disk is set up as a single large drive, designated by drive C:. Unless you can scrounge up a second hard disk for your PC, or you already have a second disk, your first task is to divide your one and only hard disk to make room for Red Hat Linux.

There are two ways to repartition your hard disk:

- Destroy the existing partition and create two smaller, new partitions — one for Windows and the other for Red Hat Linux. This requires you to back up and restore the existing Windows files. This is the hard way to repartition a hard disk.

- Use the *FIPS (First Nondestructive Interactive Partition Splitting)* utility program (included on the companion CD-ROMs) to resize the existing partition and free up space for a second partition in which you can install Red Hat Linux. FIPS cordons off the unused part of a hard disk and makes a new partition out of that unused part without destroying any data existing on the used part. You can also use commercial disk partitioning software such as PartitionMagic from PowerQuest (`http://www.powerquest.com/partitionmagic/index.html`).

No matter which approach you take to repartition your hard disk, do not perform this step before you back up the current contents of your hard disk. Backing up your hard disk ensures that your files are safe, in case something goes wrong with the repartitioning.

In this section, I show you how to repartition your hard disk by using FIPS (the easiest way to create a new partition for Red Hat Linux). The idea is to shrink the existing DOS partition and to create room for the Linux partition. Later on, during Red Hat Linux installation, you have to divide the partition meant for Linux further into at least two parts: one for the Linux root file system and the other for swap space.

Although you have no guarantee that FIPS will split a DOS partition successfully, you should consider using it to create room for Red Hat Linux — especially if you have a brand-new PC with only DOS and Windows installed on the hard disk. In this case, even if something goes wrong with FIPS, you can reinstall Windows and the applications.

The `FIPS.EXE` program and related files are in the `\DOSUTIL` subdirectory of the companion CD-ROMs. To use FIPS, follow these steps:

1. For FIPS to work, all used areas of the disk must be contiguous — or at least as tightly packed as possible. You can prepare the disk for FIPS by running a defragmenter. How you defragment the hard disk depends on your current operating system. For example, in Windows 95/98, select Start ⇨ Programs ⇨ Accessories ⇨ System Tools ⇨ Disk Defragmenter.

Check the hard disk for errors by running a program such as Norton Disk Doctor in MS-DOS 6.0 or later (in Windows 95/98, use SCANDISK).

2. In MS-DOS 6.0 or later, create a bootable disk by using the command `FORMAT-A: /S`. In Windows 95/98, create a startup disk by using the Add/Remove Programs option in the Control Panel and then following the instructions on the Startup Disk tab.

3. Copy the following files from the CD-ROM to the formatted disk. (The following example assumes that D: is the CD-ROM drive.)

    ```
    COPY D:\DOSUTILS\FIPS.EXE A:
    COPY D:\DOSUTILS\RESTORRB.EXE A:
    COPY D:\DOSUTILS\FIPSDOCS\ERRORS.TXT A:
    ```

    The `FIPS.EXE` program splits partitions, and `ERRORS.TXT` contains a list of FIPS error messages. Consult this list for an explanation of any error messages displayed by `FIPS`. `RESTORRB.EXE`, which is a program that enables you to restore certain important parts of your hard disk from a backup of those areas FIPS creates.

4. Leave the bootable disk in the A: drive, and restart the PC. The PC boots from A: and displays the A\> prompt.

5. Type `FIPS`. The FIPS program runs and shows you information about your hard disk. FIPS gives you an opportunity to save a backup copy of important disk areas before proceeding. After that, FIPS displays the first free cylinder where the new partition can start (as well as the size of the partition in megabytes).

6. Use the left and right arrow keys to adjust the starting cylinder of the new partition (the one that results from splitting the existing partition) to change the partition's size. Press the right arrow to increase the starting cylinder number. This leaves more room in the existing partition and reduces the size of the new partition you create. Try to create a new partition that is 1GB or larger.

7. When you are satisfied with the size of the new partition, press Enter. FIPS displays the modified partition table and prompts you to enter **C** to continue or **R** to re-edit the partition table.

8. Press **C** to continue. FIPS displays some information about the disk and asks whether you want to write the new partition information to the disk.

9. Press **Y**. FIPS writes the new partition table to the hard disk and then exits.

10. Remove the disk from the A: drive and reboot the PC.

When the system comes up, everything in your hard disk should be intact — but the C: drive will be smaller. You have created a new partition from the unused parts of the former C: drive.

You don't do anything with the newly created partition under DOS. Later, during Red Hat Linux installation, you create two or more Linux partitions out of this new partition.

Starting the Red Hat Linux Installation

**20 Min.
To Go**

To start the Red Hat Linux installation, put the Red Hat boot disk in your PC's A: drive and restart your PC. (In MS-DOS 6.0 or later, press the reset button or press Ctrl+Alt+Delete; in Windows 95/98, select Start ➪ Shutdown and then select Restart from the dialog box.) Your PC goes through its normal startup sequence, such as checking memory and running the ROM BIOS code. Then the PC loads Red Hat Linux from the boot disk and begins running the Red Hat installation program. The rest of the installation occurs under the control of the installation program.

As you power up or reboot the PC with the Red Hat boot disk, place this book's companion CD-ROMs in the CD-ROM drive. That way the installation program can find and use the Red Hat Linux CD-ROMs to start the installation in graphical mode. Otherwise, the installation program will start in text mode initially and prompt for the CD-ROM. Only then will it start the X Window System and switch to a graphical installation screen.

A few moments after you start the boot process, an initial screen appears. The screen displays a welcome message and ends with a boot: prompt. The welcome message tells you to press one of the function keys F1 through F5 to see more available information.

If you want to read the help screens, press the function key corresponding to the help you want. If you don't press any keys after a minute, the boot process proceeds with loading the Linux kernel into the PC's memory. To start booting Red Hat Linux immediately, press Enter. After the Linux kernel loads, it automatically starts the Red Hat Linux installation program. This, in turn, starts the X Window System, which provides a graphical user interface for the installation.

If you have all the configuration information (such as video card, monitor, network card details, IP addresses, and host names for the TCP/IP network configuration) and all goes well, installing Red Hat Linux from the companion CD-ROMs on a fast (200MHz or better) Pentium PC should take 30 to 40 minutes. (This is assuming that you select nearly all packages.) For example, on a 200MHz Pentium PC with 64MB RAM and a 1GB-disk partition devoted to Red Hat Linux, the installation takes about 35 minutes. On older 486 PCs, the installation process may take somewhat longer.

During installation, the Red Hat installation program probes — attempts to determine the presence of — specific hardware and tailors the installation steps accordingly. For example, if the installation program detects a network card, the program automatically displays the full-screen dialog boxes in which you can configure the TCP/IP network. This means you may see some variation in the sequence of steps, depending on your specific hardware configuration.

If you run into any problems during the installation, refer to Session 4 to learn how to troubleshoot common installation problems.

As you get ready to install Red Hat Linux, you go through the following steps before moving on to disk setup in the next section and the actual installation of various packages in Session 3:

1. Assuming you have already placed this book's companion CD-ROMs in the CD-ROM drive *before* starting the installation, the installation program starts the X Window System and displays a list of languages in a graphical installation screen. Use your mouse to select the language you want and then click the Next button to proceed to the next step.

In the graphical mode installation, each dialog box has online help available on the left side. You can read the help message to learn more about what you are supposed to select on a specific screen.

2. The installation program displays a list of keyboard types, as shown in Figure 2-1. Select a keyboard model that closely matches your PC's keyboard. If you don't see your keyboard model listed, select one of the generic models: Generic 101-key PC or Generic 104-key PC. (Newer keyboards with the Windows keys match this model.) Next, select a keyboard layout that corresponds to your language's character set (for example, English in the United States). Finally, select the Enable dead keys option if the language you select has special characters that must be composed by pressing multiple keys in sequence. For the English language, you can safely select the Disable dead keys option.

3. The installation program displays a screen (see Figure 2-2) from which you can configure the mouse in your system. The various mouse types are listed in a tree structure the manufacturer organizes alphabetically. You need to know your mouse type and whether it is connected to the PC's serial port or the PS/2 port (a small round connector). If your mouse type appears in the list, select it. Otherwise, select a generic mouse type. Most new PCs have a PS/2 mouse. Finally, for a two-button mouse, select the Emulate 3 Buttons option. Because many X applications assume that you use a 3-button mouse, go ahead and select this option. On a typical 2-button mouse, you can simulate a middle-button click by pressing both buttons simultaneously. On a Microsoft Intellimouse, the wheel acts as the middle button.

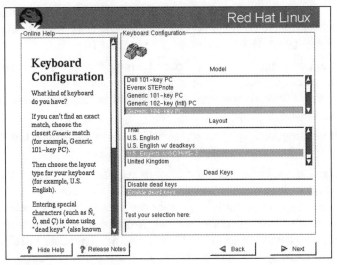

Figure 2-1
Selecting a keyboard type during Red Hat Linux installation

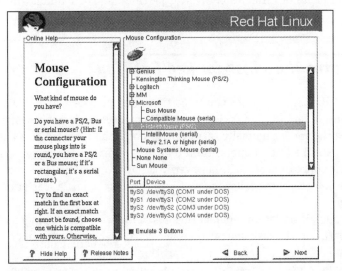

Figure 2-2
Configuring your mouse during Red Hat Linux installation

If you select a mouse with a serial interface, you are asked to specify the serial port where the mouse is connected. For COM1, specify /dev/ttyS0 as the device; for COM2, the device name is /dev/ttyS1.

4. The installation program displays a welcome message that provides some helpful information, including a suggestion that you access the online manuals at http://www.redhat.com. Click the Next button to proceed to the next step.

5. The installation program displays a screen asking if you want to install a new system or upgrade an older Red Hat installation.

   For a new installation, the installation program requires you to select the installation type — *Workstation*, *Server, Laptop* or *Custom*. The Workstation and Server installations simplify the installation process by partitioning the disk in a predefined manner. A Workstation-class installation deletes all existing Linux-related partitions. A Server-class installation deletes all existing disk partitions, including any existing Windows partitions. For maximum flexibility (so you can specify how the disk is used), select the Custom installation.

The next major phase of installation involves partitioning the hard disk for use in Red Hat Linux.

Partitioning the Hard Disk for Red Hat Linux

Like MS-DOS, Red Hat Linux requires you to partition and prepare a hard disk before you can install Red Hat Linux. For a new PC, you usually do not perform this step because the vendor normally takes care of preparing the hard disk and installing Windows and all other applications on the hard disk. Because you are installing Red Hat Linux from scratch, however, you have to perform this crucial step yourself. As you see in the following sections, this task is just a matter of following instructions.

The Red Hat Linux installation program runs *Disk Druid* — a utility program that enables you to partition the disk and, at the same time, specify which parts of the Linux file system you want to load on which partition.

Before you begin to use Disk Druid to partition your disk, you need to know how to refer to the disk drives and partitions in Linux. Also, you should understand the terms *mount points* and *swap partition*. In the next three sections, you learn these terms and concepts and then proceed to use Disk Druid.

Naming disks and devices

The first step is to understand how Red Hat Linux refers to the various disks. Linux treats all devices as files and has actual files that represent each device. In Red Hat Linux, these *device files* are in the /dev directory. If you are new to UNIX, you may not yet know about UNIX filenames. But you will learn more as you continue to use Red Hat Linux. If you know how MS-DOS filenames work, you will find that Linux filenames are similar. However, they have two exceptions: they do not use drive letters (such as A: and C:) and they substitute the slash (/) for the MS-DOS backslash (\) as the separator between directory names.

Because Linux treats a device as a file in the /dev directory, the hard disk names start with /dev. Table 2-1 lists the hard disk drive and floppy drive names that you may have to use.

Table 2-1
Hard Disk and Floppy Drive Names

Name	Description
/dev/hda	First Integrated Drive Electronics (IDE) hard disk drive (the C: drive in DOS and Windows)
/dev/hdb	Second hard disk drive
/dev/sda	First Small Computer System Interface (SCSI) drive
/dev/sdb	Second SCSI drive
/dev/fd0	First floppy drive (the A: drive in DOS)
/dev/fd1	Second floppy drive (the B: drive in DOS)

When Disk Druid displays the list of partitions, the partition names take the form hda1, hda2, **and so on. Linux constructs each partition name by appending the partition number (1 through 4 for the four primary partitions on a hard disk) to the disk's name. Therefore, if your PC's single IDE hard drive has two partitions, notice that the installation program uses** hda1 **and** hda2 **as the names of these partitions.**

Mounting a file system on a device

In Red Hat and other distributions of Linux, you use a physical disk partition by associating it with a specific part of the file system. This is a hierarchical arrangement of directories — a *directory tree*. If you have more than one disk partition (you may have a second disk with a Linux partition), you can use all of them in Red Hat Linux under a single directory tree. All you have to do is decide which part of the Linux directory tree should be on each partition — a process known in Linux as *mounting a file system on a device.* (The disk partition is a device.)

 The term *mount point* refers to the directory you associate with a disk partition or any other device.

Suppose that you have two disks on your PC and have created Linux partitions on both disks. Figure 2-3 illustrates how you can mount different parts of the Linux directory tree (the *file system*) on these two partitions.

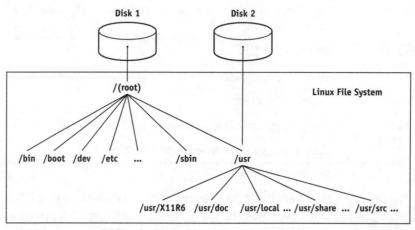

Figure 2-3
An example of mounting the Red Hat Linux file system on two disk partitions

Understanding a swap partition

Most advanced operating systems support the concept of *virtual memory*, in which part of your system's hard disk functions as an extension of the physical memory (RAM). When the operating system runs out of physical memory, it can move (or swap out) the contents of currently unneeded parts of RAM to make room for a program that needs more memory. When the operating system needs to access anything in the swapped-out data, it has to find something else to swap out, and then it swaps in the required data from disk. This process of swapping data back and forth between the RAM and the disk is also known as *paging*.

Because the disk is much slower than RAM, the system's performance is slower when the operating system has to perform a lot of paging. However, virtual memory enables you to run programs that you otherwise can't run.

Red Hat Linux supports virtual memory and can make use of a swap partition. When you create the Linux partitions, create a swap partition as well. With the Disk Druid utility program, described in the next section, it is simple to create a swap partition. Simply mark a partition type as a swap device, and Disk Druid performs the necessary tasks.

Preparing disk partitions for Red Hat Linux

**10 Min.
To Go**

After you select the installation type, a screen prompts you for the method you want to use to partition the disk — the choices are Automatically partition and REMOVE DATA, Manually partition with `fdisk` (experts only), or Manually partition with Disk Druid. Select Manually partition with Disk Druid and click the Next button. This displays the Disk Druid screen (see Figure 2-4).

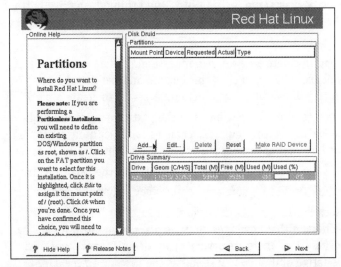

Figure 2-4
The Disk Druid screen from the Red Hat Linux installation program

Disk Druid gathers information about the hard drives on your system and displays a list of disk drives in the lower part of the screen and the current partition information for one of the drives in the Partitions list in the upper part of the screen. For each partition, Disk Druid shows five fields:

- **Mount Point** indicates the directory where the operating system will mount the partition. For example, if you have only one partition for the entire Linux file system, the mount point will be the root directory (/). For the swap partition, this field shows <Swap>. If this field appears as <not set>, you have to specify a mount point. To do so, select the partition and click the Edit button.

- **Device** refers to the partition's device name. For example, hda1 is the first partition on the first IDE drive.

- **Requested** field shows how much space the partition has. For example, if the partition has 256MB of space, this field appears as 256M.

- **Actual** field shows the amount of disk space the partition is using. Usually, the Requested and Actual fields are the same, but they may differ for partitions that can grow in size.

- **Type** field shows the partition's type, such as Linux Native or DOS.

If there are no partitions defined, the table in the Partitions list is empty. You have to add new partitions by clicking the Add button.

You perform specific disk setup tasks in Disk Druid through the five buttons that run across the middle of the screen. Specifically, the buttons perform the following actions:

- **Add** enables you to create a new partition, assuming there is enough free disk space available. When you click this button, another dialog box appears in which you can fill in information necessary to create a partition.

- **Edit** enables you to alter the attributes of the partition currently highlighted in the Partitions list. You make changes to the current attribute in another dialog box that appears when you click the Edit button.

- **Delete** removes the partition currently highlighted in the Partitions list.

- **Reset** causes Disk Druid to ignore any changes you may have made.

- **Make RAID Device** sets up a *RAID (Redundant Array of Inexpensive Disks)* device — a technique that combines multiple disks to improve reliability and data transfer rates. There are several types of RAID configurations. This button is active only if your system has the hardware necessary to support a RAID device.

Exactly what you do in Disk Druid depends on the hard drives in your PC and the partitions they already have. For this discussion, I assume that you have created the necessary hard disk space for Linux by using one of the following methods:

- You start with a single hard drive with a single partition (only the C: drive in Windows). Then you use FIPS to split that partition in two. (Refer to the "Repartitioning Your Hard Drive with FIPS" section.) After partitioning, you end up with two DOS partitions.

- Your PC has a single, large hard drive (greater than 2GB) that has two partitions (C: and D: drives in Windows). In this case, the second partition has an extended partition that contains the logical drive D:. You want to install Red Hat Linux on the extended partition that used to be the D: drive in Windows.

Both of these situations call for the same sequence of steps, as outlined in the next two sections.

Setting Up the Partitions

To prepare an existing DOS partition for Linux, you have to perform the following steps in Disk Druid:

1. Delete the DOS partition you want to use for Linux. To do this, select the partition (typically the one with Device name hda2) from the Partitions list on the Disk Druid screen and then click the Delete button. Before deleting the partition, remember to make a note of the partition's size from the Partitions list.

2. Create a new partition for the Linux file system. To do this, press the Add button on the Disk Druid screen. You should see a dialog box (see Figure 2-5) where you can fill in / as the mount point and enter the size in megabytes. To compute the size, simply subtract the size of the swap space (32MB or the amount of RAM in your PC, whichever is more) from the original size of the partition. Select the OK button, and then press Enter to complete this step and return to the Disk Druid screen.

3. Create another new partition and set it as a Linux swap space. To do this, click the Add button on the Disk Druid screen (see Figure 2-4). In the dialog box (see Figure 2-5), enter the size of the partition. Click the list of partition types, and use the mouse to select Linux Swap as the type. When you do so, the text <Swap Partition> appears in the Mount Point field. Next, click the OK button to define the new partition and return to the Disk Druid screen.

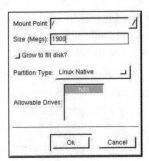

Figure 2-5
The dialog box in which you fill in the attributes of a new partition

4. If you want to access the DOS partition under Linux, make sure you assign a mount point for this partition. Basically, you assign a Linux directory name where the DOS partition will appear. For example, you can use /dosc as the mount point for the DOS partition; then you can access the DOS files in the /dosc directory in Linux. This mnemonic is good because the name dosc should remind you that this drive is the C: drive under DOS or Windows. To assign the mount point, select the DOS partition (typically listed as device hda1 in the Partitions list), and click the Edit button to edit the attributes. The Edit dialog box appears. Type the mount point (for example, /dosc), and click the OK button to return to the Disk Druid screen.

5. After making the changes, click the Next button on the Disk Druid screen to proceed to the next installation step.

Selecting Partitions to Format

After you finish specifying the partitions in Disk Druid, the Red Hat installation program displays a screen (see Figure 2-6) listing the partitions that you may have to format for use in Linux. If you have only one disk partition for Red Hat Linux, the list shows only one partition.

To format the partition, click the button next to the partition's name. Also click the button next to the option marked Check for bad blocks while formatting so that the formatting process marks any areas of the disk that may be physically defective.

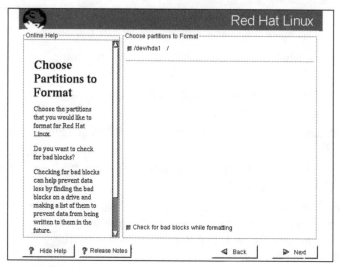

Figure 2-6
Selecting partitions to format for use in Red Hat Linux

If you have multiple disk partitions mounted on different directories of the Linux file system and you are upgrading an existing installation, you do not have to format any partitions in which you want to preserve existing data. For example, if you have all user directories on a separate disk partition mounted on the /home directory, you do not have to format that partition.

This completes the disk preparation phase of the installation. The installation program performs the actual formatting of the partitions after it asks for more configuration information, including the packages you want to install.

Done!

REVIEW

This session started by showing you how to set aside disk space for Red Hat Linux installation. Then you started the installation by using the Red Hat boot disk you prepared in the previous session. Through a graphical user interface, you specified the language, keyboard, and mouse and created the disk partitions for use in Red Hat Linux. You also learned the meaning of terms such as swap partition and the significance of mounting a file system on a disk partition.

QUIZ YOURSELF

1. What is FIPS and what can you do with it? (See "Repartitioning Your Hard Drive with FIPS.")

2. What information does the Red Hat installation program use to tailor the installation steps? (See "Starting the Red Hat Linux Installation.")

3. What does it mean to mount a file system? (See "Mounting a File System on a Device.")

4. What is Disk Druid, and what are you supposed to do with it? (See "Preparing Disk Partitions for Red Hat Linux.")

5. If you have all user directories on a separate disk partition mounted on the /home directory, do you have to reformat that partition when you perform a custom installation of Red Hat Linux? (See "Selecting Partitions to Format.")

Installing Linux

Session Checklist

✔ Configuring Red Hat Linux

✔ Selecting packages to install

✔ Completing the Red Hat Linux installation

**30 Min.
To Go**

I n the previous session, you set aside disk space for Red Hat Linux, started the installation program, and prepared the disk partitions, including a swap partition. In this session, you finish installing Red Hat Linux. You learn how to configure Red Hat Linux, select the packages to install, and let the installation program complete the remaining installation chores.

Configuring Red Hat Linux

After you prepare the disk partitions with Disk Druid and specify which partitions to format, the installation program moves on to some configuration steps. The typical configuration steps are as follows:

- Install LILO
- Configure the network

- Set the time zone
- Set the root password and add user accounts
- Configure password authentication

The following sections guide you through each of these configuration steps.

Install LILO

LILO stands for *Linux Loader* — a program that resides on your hard disk and starts Linux from the hard disk. If you have Windows 95/98 on your hard disk, you can configure LILO to load these operating systems as well. LILO is also known as the *bootloader*.

The Red Hat installation program displays the LILO Configuration screen (see Figure 3-1), which asks you where you want to install LILO. For systems with Windows 95/98 and Red Hat Linux residing on a single hard disk, it is best to install LILO on the master boot record.

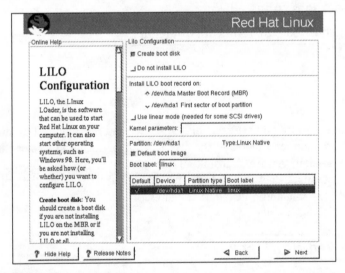

Figure 3-1
The LILO Configuration screen enables you to specify where to install LILO and whether to create a boot disk.

The first button on this screen asks if you want to create a boot disk. This is different from the installation boot disk; you can use this disk to boot your Linux system if the Linux kernel on the hard disk is damaged or if LILO — the Linux

Loader — does not work. The Create boot disk button is the default, and you should leave it that way. Later on, the installation program prompts you to insert a blank floppy into your PC's A: drive.

You can use the next button, labeled Do not install LILO, to turn off LILO installation. If you choose not to install LILO, you should definitely create a boot disk. Otherwise, you can't start Red Hat Linux when you reboot the PC.

The next part of the LILO Configuration screen gives you the option to install LILO in one of two locations:

- Master Boot Record (MBR), which is located in the first sector of your PC's hard disk (the C: drive)
- First sector of the partition where you loaded Red Hat Linux

You should install LILO in the MBR, unless you are using another operating system loader such as System Commander or OS/2 Boot Manager. The screen includes a text field labeled Kernel parameters that enables you to enter any special options that Red Hat Linux may need as it boots. Your need for special options depends on the hardware you have. On my PC I have a 3Com 3C503 Ethernet card that uses an external transceiver. When Red Hat Linux loads the driver software for the 3Com 3C503 card, I need to specify the option xcvr=1 to make sure the driver uses the external transceiver. I enter that option on the Kernel parameters text field.

 Do not use the command fdisk /mbr **in Windows after installing LILO. Doing so removes LILO from the MBR, and it will be impossible to restore LILO once it is deleted.**

The remainder of the LILO Configuration screen gives you the option to select the disk partition from which you want to boot the PC. A table then lists the Linux partition and any other partitions that may contain another operating system. If your system has a Linux partition and a DOS partition (that actually has Windows 95/98 installed on it), the table shows both of these entries. Each entry in the table is an operating system that LILO can boot.

After you install LILO, whenever your PC boots from the hard disk, LILO runs and displays a boot: prompt. At the prompt, you may type the name of an operating system to boot. (The Boot label column in the table in the bottom right section of Figure 3-1 shows the names you may enter at the LILO prompt). If the list shows two entries labeled linux and dos, type linux to boot Linux and dos to boot from the DOS partition (which should start Windows 95/98, if that's what you have installed on that partition). If you press Tab at the LILO prompt, LILO displays the boot labels.

When rebooting the PC, if you enter nothing at the LILO prompt, LILO waits for a few seconds and boots the default operating system. The default operating system is the one with a check mark in the Default column in Figure 3-1. In this case, Linux is the default operating system.

All this is for your information. You can essentially accept the default selections on this screen and click the Next button to proceed to the next configuration step.

Configure the network

Assuming the Linux kernel detected a network card, the Red Hat installation program displays the Network Configuration screen (see Figure 3-2) that enables you to configure the local area network (LAN) parameters for your Linux system.

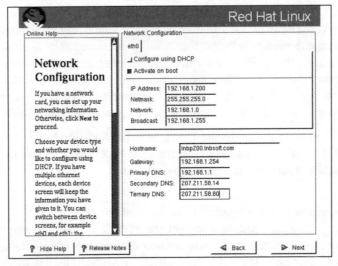

Figure 3-2
The Network Configuration screen enables you to configure the local area network.

This step is not for configuring the dial-up networking. You need to perform this step if your Linux system is connected to a TCP/IP LAN through an Ethernet card or other high-speed data network rather than just a modem connected to an ISP.

If the Red Hat installation program does not detect your network card, you should restart the installation and type expert **at the boot prompt. Then you can manually select your network card. See Session 4 for more information.**

The Network Configuration screen (Figure 3-2) displays tabbed dialog boxes—one for each network card installed on your system and detected by the Linux kernel. These tabs are labeled eth0, eth1, and so on. If your system has only one Ethernet card, you see only the eth0 tab. Figure 3-2 has only one tab. Each tab offers two choices for specifying the IP (Internet Protocol) address for the network interface:

- Use DHCP— Click the button labeled Configure using DHCP if your PC obtains its IP address and other network information from a *Dynamic Host Configuration Protocol (DHCP)* server.

- Provide static IP address — Fill in the necessary network-related information manually.

You should select DHCP only if a DHCP server is running on your local area network. If you choose DHCP, the DHCP server sets your network configuration automatically, and you can skip the rest of this section. You should leave the Activate on boot button selected so that the network is configured whenever you boot the system.

To provide static IP address and other network information, you have to enter certain parameters for TCP/IP configuration in the text input fields that appear on the Network Configuration screen (refer to Figure 3-2).

The Network Configuration screen asks for the following key parameters:

- IP address of the Ethernet interface

- The host name for your Linux system (For a private LAN, you can assign your own host name without worrying about conflicting with any other systems on the Internet.)

- IP address of the *gateway* (the system through which you might go to any outside network)

- IP address of the primary name server

- IP address of a secondary name server

- IP address of a ternary name server

If you have a private LAN (one that is not directly connected to the Internet), you may use an IP address from a range designated for private use. Common IP addresses for private LANs are the addresses in the range 192.168.1.1 through 192.168.1.254. Session 12 provides more in-depth information about TCP/IP networking and IP addresses.

After you enter the requested parameters, click the Next button to proceed to the firewall configuration step. The firewall configuration screen gives you three security-level choices. The default is High and is appropriate for now. Click on the Next button to continue.

Set the time zone

**20 Min.
To Go**

After completing the firewall configuration, you have to select the default language you want to use on your Red Hat system. Choose the language by clicking on it from the list and then click on the Next button. Now you will set the *time zone* — the difference between the local time and the current time in Greenwich, England, which is the standard reference time. The time zone is also known as *Greenwich Mean Time (GMT)* or UTC, which the International Telecommunication Union (ITU) selected as a standard abbreviation for *Coordinated Universal Time*. The installation program shows you the Time Zone Selection screen (see Figure 3-3) from which you can select the time zone, either in terms of a geographic location or as an offset from the UTC. Figure 3-3 shows the selection of a time zone in a geographic location.

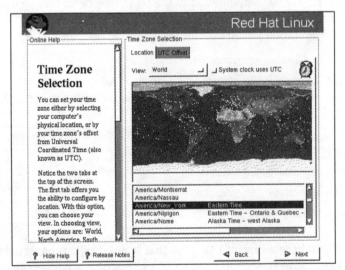

Figure 3-3
Selecting your time zone in terms of a geographic location

Notice that there are two tabs on the Time Zone Selection screen — Location and UTC Offset. Initially, the screen shows the Location tab. This tab enables you to pick a time zone by simply clicking your geographic location. As you move the mouse over the map, the currently selected location's name appears in a text field. If you want, you can also select your location from a long list of countries and regions. If you live on the East Coast of the United States, for example, select USA/Eastern. Of course, the easiest way is to click eastern USA on the map.

If the worldview of the map is too large for you to select your location, click the View button on top of the map. A drop-down list of views appears with several choices. You can then click the view appropriate for your location.

The other way to set a time zone is to specify the time difference between your local time and UTC. Click the UTC Offset tab to select the time zone this way.

For example, if you live in the eastern part of the United States, select UTC-05:00 as the time zone. This tab also enables you to activate Daylight Saving Time, which applies to USA only. After you select your time zone, click the Next button to proceed to the next configuration step.

Set the root password and add user accounts

After you complete the time zone selection, the installation program displays the Account Configuration screen (see Figure 3-4) in which you can set the root password and add one or more user accounts.

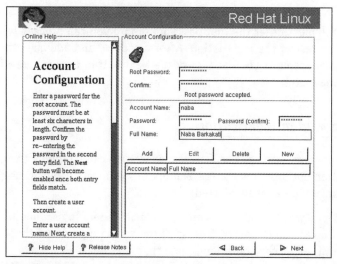

Figure 3-4
Setting the root password and adding other user accounts

The root user is the *super user* in Linux. Because the super user can do anything in the system, you should assign a password you can remember — but that others cannot guess easily. Typically, make the password at least eight characters long, include a mix of letters and numbers, and (for good measure) throw in some special characters such as + or *. Remember the password is also case sensitive.

Type the password on the first line and then re-enter the password on the next line. Each character in the password appears as an asterisk (*) on the screen. Both entries must match before the installation program accepts the password. The installation program displays a message when it accepts the root password. Passwords should be at least six characters in length and be a combination of numbers and letters. Do not use proper names or any words from a dictionary. After you type the root password twice, you might also want to add one or more user accounts.

You should always add a user account, even if you are the only one using the PC. If you log in as root, it is very easy to make a mistake and cause irreparable damage to the system because root has free access to the system. By logging in as a user, you are ensuring that you can't damage the system by mistake. To add a user account, fill in the Account Name, Password, and Full Name fields and then click the Add button. The new account information then appears in the table underneath the Add button. You do not have to add all the user accounts at this time. Later on, you can use the Linuxconf tool (which comes with Red Hat) to add more user accounts.

 You must enter the root password before you can proceed with the rest of the installation. After you do so and add any other user accounts you need, click the Next button to continue with the installation.

Configure password authentication

The installation program displays a screen from which you can configure the password authentication options. There are several options you can enable or disable. Of these, the first two are already selected:

- **Enable MD5 passwords:** Select this option to enable users to use long passwords of up to 256 characters instead of the standard password that can be, at most, eight characters long. Note that *MD5* refers to *Message Digest 5*, an algorithm developed by RSA, Inc. to developed to compute the digest of the entire data of a message. Essentially, MD5 reduces a message to a digest consisting of four 32-bit numbers. This allows you to enter a passphrase rather than just a password. You can enter anything that you can remember, such as a complete sentence, or a poem, that is much more difficult for someone to guess.

- **Enable shadow passwords:** This option replaces the /etc/psswd file with /etc/shadow, which only the super user (root) can read. This provides an added level of security.

You should use these default settings for increased system security. Click the Next button to proceed to the next configuration step.

Selecting the Package Groups to Install

After you complete the key configuration steps, the installation program displays a screen from which you can select the Red Hat Linux package groups you want to install. After you select the package groups, you can take a coffee break, and the Red Hat installation program can format the disk partitions and copy all selected files to those partitions.

Red Hat uses special files called *packages* to bundle a number of files that make up specific software. For example, all configuration files, documentation, and binary files for the Perl programming language come in a Red Hat package. You use a special program called *Red Hat Package Manager (RPM)* to install, uninstall, and get information about packages. Session 23 shows you how to use RPM. For now, just remember that a package group is made up of several Red Hat packages.

Figure 3-5 shows the Package Group Selection screen with the list of package groups you can elect to install. An icon, a descriptive label, and a button prefix identify each package group.

Some of the components are already selected, as the pressed-in buttons indicate. These are the minimal sets of packages Red Hat recommends for installation for the class of installation (Workstation, Server, or Custom) you have chosen. You can, however, choose to install any or all of the components. Use the mouse to move up and down in the scrolling list, and click the mouse on an entry to select or deselect that package group.

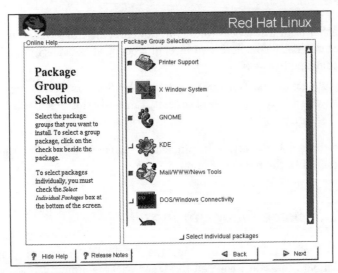

Figure 3-5
*The Package Group Selection screen from which you select the components
to install*

**In an actual Red Hat Linux installation, you install exactly those
package groups that you need. However, for the purpose of this
crash course, you choose many different package groups because
you need them to go through all the sessions. Each package
group requires specific packages to run. The Red Hat installation
program automatically checks for any package dependencies and
shows you a list of packages required that you have not selected.
In this case, you should install the required packages.**

Because each package group is a collection of many different Red Hat packages,
the installation program also gives you the option to select individual packages. If
you select the item labeled Select individual packages that appears below the
list in Figure 3-5 and then click the Next button, the installation program takes
you to other screens where you can select individual packages. If you are installing
Red Hat Linux for the first time, you really do not need to go down to this level of
detail to install specific packages. Simply pick the components you think you need
from the screen shown in Figure 3-5. After you select the components you want,
click the Next button to continue with the rest of the installation.

You can always install additional packages later on with the RPM
utility program, described in Session 23.

Completing the Installation

**10 Min.
To Go**

After you complete the key configuration steps and select the components to
install, the installation program configures the X Window System. The installation
program uses an X server with minimal capability that can work on all video cards.
In this step, the installation program prepares the configuration file that the X
server uses when your system reboots.

The installation program tries to detect the video card and displays an X
Configuration screen indicating a successful or nonsuccessful probe. If your video
card is not detected, you can choose it from the list, or pick a generic VGA driver.
Next the installation tries to detect your monitor and displays the X Configuration
screen (see Figure 3-6) with the result, whether it succeeds.

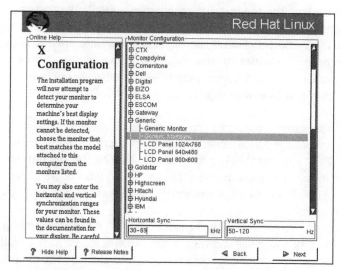

Figure 3-6
The result of detecting the monitor displayed on the X Configuration screen

If the installation program displays a wrong monitor or a generic one as the choice, you should enter a range of values for the two parameters that appear along the bottom of the screen:

- **Horizontal Sync** — the number of times per second the monitor can display a horizontal raster line, in kilohertz (kHz). A typical range might be 30–64 kilohertz (kHz).
- **Vertical Sync** — the number of times per second the monitor can display the entire screen, in Hertz (Hz). Also known as *vertical refresh rate*, the typical range is 50–90 Hertz (Hz).

Typically, the monitor's documentation includes all this information. Other places to get information about your monitor include: your Microsoft Windows setup, your system's Windows driver, your computer vendor's Web site, or the Norton System Information tool.

Do not specify a horizontal synchronization range beyond the capabilities of your monitor. A wrong value can damage the monitor.

After selecting the monitor, the installation program presents the Custom Configuration screen from which you can choose the color depth and screen resolution. The installation program chooses the values it determines are best for your system. You may change the values by clicking on the arrows to open a drop-down box from which you may choose different values. You can also choose to have your system start in text or graphical mode by checking the appropriate box at the bottom of the screen.

After you finish selecting X configuration options, click the Next button. The installation program displays an informative message telling you that a log of the installation is in the /tmp/install.log file. That file lists all the Red Hat packages installed in your system. You can review the install log later on and keep the file for future reference. The content of the install log depends on the exact packages you choose to install.

Click the Next button to proceed with the installation. The Red Hat installation program formats the disk partitions and then installs the packages. As it installs packages, the installation program displays a status screen showing the progress of the installation with information such as the total number of packages to install, the number installed so far, an estimated amount of disk space needed, and an estimated time remaining to install. Formatting and installation both take awhile.

After installing all the packages, the installation program displays a screen that prompts you to insert a blank floppy into your PC's A: drive. This floppy is the emergency boot disk you can use to start Red Hat Linux if something happens to the hard disk or you do not install the LILO.

Insert a blank floppy into your PC's A: drive, and click the Next button. The installation program copies the Linux kernel and some other files to the floppy. After preparing the boot disk, the installation program displays a message informing you that installation is complete.

When you insert a blank floppy into your PC's A: drive, during the process of copying the Linux files to the drive all previous data on the floppy is destroyed.

Done!

The message goes on to remind you to remove the floppy from drive A: before exiting the installation program. Do so, label the floppy appropriately, and save it for future use. Then click the Exit button to reboot your PC. When it finishes rebooting, you should get the Red Hat Linux graphical login screen. You are now all set to explore and learn Linux.

REVIEW

In this session, you continued with the Red Hat Linux installation steps you started in the previous session. The installation program enabled you to configure a number of items, including the Linux Loader (LILO), the LAN, the time zone, and the password of the root user. Then you selected the package groups to install and configured the X Window System. After that, the installation program took over — it formatted the disk partitions and copied all necessary files from the CD-ROM to the disk. You also prepared a boot disk for use in an emergency when LILO fails to boot Red Hat Linux.

QUIZ YOURSELF

1. What is LILO and what does it do? (See "Install LILO.")
2. What is the root user? (See "Set the root Password and Add User Accounts.")

3. What parameters do you have to specify in the Network Configuration screen? (See "Configure the Network.")

4. What happens if you do not select any package groups to install? (See "Selecting the Package Groups to Install.")

5. What parameters do you have to specify if the installation program cannot correctly detect your monitor? (See "Completing the Installation.")

SESSION
4

Running Linux for the First Time

Session Checklist

✔ Troubleshooting and installing Red Hat Linux in text mode

✔ Troubleshooting and installing Red Hat Linux in expert mode

✔ Configuring the X Window System

✔ Logging in and out

✔ Exploring GNOME and KDE

**30 Min.
To Go**

In the last three sessions, you installed Red Hat Linux from this book's companion CD-ROMs. The Red Hat Linux installation program attempts to detect key hardware components automatically such as a SCSI controller and network card. Based on the detected hardware, the installation program takes you through a sequence of steps to configure the detected hardware. For example, if the installation program fails to detect the network card correctly, it skips the network configuration step. The installation program also tries to simplify the installation by skipping some system configuration steps such as setting up a printer. You can recover from most of the installation and configuration problems because there are other ways to perform these tasks. This session shows you several troubleshooting approaches for some common installation and configuration problems.

Installing Red Hat Linux in Text Mode

The Red Hat installation program attempts to use a minimal X Window System (X) to display the graphical user installation screens. If the program fails to detect a video card, X does not start. If — for this reason or any other reason — X fails to start, you can always fall back on the older text mode installation program to specify the video card manually. You can also use the text mode installation if you are comfortable with the older installation program.

To use text mode installation, type text at the boot: prompt after you start the PC from the Red Hat Linux boot floppy. From then on, the basic sequence is similar to that of the graphical installation described in Session 2. However, many small details are different. You should be able to respond to the prompts and perform the installation.

In text mode, when the installation program fails to detect the video card, it displays a list of video cards. Select one video card from the list. Because of your help in selecting the video card, X may work when you install in text mode. If it does not, you can configure X using the information in the "Configuring X" section that appears later in this session and in session 5.

Installing Red Hat Linux in Expert Mode

If the Red Hat installation program does not detect your SCSI controller or network card, you can specify these devices manually by running the installation in expert mode. Look for any indication of SCSI or network devices in the messages displayed by the Linux kernel as it boots. To view these boot messages, press Ctrl+Alt+F4. This switches to a text-mode virtual console where the messages appear. A *virtual console* is a screen of text or graphical information stored in memory that you can view on the physical screen by pressing the appropriate key sequence.

To run the installation in expert mode, type expert at the boot: prompt in the initial text screen that appears during the Red Hat Linux installation. The installation program then displays another text screen that asks for a driver disk, if you have one.

Your hardware vendor provides a floppy disk with Linux drivers. If you have that disk, press Enter, and a dialog box prompts you to insert the disk into the A: drive. After you do so, press Enter, and the installation program loads the driver and guides you through steps necessary to install the driver.

If you do not have a driver disk, select Cancel. The installation program then goes through two more screens in which you select the language and the keyboard layout. Then the installation program prompts for the media containing the packages to be installed.

Next, the installation program displays a dialog box that gives you another opportunity to add devices. Press Tab to highlight the Add Device button, and then press Enter. The installation program then displays a dialog box that prompts for the type of device — SCSI or Network.

If you have any SCSI devices, such as a SCSI hard drive, select SCSI and press Enter. Then, the installation program displays a list of SCSI controllers from which you should select the one on your system and press Enter. The installation program then loads that driver module.

The SCSI driver automatically probes and determines the SCSI controller's settings, such as interrupt request (IRQ) and I/O port address. If the driver has problems detecting the SCSI controller's settings, you can specify these parameters manually. To do so, select the check box labeled Specify module parameters, and press Enter. The installation program then prompts you for the module parameters.

You can then enter a line such as aha152x=0x340,11,7 to specify the parameters for the driver module. See the sidebar "Specifying SCSI Controller Settings" later in this session for more information on these settings.

After you add any SCSI controllers, you return to the dialog box that enables you to select a device type. You can add network cards from this dialog box as well. In the dialog box, select Network from the list, and press Enter. The installation program then displays a list of network cards from which you can select your network card.

When you press Enter, the installation program loads the driver module for the selected network card. That driver probes and determines the network card's settings.

Once you return to the screen from which you select SCSI or network device, select Back and press Enter. This takes you to the dialog box that asks you about adding devices. Select Done and press Enter. The installation program then switches to graphics mode and guides you through the rest of the installation, as outlined in Sessions 2 and 3.

Configuring the X Window System

If the installation program cannot detect your video card during the X configuration step, you can skip that step and configure X after completing the rest of the installation.

Specifying SCSI Controller Settings

If you have a SCSI controller in your system, the Red Hat installation program loads a SCSI driver module for that controller. You have to identify the type of SCSI controller (such as Adaptec 1542 or Adaptec 2940). The installation program can attempt to determine the controller settings, such as the IRQ and the I/O port address, by probing various I/O port addresses. However, if the installation program fails to determine the SCSI controller settings, you have to specify these parameters — IRQ and I/O address — as options for the driver module. The exact formats of these options vary from one module to another. For example, the driver for an Adaptec AHA 152x card accepts the options in the following format:

```
aha152x=IOPORT,IRQ,SCSI_ID[,Reconnect,Parity]
```

where *IOPORT* is the I/O port address, *IRQ* is the interrupt request number, and *SCSI_ID* is the SCSI ID of the SCSI controller. The last two items are optional. A typical module option for the aha152x module might be:

```
aha152x=0x340,11,7
```

After the installation is complete and you reboot the PC, you get a text login screen. Log in as root and type Xconfigurator to run a utility program with that name. The Xconfigurator utility enables you to create a configuration file that the X server needs.

The Xconfigurator program starts with a Welcome dialog box that displays a message about the X configuration file. After reading the message, press Enter to continue with the configuration process.

Xconfigurator automatically detects the chipset your video card uses and displays a summary message, as shown in Figure 4-1.

In this case, Xconfigurator finds a video card based on the S3 ViRGE/DX (or /GX) chipset and recommends the SVGA X server. In fact, the message from Xconfigurator is somewhat cryptic. The SVGA X server refers to the X server program with the full name XF86_SVGA installed in the /usr/X11R6/bin directory. Because the dialog box in Figure 4-1 is for your information only, press Enter to continue with the rest of the configuration. A dialog box then appears that enables you to select your monitor from a list.

Figure 4-1
The message that results from the Xconfigurator's probing of the video card

Press the up and down arrow keys to browse through the list. If you find your monitor model listed, position the cursor on that monitor and then press Enter. Otherwise, select Custom and press Enter. If you choose Custom, Xconfigurator displays another dialog box in which you have to provide two critical parameters for your monitor:

- *Horizontal synchronization frequency*—the number of times per second the monitor can display a horizontal raster line, in kilohertz (kHz)

- *Vertical synchronization rate* or *vertical refresh rate*—the number of times per second the monitor can display the entire screen

You can find the parameters for the frequencies in your monitor's manual. Press Enter to continue. Xconfigurator displays a list of predefined horizontal synchronization ranges.

Typically, one of the items from this list should match your monitor's specifications. If you need to guess your monitor's capabilities, be conservative. Do not specify a horizontal synchronization range beyond the capabilities of your monitor. A wrong value of horizontal synchronization frequency can damage your monitor. If you are configuring a display for a laptop, choose the generic LCD display setting that matches the resolution of your display.

For example, if your monitor's manual says your monitor is capable of displaying 1,280 by 1,024 resolution at 60Hz, you should pick the item that matches this specification. After selecting the horizontal synchronization capabilities, press Enter.

Xconfigurator now prompts you for the vertical synchronization rate of your monitor. Pick the vertical synchronization range nearest to your monitor's specifications and press Enter.

If Xconfigurator is unable to detect the amount of video memory on your video card, it displays a dialog box that prompts you to select the amount of video memory from a list. Select the amount closest to your video card's memory and press Enter.

Xconfigurator prompts you to identify the clock chip — a timing device on the video card. You can safely press Enter to accept the default selection labeled No Clockchip Setting (recommended).

Xconfigurator then displays a Select Video Mode dialog box with a list of video modes in terms of pixel resolution such as 1,280 × 1,024 and color such as 16 bits per pixel, as shown in Figure 4-2.

**20 Min.
To Go**

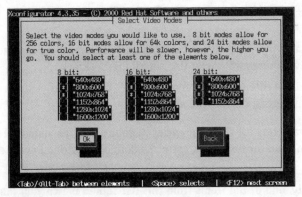

Figure 4-2
Selecting one or more video modes

Press Tab to move the cursor to a video mode, and press the Spacebar to select that mode. You can choose as many modes as you want. Then press Tab to select the OK button and press Enter.

Next, Xconfigurator gives you the option of starting X to test your configuration. You should press Enter. A graphical X screen appears, and Xconfigurator shows a dialog box that asks if you can read the text. Click to close the dialog box.

Xconfigurator then writes the XF86Config file in the /etc/X11 directory and completes the X configuration. The next time you reboot the PC, X should start, and you should get a graphical login screen.

Now that you have installed Red Hat Linux from this book's companion CD-ROMs, you are ready to explore and learn it. First, you learn how to log in, log out, and shut down your Linux system. Then you power up again and take a quick tour of the GNOME and KDE *graphical user interfaces* (*GUIs* — pronounced "goo-ease").

Starting Linux

After the installation is complete, the Red Hat Linux installation program automatically reboots the system. The PC goes through its normal power-up sequence and loads LILO from the C: drive; a screen appears with the names of the partitions that LILO can boot. If you do nothing, LILO proceeds to boot from the partition that you designated as the default when you configured LILO in Session 1. If you press Ctrl+X, the following prompt appears:

```
LILO boot:
```

When you install LILO, if you specify the Linux partition as the default, you can simply wait; after a few seconds, LILO boots Linux.

If you want to boot from another partition (such as Windows), press the Tab key. LILO displays the names of the available bootable partitions. For example, a typical display might be:

```
linux dos
```

You can then type the name of the partition you want to boot or press Enter to boot from the first partition.

After LILO boots Linux, you should see a long list of opening messages — including the names of the devices Linux detects. At the end of all the messages, you see a graphical login screen, as shown in Figure 4-3.

The window in the middle of the screen displays a welcome message with your system's host name — the name you assign to your system when you configure the network. If the network is not configured, `localhost.localdomain` is used as the host name.

You can log in using any of the accounts, including root, which you define during the installation. For example, to log in as root, type `root` (move the mouse over the login window before you begin typing) in the text field and press Enter. Then type the root password (the one you set during installation) to log in as the super user.

Figure 4-3
The graphical login screen in Red Hat Linux

Because the default GUI is GNOME, the GNOME desktop appears with a warning dialog box from the GNOME File Manager. Click the OK button to dismiss the warning dialog box. The GNOME Hints window appears, and you get a desktop (as shown in Figure 4-4).

You will explore the GNOME desktop in a few minutes. For now, I want to show you how to log out and shut down your Linux system.

Logging out

Before you explore the GNOME GUI, you should learn how to log out. To log out, select Main Menu — the stylized foot icon at the left edge of the GNOME Panel in the GNOME desktop (see Figure 4-4) — and then select Log Out from the menu. The screen grays out, and a dialog box prompts to see if you really want to log out and also gives you the option to halt or reboot the PC. Click the Yes button to log out. After a few moments, the graphical login screen (see Figure 4-3) appears so that another user (or you again) can log in and use the system.

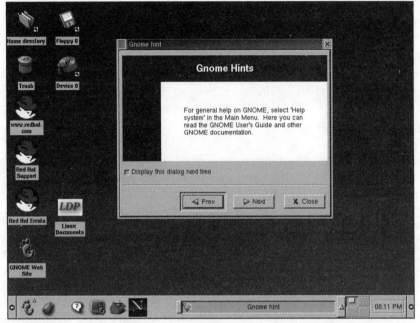

Figure 4-4
The initial GNOME desktop after logging in as root

Shutting down Red Hat Linux

When you are ready to shut down Red Hat Linux, you must do so in an orderly manner. Even if you are the sole user of a Linux system, several other programs are usually running in the background. Also, operating systems such as Linux try to optimize the way they write data to the disk. Because disk access is relatively slow (compared with the time needed to access memory locations), data generally is held in memory and written to the disk in large chunks. Therefore, if you turn the power off, you run the risk of some files not updating properly.

Any user (you do not have to be logged in) can shut down the system from the desktop or the graphical login screen. The System menu in the login dialog box provides menu options for rebooting or halting the system. To shut down the system, simply select System ⇨ Halt in the graphical login screen shown in Figure 4-3.

Another dialog box asks you to confirm if you really want to halt the system. Click the Yes button. The system then shuts down in an orderly manner.

As the system shuts down, you see messages about processes being shut down. You may be surprised how many processes there are — even though no one is explicitly running any programs on the system. If your system does not automatically turn the power off on shutdown, you can manually turn off the power.

Exploring GNOME

Power up the PC again, and log in after you get the graphical login screen. You should again get the GNOME desktop because it's the default. In this section, you spend some time exploring the GNOME desktop.

The exact appearance of the GNOME display depends on the current session. A *session* is nothing more than a set of applications (including a window manager) and the state of these applications. GNOME stores the session information in a file named session **in the** .gnome **subdirectory of your home directory. This is a text file; if you are curious, you can browse the file with the command** more ~/.gnome/session**. Don't worry about the command's syntax right now; you learn more about Linux commands in Sessions 6, 7, and 8.**

What Is GNOME?

GNOME stands for *GNU Network Object Model Environment*; *GNU*, as you probably know, stands for *GNU's Not UNIX*. GNOME is a graphical user interface (GUI) and a programming environment. From the user's perspective, GNOME is like the Motif-based *Common Desktop Environment (CDE)* or Microsoft Windows. Behind the scenes, GNOME has many features that enable programmers to write graphical applications that can work together well. In this session, I only point out some key features of the GNOME GUI, and I leave the details to you to explore on your own.

You can always find out the latest information about GNOME by visiting the GNOME home page at http://www.gnome.org.

The initial GNOME desktop (see Figure 4-4) produced by the default session description is very similar to the Windows 95/98/NT/2000 desktop. It includes the GNOME panel (similar to a Windows taskbar) and the Sawfish window manager, resulting in a desktop similar to the one shown in Figure 4-4.

As you can see from the icons appearing on the left side of the GNOME desktop (refer to Figure 4-4), GNOME enables you to place folders and applications directly on the desktop. This is similar to the way you can place icons directly on the Windows 95/98/NT/2000 desktop.

You can move and resize the windows just the way you do in Microsoft Windows. Also, as in the window frames in Microsoft Windows 95/98/NT/2000, the right-hand corner of the title bar includes three buttons. The leftmost button reduces the window to an icon, the middle button maximizes the window to fill up the entire screen, and the rightmost button closes the window.

A key feature of the GNOME desktop is the long bar along the bottom edge of the screen. This is known as the *GNOME panel* or simply the *panel*. The panel is a separate GNOME application. As Figure 4-5 shows, it provides a display area for menus and small panel applets. Each panel applet is a small program designed to work inside the panel. For example, the clock applet on the panel's far right displays the current time.

Figure 4-5
The GNOME panel

Notice the two outward-pointing arrows at the left and right ends of the panel. Click the arrow and see that the panel slides away, reducing its display area down to a small sliver along the edge of the screen. This frees up more desktop area for windows. Click the arrow again and the panel reappears.

The panel includes several other applets:

- **The GNOME pager applet:** This provides a virtual desktop larger than the physical dimensions of your system's screen. In Figure 4-5, the pager displays four pages in a small display area. Each page represents an area equal to the size of the X display screen. To go to a specific page, click that page in the pager window. The GNOME pager applet also displays buttons for each window displayed in the current virtual page.

- **Launcher applets:** These are the buttons to the right of the foot icon.
  Each displays a button with the icon of the application that the button
  starts. Clicking a button starts (launches) that application. Try clicking
  each of these buttons to see what happens. The question mark (?) button
  launches the GNOME Help Browser; the toolbox button launches the GNOME
  Control Center; the terminal icon launches a terminal window; and the
  icon with the earth icon launches Netscape Communicator. The lock icon
  starts the screensaver and requires you to enter the password to get back
  to the desktop.

- **Main Menu button:** The GNOME panel also displays the Main Menu button
  that behaves like the Windows Start menu. This is the button at the left-
  hand side of the panel (see Figure 4-5) with the image of a stylized foot
  (the GNOME logo). That foot is the Main Menu button. As with the Start
  button in Windows 95/98/NT/2000, you can launch applications from the
  menu that pops up when you click the left mouse button on the foot.
  Typically, this menu lists items that start an application. Some of the
  menu items have an arrow. Another pop-up menu appears when you place
  the mouse pointer on an item with an arrow.

When time permits, you should explore all the items in the Main menu to see
all the tasks you can perform from this menu. At this point, select Main Menu
(foot) ⇨ Log Out to log out so you can begin a KDE session.

Exploring KDE

To try the KDE GUI, you have to install the KDE package when you install Red Hat
Linux during the first three sessions on Friday. Typically, the installation program
makes GNOME your default GUI. For now, you can change the GUI for the next session by selecting Session ⇨ KDE from the graphical login window.

**In Session 17, you learn how to change the default GUI from
GNOME to KDE and vice versa.**

**10 Min.
To Go**

When you log in, you should get the KDE desktop for this session. The next
time you log in, the system reverts to GNOME (assuming that is your default GUI).

What Is KDE?

KDE stands for the *K Desktop Environment*. The KDE project started in October 1996 with the intent to develop a common GUI for UNIX systems that use the X Window System. The first beta version of KDE was released a year later in October 1997, and KDE version 1.0 was released in July 1998.

From the user's perspective, KDE provides a graphical desktop environment that includes a window manager (kwm); a file manager (kfm); a panel (kpanel) for starting applications; a help system; configuration tools; and many applications, including an image viewer, PostScript viewer, and mail and news programs.

From the developer's perspective, KDE has class libraries and object models for easy application development in C++. KDE itself is a large development project.

You can always find out the latest information about KDE by visiting the KDE home page at http://www.kde.org/.

After you select KDE as the GUI for the session and login, you see an initial KDE desktop similar to the one shown in Figure 4-6.

KDE is easy to use and shares many similarities with the Windows 95/98/NT/2000 GUI. You can start applications from a menu similar to the Start menu in Windows. KDE also enables you to place folders and applications directly on the desktop.

The KDE panel appearing along the bottom edge of the screen starts applications. The left and right ends of the panel show outward-pointing arrows. You can click these arrows to hide the panel and make more room on the desktop for applications. When the panel is hidden, it still shows a small bar with an arrow. To view the entire panel again, click that arrow, and the panel slides out.

The KDE desktop also includes a menu bar along the top of the desktop. From the pull-down menus on this menu bar, you can perform a number of tasks, such as log out, configure the desktop, and get help. You can perform all of these tasks through the K button on the KDE panel as well.

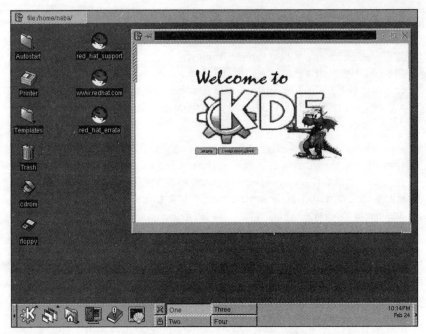

Figure 4-6
The initial KDE desktop for a typical user

The following is a list of a few of the buttons on the KDE panel. If you don't know what a button does, simply move the mouse over the button, and a small pop-up window displays a brief message about that button.

- **Start button/Main menu:** The most important component of the panel is the K button on the left-hand side of the panel. That button is like the Start button in Windows 95/98/NT/2000. When you click the K button, a pop-up menu appears. From this menu, you can get to other menus by moving the mouse over items with a rightward pointing arrow. You can start applications from this menu. That's why the KDE documentation calls the K button the *Application Starter*.

- **On-line help:** To read the online help on KDE, click the button with an icon of a book.

- **File manager:** To view the contents of your home directory, click the button with the icon of a folder and a home.

- **Virtual desktop:** KDE supports a virtual desktop. By default, you get four virtual desktops. You can click one of the buttons labeled 1, 2, 3, or 4 to switch to a specific desktop. You can use the desktops to organize your application windows. You do not need to clutter a single desktop with many open windows. When a desktop gets crowded, simply switch to another desktop and open the applications there.

- **Terminal emulation:** The KDE panel also includes a button with the icon of a terminal covered by a shell. Click this button to run a terminal emulation program and get a terminal window. You can type Linux commands at the shell prompt in the terminal window.

- **KDE control center:** Click on the button with an icon of a terminal covered by a circuit board to start the KDE control center. The control center enables you to configure various aspects of the KDE desktop.

Done!

To log out of KDE, select K ⇨ Logout, and click the Logout button on the resulting dialog box.

REVIEW

This session showed you how to overcome some common installation problems by running the installation in different modes. You learned how to use the text mode installation and how to use expert mode to install devices that the installation program does not detect. You also learned how to configure X to enable graphical logins. Next, you learned how to log in, log out, and shut down the system. Then you powered up the system again, logged in, and explored the key features of the GNOME desktop. Next, you learned how to select KDE as your GUI for a session and explored the key features of KDE. For both GUIs, you discovered how to start applications. In particular, you learned to open a terminal window where you can type Linux commands. You use these terminal windows to try out various Linux commands in future sessions.

QUIZ YOURSELF

1. How do you start the installation in text mode? (See "Installing Red Hat Linux in Text Mode.")

2. What do you do if the Red Hat installation program does not detect your network card? (See "Installing Red Hat Linux in Expert Mode.")

3. When would you manually configure the X Window System? (See "Configuring the X Window System.")

4. Why must you shut down a Linux system in an orderly manner? (See "Shutting Down Red Hat Linux.")

5. How do you switch your GUI to KDE? (See "Exploring KDE.")

PART

I

Friday Evening

1. How do you find out information about your PC's hardware before beginning to install Red Hat Linux from this book's companion CD-ROM?

2. Why do you need a boot disk to install Red Hat or other distributions of Linux? How would you create the Red Hat boot disk from the companion CD-ROM?

3. Why do you usually have to repartition your hard disk before installing Linux? What are the different ways to repartition the hard disk? Which approach do you use to create room on your hard disk for the Linux partitions?

4. What are the different types of installation options for Red Hat Linux? What happens if you select a Server class installation?

5. What are the names of IDE and SCSI disk devices in Linux? What are some of the partition names?

6. How does Linux make use of the swap partition? How much swap space should you set aside for Linux?

7. Suppose you have a single disk partition, besides the swap partition, for installing Linux. What mount point must you specify for this partition in Disk Druid before you can install Linux?

8. How do you mount a DOS partition during Linux installation?

9. Suppose your PC has both Windows 95/98 installed and you are now installing Red Hat Linux. During installation, how do you make sure that the Linux Loader (LILO) boots Windows by default?

10. Can you add normal user accounts during Red Hat Linux installation? Is there any limit on how many user accounts you can add? How do you add a user account?

11. What are package groups? Can you select individual packages in a package group?

12. Suppose you are installing Red Hat Linux on a PC that's on a network where a Dynamic Host Configuration Protocol (DHCP) server dynamically assigns the IP addresses. How do you perform the network configuration when installing Red Hat Linux on this PC?

13. What are the two ways in which you can specify the time zone during Red Hat Linux installation? How do you enable Daylight Saving Time?

14. How do you start the Red Hat Linux installation with the text mode interface? Why might you use the text mode installation?

15. Explain the situations in which you have to use the expert mode installation. How do you begin installing Red Hat Linux in the expert mode?

16. What are the typical parameters you may have to specify for a SCSI adapter or network card when installing in expert mode? Show a sample specification of parameters for a SCSI adapter.

17. If the Red Hat installation program does not detect the video card correctly, how do you troubleshoot this problem? What utility do you use?

18. When you configure X, you specify the horizontal synchronization frequency and vertical refresh rate of the monitor. What do these terms mean? How might you find the values of these parameters for your monitor?

19. Suppose you want to connect a printer to your PC's parallel port and configure it for printing in Linux. How do you determine if Linux detects your PC's parallel port?

20. What types of printers can you set up with Linux? Can you configure your Linux system to print on a printer attached to a Windows system on the local area network? If so, what is that type of printer?

☑ Friday

☑ **Saturday**

☐ Sunday

PART

II

Saturday
Morning

Configuring the X Window System

Session Checklist

✔ Setting up the X Window System

✔ Running and controlling the X Window System

**30 Min.
To Go**

This morning's sessions focus on various system administration tasks, such as configuring X; learning the Linux boot sequence; installing new software packages from RPM and tar files; building a new kernel; scheduling jobs to run at specific times; and performing system backups. This session shows you the steps involved in configuring the X Window System, or X for short. It's important to learn how to configure X because graphical desktops such as GNOME and KDE require X to work.

Setting Up the X Window System

The term *X Window System,* or *X* for short, is loosely applied to several components that facilitate window-based graphics output (or a graphical interface) on a variety of bitmapped displays. A bitmapped display has two distinct components: a *video monitor* on which the graphics output appears and a *video card* (or *graphics card*) — either a plug-in card or some circuitry built into the system's motherboard — that causes the output to appear on the monitor.

The X Window System for Linux comes from the *XFree86 project* — a cooperative project of programmers who bring X to the PC. (You can access the XFree86 home page at http:// www.xfree86.org/**.) As a result, the Linux version of X is called XFree86.**

Understanding the X server

At the heart of X is the *X server* — a process (computer program) running on a computer that has a bitmapped display, a keyboard, and a mouse. Applications (*X clients*) that need to display output do so by communicating with the X server via one of several possible interprocess communication mechanisms.

When you run X on your system, the X server runs on your computer and controls the monitor, keyboard, and mouse. The server responds to commands X clients send that open windows and draw in those windows. The X clients may run locally or on remote systems.

The X server configures the display (number of colors, resolution in terms of number of pixels horizontally and vertically), mouse, and keyboard based on information stored in a configuration file. Linux comes with two versions of XFree86 — 3.3.6 and 4.0.1. Depending on your video card, the installation program selects an X server from one of these versions of XFree86. Each version has a different configuration file. For XFree86 3.3.6, the configuration file is /etc/X11/XF86Config. For XFree86 4.0.1, the configuration file is /etc/XFree86Config-4.

Configuring X requires you to prepare the configuration file. The configuration file contains information about your video card, monitor, keyboard, and mouse. Red Hat Linux comes with a utility program called xf86config (same name as the configuration file, but in lowercase) that enables you to create the XF86Config working configuration file.

You don't need to create the X configuration file with the xf86config **program if when you install Red Hat Linux (following the instructions outlined in Sessions 1 through 3) the installation program automatically detects your system's video chipset and enables you to configure X through a number of dialog boxes. Additionally, Session 4 shows you how to run the** Xconfigurator **utility to create the X configuration file.**

This session walks you through the X configuration process by using the xf86config program so that you can see the configuration options in detail and understand the format and purpose of various items of information stored in the configuration file. In particular, when you configure X with xf86config, you see the list of over 600 video cards the latest version of XFree86 supports. If X is not configured correctly during Linux installation, you can select your card from this list and create a working X configuration file.

Using the xf86config program

**20 Min.
To Go**

The xf86config program asks you questions. You need to have some information about your PC's video card and monitor to answer these questions.

To run xf86config, log in as root and type xf86config at the shell command prompt. The xf86config program displays a screen of text with some helpful information. Press Enter to continue.

The xf86config program asks you to specify a mouse protocol that determines how the X server communicates with the mouse. The program shows you a numbered list of mouse types. Type the number that corresponds to your mouse type; then press Enter.

The xf86config program then asks the following:

```
Please answer the following question with either 'y' or 'n'.
Do you want to enable Emulate3Buttons?
```

If your mouse has two buttons, xf86config suggests that you enable Emulate3Buttons. Enter y. If you enable Emulate3Buttons, you can simulate a middle button click by pressing both buttons simultaneously. Many X applications assume that the mouse has three buttons, so this feature comes in handy in the PC world, where a mouse typically has two buttons.

Next, you have to specify the full device name for the mouse. During Red Hat Linux installation, you configure the mouse, and the installation program creates a link between your mouse device and the standard name /dev/mouse. Therefore, you can press Enter.

The xf86config program displays a list of keyboard types and prompts you for the one that matches your keyboard. Enter the number from the list. If none of the types match, you can always select 1, which represents Generic 101-key PC keyboard.

The xf86config program then asks you for the country for which the keyboard should be configured. Again, you have to pick from a list displayed by the program.

Next, xf86config informs you that it needs two critical parameters of your monitor:

- *Horizontal synchronization frequency* — the number of times per second the monitor can display a horizontal raster line, in kilohertz (kHz)
- *Vertical synchronization rate* — the number of times per second the monitor can display the entire screen, in Hertz (Hz)

You can find this information in your monitor's manual.

Press Enter to continue. The xf86config program displays a number of ranges for horizontal synchronization frequency, or you can type 11 to enter your own range of values.

Do not specify a horizontal synchronization range beyond the capabilities of your monitor. A wrong value can damage the monitor.

To enter a range of values, type 11 and then press Enter. The program prompts you for the range. Enter the range as two values separated by a minus sign (-). My monitor's documentation says the horizontal synchronization range is 30–69 kHz, so I enter the following:

```
Horizontal sync range: 30-69
```

Next, xf86config prompts you for the vertical synchronization rate and gives you a range of values; or you can type 5 to enter your own range of values. If you know the range, type 5 and then press Enter. At the next prompt, enter the range for the vertical synchronization. My monitor's documentation shows this range to be 50–120 Hz, so I enter the following:

```
Vertical sync range: 50-120
```

Next, enter an identifier for your monitor's definition. Typically, you enter your monitor's make and model. You can enter anything here. This identifier is used to refer to the monitor in another part of the configuration file. For my system's monitor, I respond as follows:

```
Enter an identifier for your monitor definition: Micron700FGx
```

The next task is to configure the video-card settings. The xf86config program displays an explanatory message and asks this question:

```
Do you want to look at the card database? y
```

Type y and then press Enter. The program then displays a list of several hundred cards. (The numbering starts at zero and goes on to over 600.) Press Enter after each screen to see the entire list. The make, model, and chipset of the video card are crucial pieces of information you need to select the correct XFree86 X server and to configure it properly.

Select your video card by typing the appropriate number. One of my PCs, for example, has a Diamond Stealth 3D 2000 PRO video card with the S3 ViRGE/DX chipset. I notice the following line on one of the screens:

```
240   Diamond Multimedia Stealth 3D 2000 PRO      S3 ViRGE/DX
```

I type 240 — the number corresponding to my video card — and press Enter.

Each new release of XFree86 supports more video cards. For example, XFree86 4.0.1 supports 749 cards. (As a point of reference, Version 3.1.2 supported only 124 entries, Version 3.3.1 supported 382 cards, and Version 3.3.6 supported 671 cards.) If your video card's vendor and model do not appear in the list but you know the video chipset, try selecting the entry that corresponds to the generic chipset.

After you enter your selection, xf86config displays some information (and any appropriate instructions) about your chosen video card.

After you press Enter to continue, xf86config asks how much video memory your video card has. Most current video cards have anywhere from 4MB (4,096KB) to 32MB (32,768KB) of video memory. You need at least 1MB of video memory to display 256 colors at 1,024 × 768 resolution (1,024 pixels horizontally by 768 pixels vertically). Type the number that corresponds to the amount of memory in your video card and then press Enter.

Now you have to provide an identifier for your video card. Type the appropriate information for your card. The following is what I enter for my PC's video card:

```
Enter an identifier for your video card definition: Diamond Stealth 3D 2000 PRO
```

The program next asks you to enter the default color depth in terms of number of bits per pixel. The choices range from monochrome (1 bit per pixel) to millions of color (24 bits per pixel). Enter the number corresponding to the depth you want and then press Enter.

This step completes your session with xf86config. The program displays the following message asking whether it can write the XF86Config file in the current directory:

```
I am going to write the XF86Config file now. Make sure you don't accidentally
overwrite a previously configured one.

Do you want it written to the current directory as 'XF86Config'? n

Please give a filename to write to: /etc/X11/XF86Config
```

**10 Min.
To Go**

Answer n in response to the first question; then type /etc/X11/XF86Config and press Enter. The xf86config program writes the configuration file and exits.

Running and Controlling the X Window System

After you have a complete XF86Config file, your X server should be ready to run. Typically, you select a graphical login option during Linux installation, so X starts automatically whenever your system restarts.

If you do not opt for a graphical login option, you can start the X server by running the startx script, which is a file that contains shell commands. This shell script is in the /usr/X11R6/bin directory, but that directory should be in your PATH environment variable. Therefore, to run that script, type startx at the shell prompt.

There are some special keystrokes you can use to control the X server. The following sections describe these methods of controlling X.

Aborting X with Ctrl+Alt+Backspace

If you create a new XF86Config file to try out some new video modes, you can abort the X server by pressing Ctrl+Alt+Backspace to kill the X server. (In UNIX, the term *kill* refers to exiting a program abnormally. UNIX even has a `kill` command that stops errant programs.)

If you select the graphical login option upon installing Red Hat Linux, the X server immediately restarts — but this time with the configuration options in the new `XF86Config` file. If your system is not set up for a graphical login screen, you return to the text display.

If you enable the graphical login screen and X does not work properly because of erroneous configuration options in the `XF86Config` file, press Ctrl+Alt+F1 to get a text-mode login screen. Then log in as root, and follow the procedures in the preceding section for setting up X. Press Ctrl+Alt+F7 to get back to the graphical login screen, and press Ctrl+Alt+Backspace to kill the X server and force it to restart with the new configuration options.

Switching screen modes with Ctrl+Alt+Keypad keys

To exemplify how to switch screen modes, look at the Screen section that applies to your X server in your `XF86Config` file. Notice there are several Display subsections. Each Display subsection lists the video modes supported for a specific depth — the number of bits in each pixel's value. The Display subsections list the video modes in terms of the display resolution, which is expressed in terms of the number of pixels horizontally and vertically. For example, here is a partial listing of a Screen section of the X configuration file for an SVGA X server:

```
# The svga server
Section "Screen"
    Driver      "svga"
    Device      "Diamond Stealth 3D 2000 PRO"
    Monitor     "Micron700FGx"

    Subsection "Display"
        Depth       8
        Modes       "640x480" "800x600" "1024x768" "1280x1024"
        ViewPort    0 0
    EndSubsection
```

```
Subsection "Display"
    Depth       16
    Modes       "640x480" "800x600" "1024x768" "1280x1024"
    ViewPort    0 0
EndSubsection


    ...
EndSection
```

When the X server starts, it configures the video card at the default resolution (in this case, 640 × 480, or 640 pixels horizontally by 480 pixels vertically) that corresponds to the first mode shown in the Modes entry of the first Display subsection.

You can try the other modes without having to exit the X server. Press Ctrl+Alt+Keypad +. (*Keypad* + means the plus key in the numeric keypad.) The X server switches to the next mode — in this case, 800 × 600. Press Ctrl+Alt+Keypad + again, and the X server switches to 1,024 × 768 mode. When you press Ctrl+Alt+Keypad +, the X server cycles forward to the next mode listed in the Modes entry.

Press Ctrl+Alt+Keypad + several times to make sure the X server works in all video modes.

To cycle backward to the preceding mode, press Ctrl+Alt+Keypad –. (*Keypad* – means the minus key in the numeric keypad.) Therefore, if the X server is displaying in 800 × 600 mode and you press Ctrl+Alt+Keypad –, the server switches to 640 × 480 mode.

You can make the X server start in any of the supported modes. If you want the X server to start at the highest-resolution mode, simply change the Modes entry in the Screen section that corresponds to your X server (the Driver entry in the Screen section indicates the X server type) to the following:

```
Modes       "1024x768" "800x600" "640x480"
```

This change makes X start in 1,024 × 768 mode, which gives you much more screen area than 640 × 480 mode. Some applications require the X server to run in 16-bit color depth. To learn how to run the X server in 16-bit color depth, see the sidebar.

Done!

Running the X Server in 16-Bit Color

Some applications, such as the Applixware office suite, require you to run the X server in 16-bits per pixel mode (also referred to as a 16-bit color depth). To make the X server start with a 16-bit color depth, perform the following steps:

1. Open the `/etc/X11/XF86Config` file by using your favorite text editor. (In Caldera and SuSe the file is `/etc/XF86config`.)

2. Locate the Screen section corresponding to the X section that corresponds to your X server. For example, if you use the SVGA server, look for the Screen section that has `svga` as the `Driver` entry.

3. Just before the first Display subsection, insert the following line:

   ```
   DefaultColorDepth 16
   ```

   This forces the X server to use a 16-bit color depth. The server uses the information from the Display subsection that specifies `Depth` as 16.

4. Save the `XF86Config` file.

5. If X is running (and assuming you have enabled the graphical login screen), press Ctrl+Alt+Backspace to stop the X server and to force it to restart. It should now use a 16-bit color depth.

REVIEW

This session showed you how to configure the X Window System by using the `xf86config` program. You familiarized yourself with the organization of the `XF86Config` file — the X configuration file — that resides in the `/etc/X11` directory of your Linux system. You also learned how to control the X server with special keystrokes and how to change the default color depth of the display.

QUIZ YOURSELF

1. What is the X server and what does it do? (See "Setting Up the X Window System.")

2. What is `xf86config` and how do you start it? (See "Using the xf86config Program.")

3. How do you kill the X server? (See "Aborting X with Ctrl+Alt+Backspace.")

4. What keystroke causes the X server to use the next available screen resolution? (See "Switching Screen Modes with Ctrl+Alt+Keypad Keys.")

5. How do you ensure the X server runs using a 16-bit color depth? (See "Running the X Server in 16-Bit Color Depth.")

Installing a Printer

Session Checklist

✔ Configuring printers

✔ Understanding the basics of printing in Linux

✔ Configuring a printer in Red Hat Linux

✔ Configuring a printer in Caldera Open Linux

✔ Configuring a printer in SuSe Linux

**30 Min.
To Go**

I n this session, you will learn to configure a printer to work with three distributions of Linux. First, you will check if Linux can detect the parallel port of your PC. Then you will learn how printing works in Linux and what types of printers Linux supports. Finally, you'll configure a printer to work with Red Hat Linux, Caldera Open Linux, and the SuSe distribution.

Configuring Printers

The installation programs for the major distributions do not include a printer-configuration step. However, as long as the Linux kernel can detect your PC's parallel port, it is easy to configure a printer from an X utility program. To see if Linux detected the parallel port, type dmesg | grep par in a terminal window. The dmesg command provides information about kernel parameters. In this instance the parameter you want to see is the parallel port. Here is typical output from this command:

```
parport0: PC-style at 0x378 [SPP,PS2]
parport0: no IEEE-1284 device present
lp0: using parport0 (polling)
```

The first line starts with the word parport0, which is how Linux identifies the first parallel port. The remainder of the line specifies the characteristics and address of the port, which in this case is a PC-style located at 0x378. Parallel ports are typically at 0x378 and, although not shown, interrupt 7.This line essentially indicates that the operating system has detected the parallel port.

Linux Printing Basics

Under Linux, print jobs are typically sent to the printer through print queues. Data sent to the printer is first buffered in a print queue and then sent to the printer by a program called a print spooler. The print spooler also ensures that print jobs sent simultaneously to the print queue are sent sequentially to the printer to avoid causing printer conflicts.

Data to be printed is usually in a form that the printer cannot understand, and a program known as a print filter usually translates data. The print filter translates the data to a standard print language such as ASCII text, PostScript, PCL 3, PCL 5, or PCL 6.

PostScript is the standard Unix/Linux print language. Because PostScript printers are somewhat expensive, Linux uses a filter program called Ghostscript to translate PostScript data into PCL 3, 5, or 6. HP and other compatible inkjet printers use PCL 3. Many laser printers use PCL 5 and 6.

Therefore, it is possible to use almost any printer as long as it understands one of the languages mentioned here. However, if the printer does not recognize one of the standard languages just discussed, that printer usually will not work with Linux and will only work with the operating system for which it was designed. These printers are known as GDI printers (sometimes called Winprinters) and will only work with Microsoft Windows. If you are considering buying a printer to use with Linux, be sure it is not a GDI printer. Check the Printer Compatibility How-To before buying any printer for use with Linux.

We'll start by configuring a printer in Red Hat Linux, and then we'll take a look at configuring a printer in the Caldera and SuSe distributions. Regardless of the distribution, we need to be running X to set up the printer. We'll use the GNOME desktop for setting up the printer in Red Hat Linux and the KDE desktop for the other distributions.

Configuring a Printer in Red Hat Linux

From the graphical login screen, log in as root and select Main Menu ➪ Programs ➪ System ➪ Printer Tool from the Gnome desktop. (If you are not logged in as root, type su in a terminal window, enter the root password, and then type printtool to run the print tool.)

The main window of the print tool, formally known as Red Hat Linux Print System Manager, appears (as shown in Figure 6-1). If you have not installed the IPX/Netware Connectivity package group, you see a dialog box with a message informing you that a package named ncpfs is not installed; therefore, you cannot print to a Netware printer. You can click the Ignore button to dismiss this dialog box and work with the main window of the print tool.

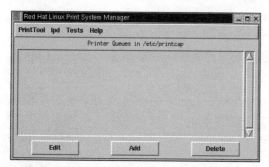

Figure 6-1
The Red Hat Linux Print System Manager window enables you to manage the print queue and to add a new printer.

You can manage the printer queue and add a new printer through the print tool utility. Click the Add button to configure a new printer. The print tool displays the Add a Printer Entry dialog box, asking you to select the type of printer, as shown in Figure 6-2.

Figure 6-2
Selecting the type of printer

**20 Min.
To Go**

You can select from five types of printers:

- **Local Printer:** Refers to a printer connected directly to a parallel or serial port of the PC where you install Red Hat Linux

- **Remote Unix (lpd) Queue:** Refers to a printer physically connected to another Linux system on the local network (lpd refers to the Linux printer daemon — the process that manages the printer queue.)

- **SMB/Windows 95/NT Printer:** Refers to a printer connected to another PC that is on the local network and that runs the LAN Manager protocol (typically used to share resources such as disks and printers among PCs running Windows 95/98 or Windows NT)

- **NetWare Printer (NCP):** Refers to a printer connected to a Novell Netware server on the local area network

- **Direct to port printer:** Refers to a network-connected printer that prints data received at a specific TCP/IP port (typically port number 9100)

Specify the printer connection that applies to your configuration. For this discussion, assume you are connecting a printer to the PC's parallel port, which means you should select the Local Printer button in the Add a Printer Entry dialog box. After you select the Local Printer button and click OK, the print tool displays a dialog box with information about the detected parallel ports. Click OK to continue with the printer configuration. Next, the Edit Local Printer Entry dialog box prompts for various entries for the local printer (as shown in Figure 6-3).

The text fields are already filled in, and you can accept these as they are. You do have to select an input filter, which is a printer driver that depends on the make and model of the printer you are connecting to the parallel port. To do this, click the Select button next to the Input Filter text field. This brings up a large dialog box (see Figure 6-4) that enables you to select the printer type and to choose some other parameters such as the paper size and the resolution of the printer (typically 600 × 600 dots per inch in modern laser printers). Select the appropriate values for all the fields.

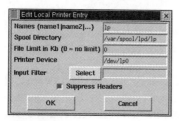

Figure 6-3
Providing information about a local printer

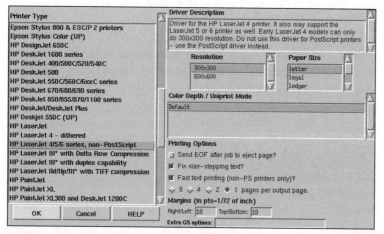

Figure 6-4
Selecting a printer type and options such as paper size and resolution

A specific item in the dialog box shown in Figure 6-4 is an option labeled `Fix stair-stepping text?` This refers to a problem that occurs when text files from Red Hat Linux are sent to the printer. In Linux text files, each line ends with a single linefeed character; in DOS and Windows, each line ends with a carriage return followed by a linefeed. The printer reacts to carriage returns and linefeeds the same way as old-fashioned typewriters — a linefeed advances to the next line and a carriage return moves to the beginning of a line. When printing a DOS text file, the lines print one after another as expected. However, when the printer prints a Linux text file with lines ending in a linefeed only, the output looks something like this:

```
Line 1 ends here
                Line 2 here
                        and so on
                                like a staircase.
```

To avoid this staircase effect, just check the box marked Fix stair-stepping text? in the dialog box you see in Figure 6-4, and Red Hat Linux takes care of the problem by sending a carriage return before each linefeed whenever you print a text file.

After you select the options shown in Figure 6-4, click OK in successive dialog boxes until you return to the Print System Manager window shown in Figure 6-1. This window should now show information about the new printer, and you can then print a test page by selecting Tests ⇨ Print ASCII test page from the menu.

Configuring a Printer in Caldera Open Linux

Be sure you are logged in as Root before starting to configure a printer in Caldera Open Linux. From the KDE desktop, click the K (main menu) in the lower-left corner, and select COAS ⇨ Peripherals ⇨ Printer. An introductory screen welcomes you to the COAS (Caldera Open Administration System) utility. Click OK to continue to the Printer Configuration dialog box, as shown in Figure 6-5.

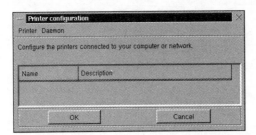

Figure 6-5
The Printer Configuration dialog box allows you to add printers and to stop and start the printer daemon.

Choose Printer ⇨ Add to open a pop-up box listing printers. Choose your printer from the list of printers. If the exact model of your printer is not listed, choose a printer compatible to yours. Some experimentation may be necessary to find a suitable driver for your printer. After selecting a printer, click OK to continue to the next dialog box and to choose a name for the printer, as shown in Figure 6-6.

Enter a name for the printer, or just click OK to accept the default name LP. The next dialog box to appear allows you to specify some attributes for the printer. Figure 6-7 shows the Printer Attributes dialog box where you can set the paper size and print resolution. You can see that the actual printer device is shown as /dev/lp0 in this dialog box.

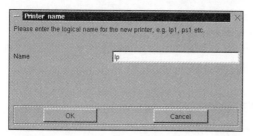

Figure 6-6
After selecting the printer, it is necessary to give it a name.

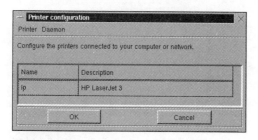

Figure 6-7
The Printer Configuration dialog box contains options for changing the paper size and print resolution.

When you've finished setting the printer's attributes, click OK to finish the setup. Figure 6-8 will appear with the printer you've just configured shown in the box.

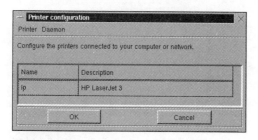

Figure 6-8
After configuring the printer, it is listed in the Printer Configuration dialog box.

To finish the printer configuration, click OK, and wait for the printer daemon to restart. After the daemon restarts, COAS informs you that the printer is now ready to be used. To be sure that the printer is configured properly, try to print from one of the KDE applications such as the Text Editor.

Configuring a Printer in SuSe Linux

**10 Min.
To Go**

To configure a printer in SuSe Linux, use the YaST2 (Yet another Setup Tool Two) program included with the distribution. The desktop installed by default with SuSe is KDE, so you can use this desktop to start YaST2. Click the K in the lower-left corner of the KDE desktop, and select SuSe ⇨ Administration ⇨ Configuration ⇨ Printer. The YaST2 printer configuration dialog box appears (see Figure 6-9) and tries to detect a printer automatically.

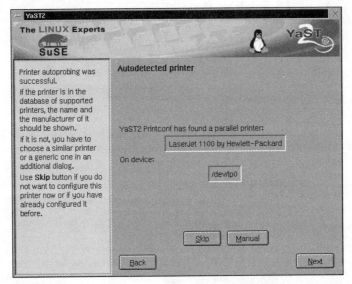

Figure 6-9
The YaST2 Printer Configuration tool will detect a printer connected to the PC automatically.

If a printer is found, its name and manufacturer, as well as the device location, will be shown. For printers not detected, you will need to choose one compatible to yours by clicking the Manual button and selecting one from the list. When you are satisfied with your choice, click Next to continue to the Printer's Settings screen shown in Figure 6-10.

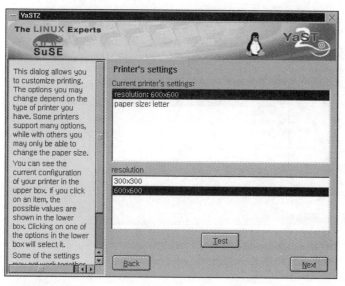

Figure 6-10
The Printer's Settings dialog box contains options for you to set the print resolution and choose a paper size.

The box near the top of the dialog box shows the printer's current settings. Select the setting you wish to change by clicking it in the top box, and then select a new setting from the choices listed in the bottom box. When you are satisfied with your choices, click the Test button, and then click OK in the dialog box that prompts you to check that the printer is ready.

If the page does not print or does not come out as expected, go back to the beginning of this section and repeat the steps to choose a different printer. If the page comes out as expected, click OK to proceed to the next dialog box shown in Figure 6-11.

After you have successfully configured a printer, it will be listed in the box titled Printers Added in This Session. If no printers were configured, this box gives you another opportunity to add one by choosing it from the bottom list and clicking Add. Clicking Finish completes the printer-configuration process. YaST2 will notify you that the configuration has been saved and that the printer is now ready for use.

Done!

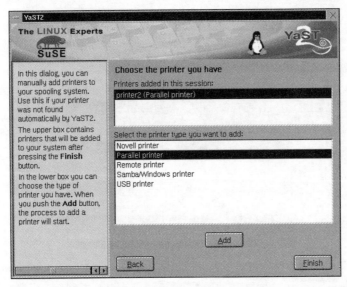

Figure 6-11
This dialog box shows the printers you have configured.

REVIEW

In this session, you learned to determine if Linux recognizes the parallel port on your PC. You learned a little about printer languages compatible with Linux. You also learned to configure a printer in three different Linux distributions: Red Hat, Caldera Open, and SuSe.

QUIZ YOURSELF

1. How do you start the utility program that enables you to configure printers in Red Hat Linux? (See "Configuring a Printer in Red Hat Linux.")

2. What does it mean to "fix stair-stepping text"? (See "Configuring a Printer in Red Hat Linux.")

3. How do you start the utility program that enables you to configure printers in Caldera? (See "Configuring a Printer in Caldera Open Linux.")

4. How do you start the utility program that enables you to configure printers in SuSe? (See "Configuring a Printer in SuSe Linux.")

5. What is a GDI printer, and will it work in Linux? (See "Linux Printing Basics.")

Linux File and Directory Structure

Session Checklist

✔ Understanding the Linux file system

✔ Using the GNOME file manager

✔ Navigating and manipulating files and directories with Linux commands

I n session 4, you learned to log in, log out, and shut down your Linux system. This session shows you how to work with files and directories. The session starts with a quick introduction to the Linux file system. It then shows you how to use the GNOME file manager and several Linux commands to work with files and directories.

**30 Min.
To Go**

Understanding the Linux File System

Like any other operating system, Linux organizes information in files and directories. The files are, in turn, contained in directories. A *directory* is a special file that can contain other files and directories, giving rise to a hierarchical structure. This hierarchical organization of files is called the *file system*.

The Linux file system provides a unified model of all storage in the system. The file system has a single root directory, indicated by a forward slash (/). Then there is a hierarchy of files and directories. Parts of the file system can reside on different physical media such as a hard disk, floppy disk, and CD-ROM. Figure 7-1 illustrates the concept of the Linux file system and how it spans multiple physical devices.

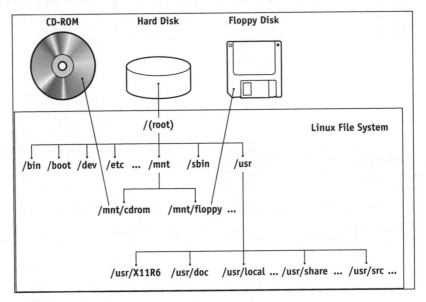

Figure 7-1
The Linux file system provides a unified view of storage that may span multiple drives.

If you are familiar with MS-DOS or Windows 95/98/NT/2000, note that there is no concept of a drive letter in UNIX. Also, filenames do not have a strict 8.3 name-extension format. (The term *8.3 filename* comes from the use of an eight-character name and three-character extension in MS-DOS.) In Linux, you can have long filenames (up to 256 characters), and filenames are case-sensitive. Often, UNIX filenames have multiple extensions such as sample.tar.Z. Here are some UNIX filenames: index.html, Makefile, kernel-2.2.15-2.5.0.i686.rpm, .bash_profile, and httpd_src.tar.gz.

To locate a file, you need more than just the file's name; you also need information about the directory hierarchy. The term *pathname* refers to the complete specification necessary to locate a file — the complete hierarchy of directories leading to the file — and the filename. Figure 7-2 shows a typical Linux pathname for a file.

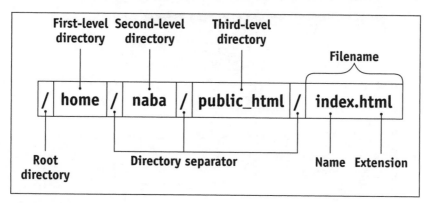

Figure 7-2
A typical Linux pathname

As you can see from Figure 7-2, a Linux pathname consists of the following parts:

1. The root directory, indicated by a forward slash (/) character

2. The directory hierarchy, with each directory name separated from the previous one by a forward slash (/) character; a / appears after the last directory name

3. The filename, with a name and one or more optional extensions

Now that you know the basics of the Linux file system, you can explore the file system. You can access the files and directories in two ways:

- By using a graphical file manager in the GNOME or KDE desktop
- By typing appropriate Linux commands in a terminal window or a text console

This session covers both the graphical file manager and the Linux commands. The graphical file manager is similar to Windows Explorer and is intuitive to use. Now we'll spend a few minutes exploring the file system by using the GNOME file manager. (The KDE file manager works in a similar manner, so I don't cover it here.)

Using the GNOME File Manager

After you log into your Linux system from the graphical login screen, you can view your home directory with the GNOME file manager by double-clicking on the file folder icon on the desktop. Figure 7-3 shows the initial display of your home directory.

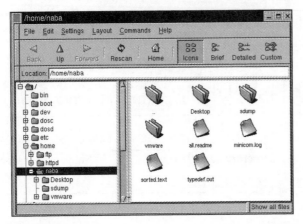

Figure 7-3
My home directory, as it appears in the GNOME file manager

Viewing files

The GNOME file manager's window is vertically divided into two panes. The left side shows a tree view of the file system in a scrolling window; the right side shows the files and directories in the currently selected directory with icons. As you can see from the tree view, Figure 7-3 shows the content of the /home/naba directory. The title bar shows the name of the currently selected directory.

If you have used Windows Explorer, you can use the GNOME file manager in a similar manner. To view the contents of another directory, first locate the directory in the tree view. For example, to view the /etc/X11 directory, click the plus sign (+) next to the etc directory. This causes the file manager to display the subdirectories in etc and to change that plus sign to a minus sign. Now click the X11 directory. The right-hand side of the window now shows the contents of the /etc/X11 directory.

The GNOME file manager displays the contents of the selected directory by using icons. Each directory appears as a folder with the name of the directory shown underneath the folder icon. Different files have different icons. Ordinary files appear as sheets of paper. Directories appear as folders.

The GNOME file manager window has the usual menu bar and a toolbar. Notice that, in Figure 7-3, the toolbar button labeled Icons is pressed. That means the directory contents are displayed using large icons. Click the Brief button; this causes the file manager to display the contents by using smaller icons in a list format.

To view more information about each file, click the Detailed button on the toolbar. The file manager now displays the size of each file or directory and the time when each was last modified. The detailed view shows the directory's contents in a tabular form with three columns labeled Name, Size, and MTime. If you click any of the information titles — Name, Size, or MTime — along the top of the detailed view, the file manager sorts the list according to the information. For example, click the MTime information title. The file manager now displays the list of files and directories sorted according to the most recent time of modification, or the MTime. Clicking the Name information title sorts the files and directories alphabetically. This feature works in the Brief and Custom view as well.

Finally, you can view the file permissions by clicking the Custom button. The file manager then displays the icons, filenames, sizes, and file permissions.

For now, ignore the meaning of the permissions. You learn about them in the next section when I discuss the Linux commands that navigate the file system.

Performing tasks

**20 Min.
To Go**

In addition to moving around the file system and viewing contents of directories, you can use the file manager to perform tasks such as moving a file from one directory to another and deleting a file. I don't show you each and every step, but you can take a few moments to try the following tasks:

- To move a file to a different directory, drag and drop the file's icon on the directory where you want the file.

- To copy a file to a new location, select the file's icon and then select File ⇨ Copy. You may also right-click the mouse on the file's icon and select Copy from the pop-up menu. A dialog box prompts you for the name of the directory to which the file should be copied.

- To delete a file or directory, right-click the icon, and select Delete from the pop-up menu. A dialog box asks you to confirm if you really want to delete the file or directory. You can click Yes to delete the selected item or No to cancel the operation.

- To rename a file or a directory, click the name in the Icon view (see Figure 7-3). Then you can type the new name or edit the name.

- To create a new directory, right-click in an empty area of the right-hand window, and select New Directory from the pop-up menu. A dialog box prompts you for the name of the new directory.

- To find files, select Commands ⇨ Find Files from the menu bar. A dialog box prompts you for what you want to find and where to start the search. After you enter this information, click OK to start the search. The results of the search appear in a new window.

Using Linux Commands to Navigate and Manipulate Files and Directories

Although the graphical file managers are easy to use, you can employ them only if you have a graphical login. Sometimes you may not have a graphical environment in which to run a graphical file manager. For example, you might be logged in through a text terminal, or X might not work on your system. In these situations, you have to rely on Linux commands to work with files and directories. The nice part is that you can always use Linux commands — even in the graphical environment. All you have to do is open a terminal window and type the Linux commands. Click the terminal icon in the GNOME panel to start a terminal emulation program that displays a terminal window.

Directory navigation

In Linux, your home directory is /root when you log in as root. For other users, the home directory is usually in the /home directory. My home directory (when I log in as naba) is /home/naba. This information is stored in the /etc/passwd file. By default, besides the super user, only you have permission to save files in your home directory, and only you can create subdirectories in your home directory to further organize your files.

Linux supports the concept of a *current directory*, which is the directory in which all file and directory commands operate. After you log in, for example, your current directory is the home directory. To see the current directory from the terminal window, type the pwd command.

To change the current directory, use the cd command. To change the current directory to /usr/doc, type the following:

```
cd /usr/share/doc
```

Then, to change the directory to the bash-2.04 subdirectory in /usr/share/doc, type this command:

```
cd bash-2.04
```

Now, if you use the pwd command, that command shows /usr/share/doc/bash-2.04 as the current directory. Therefore, you can refer to a directory's name in two ways:

- An absolute pathname (such as /usr/share/doc) that specifies the exact directory in the directory tree

- A relative directory name (such as `bash-2.04`, which represents the `bash-2.04` subdirectory of the current directory)

If you type `cd bash-2.04` in `/usr/share/doc`, the current directory changes to `/usr/share/doc/bash-2.04`. However, the same command in `/home/naba` tries to change the current directory to `/home/naba/bash-2.04`, which probably does not exist. Incidentally, typing the `cd` command without any arguments changes the current directory to your home directory.

 You can use a shortcut to refer to any user's home directory. Prefix a user's login name with a tilde (~) to refer to that user's home directory. Therefore, `~naba` refers to the home directory of the user `naba`, and `~root` refers to the home directory of the root user. If your system has a user with the login name `emily`, you can type `cd ~emily` to change to Emily's home directory.

The directory names . and .. have special meanings. A single period (.) indicates the current directory, whereas two periods (..) indicate the parent directory. If the current directory is `/usr/share/doc`, for example, you can change the current directory to `/usr/share` by typing this command:

```
cd ..
```

Essentially, this command takes you up one level in the file system hierarchy.

Directory listings and permissions

As you move around the Linux directories, you may want to know the contents of a directory. You can get a directory listing by using the `ls` command. By default, the `ls` command — without any options — displays the contents of the current directory in a compact, multicolumn format. For example, type the following commands to see the contents of the `/etc/X11` directory. (Type the commands shown in boldface; I omitted the command prompts from the listing.)

```
cd /etc/X11
ls
X  XF86Config-4  applnk  gdm  lbxproxy  proxymngr  twm  xinit
xsm  XF86Config  Xmodmap  fs  kdm  prefdm  rstart  xdm  xserver
```

From this listing, you cannot tell whether an entry is a file or a directory. To distinguish the directories from the files, use the `-F` option with `ls` as follows:

```
ls -F
X@              Xmodmap  gdm/        prefdm*    twm/    xserver/
```

```
XF86Config    applnk/   kdm/        proxymngr/   xdm/      xsm/
XF86Config-4  fs/       lbxproxy/   rstart/      xinit/
```

Now the directory names have a slash (/) appended to them. Plain filenames appear as is. The at sign (@) appended to the first filename indicates that that file is actually a link to another file (in other words, this filename simply refers to another file). An asterisk (*) is appended to executable files (for example, the prefdm file in the listing).

You can see even more detailed information about the files and directories with the -1 option.

```
ls -1
```

For the /etc/X11 directory, a typical output from ls -1 looks like the following:

```
total 76
lrwxrwxrwx  1 root    root     24 Jul 31 20:32 X -> /usr/X11R6/bin/XF86_SVGA
-rw-r--r--  1 root    root  14549 Jul 31 20:59 XF86Config
-rw-r--r--  1 root    root   1545 Jul 31 20:32 XF86Config-4
-rw-r--r--  1 root    root    491 Jul 14 14:46 Xmodmap
drwxr-xr-x  9 root    root   4096 Jul 31 15:29 applnk
```

This listing shows considerable information about each directory entry — which can be a file or another directory. Looking at a line from the right column to the left, you see that the rightmost column shows the name of the directory entry. The date and time before the name show when the last modifications to that file were made. Before the date and time is the size of the file, in bytes.

The file's group and owner appear to the left of the column that shows the file's size. The next number to the left indicates the number of links to the file. (A *link* is like a shortcut in Windows.) Finally, the leftmost column shows the file's *permission settings*, which determine who can read, write, or execute the file. The first letter of the permission setting has one of the following special meanings:

- If the first letter is 1, the file is a symbolic link to another file.
- If the first letter is d, the file is a directory.
- If the first letter is a dash (-), the file is a normal file.
- If the first letter is b, the file represents a block device such as a disk drive.
- If the first letter is c, the file represents a character device such as a serial port or a terminal.

After the first letter, the leftmost column shows a sequence of nine characters that appears as rwxrwxrwx when each letter is present. Each letter indicates a specific permission: read (r), write (w), and execute (x). A hyphen in place of a letter indicates no permission for a specific operation on the file. Thus, the string rw- means the owner has read and write permission, but not execute permission. Think of these nine letters as three groups of three letters (rwx), interpreted as follows:

- The leftmost group of rwx controls the read, write, and execute permission of the file's owner.

- The middle three rwx letters control the read, write, and execute permission of any user belonging to that file's group.

- The rightmost group of rwx letters controls the read, write, and execute permission of all other users (collectively referred to as the *world*).

Thus, a file with the permission setting rwx------ is accessible only to the file's owner. Meanwhile, the permission setting rwxr--r-- makes the file readable by the world.

Each of the three groups of letters is assigned a number value. The r is 4, the w is 2, and the x is 1. The chmod command uses these numbers to change file permissions. To set full permissions for yourself, set the first number to seven. To set full permissions to everyone, set all numbers to seven. To deny permission, set the number to zero. Following are some examples showing the command and the results.

```
chmod 700 filename     rwx
chmod 777 filename     rwxrwxrwx
chmod 644 filename     rw r  r
chmod 000 filename
```

Typically, executable programs (including shell programs) have execute permission. However, for directories, the execute permission is equivalent to a use permission — a user must have execute permission on a directory to open and read the contents of the directory.

An interesting feature of the ls command is the fact that it does not list any file whose name begins with a period. To see these files, you must use the ls command with the -a option as follows:

```
ls -a
```

**10 Min.
To Go**

File manipulation

You often may copy files from one directory to another. Use the cp command to perform this task. The cp command makes a new copy of a file and leaves the original intact. To copy the file /usr/X11R6/lib/X11/xinit/Xclients to the Xclients.sample file in the current directory (such as your home directory), type the following:

```
cp /usr/X11R6/lib/X11/xinit/Xclients Xclients.sample
```

If you want to copy a file to the current directory and retain the same name, use a period (.) as the second argument of the cp command. Thus, the following command copies the XF86Config file from the /etc/X11 directory to the current directory (denoted by a single period):

```
cp /etc/X11/XF86Config .
```

Another Linux command, mv, moves a file to a new location. The original copy is gone, and a new copy appears at the specified destination. You can use mv to rename a file. If you want to change the name of today.list to old.list, use the mv command as follows:

```
mv today.list old.list
```

On the other hand, you can move the today.list file to a subdirectory named saved with this command:

```
mv today.list saved
```

Another common file operation is deleting a file. Use the rm command to delete a file named old.list, for example, by typing the following command:

```
rm old.list
```

Be careful with the rm **command, particularly when you log in as** root**. Inadvertently using a wildcard with** rm **makes deleting files very easy.**

In addition to copying, renaming, and deleting files, you may want to view a file's contents. Use the more command to look at a text file one page at a time. To view the file /etc/X11/XF86Config-4, for example, use this command:

```
more /etc/X11/XF86Config-4
```

The more command pauses after each page, so you have to press the Spacebar to move to the next page. Press Enter to move forward one line at a time in the file. To move to the previous page, press b.

Another useful Linux command for file viewing is less. (The name is a play on words because less does more than more.)

Directory manipulation

To organize files in your home directory, you have to create new directories. Use the mkdir command to create a directory. For example, to create a directory named images in the current directory, type the following:

```
mkdir images
```

After you create the directory, you can use the cd images command to change to that directory. When you no longer need a directory, use the rmdir command to delete it. You can delete a directory only when the directory is empty.

File and directory finder

Finally, I want to introduce you to the find command because it's very useful for locating files (and directories) that meet specified search criteria. The Linux version of the find command comes from GNU, and it has more extensive options than the standard UNIX version. I show the syntax for the standard UNIX find command, however, because that syntax works in Linux and you can use the same format on other UNIX systems.

Suppose you want to find any file or directory with a name that starts with gnome. You can use find to perform this search, as follows:

```
find / -name "gnome*" -print
```

This command tells find to start at the root directory (/), look for filenames that match gnome*, and display the full pathname of any matching file.

You can use variations of this simple form of find to locate a file in any directory (as well as subdirectories in the directory). If you forget where in your home directory you stored all files named report* (names that start with the string report), you can search for the files by using the following command:

```
find ~ -name "report*" -print
```

When you become comfortable with this syntax of find, you can use other options of find. For example, to find only specific types of files (such as directories), use the -type option. The following command displays all top-level directory names in your Linux system:

```
find / -type d -maxdepth 1 -print
```

Done!

The preceding example represents using the simple form of the find command. You probably do not have to use the complex forms of find in a typical Linux system, but you can look up the rest of the find options by using this command:

    man find

REVIEW

This session began with a brief introduction to the Linux file system and discussed how files are named. Then you used the GNOME file manager to navigate the file system and look at different views of directories. You also performed some basic operations such as copying files, deleting files, and creating new directories. Next, you learned a number of Linux commands for navigating the file system and manipulating files and directories.

QUIZ YOURSELF

---

1. What is a *pathname*? (See "Understanding the Linux File System.")
2. In the GNOME file manager, how do you sort the list of files and directories alphabetically? (See "Using the GNOME File Manager.")
3. What Linux command do you use to change the current directory to your home directory? (See "Directory Navigation.")
4. What option can you use with the ls command to view all files and see the directory names listed with a / suffix? (See "Directory Listings and Permissions.")
5. What Linux command finds all files named COPYING starting in the /usr/doc directory? (See "File and Directory Finder.")

The Command Shell

Session Checklist

✔ Getting started with the Bash shell

✔ Using the Bash shell

30 Min.
To Go

As discussed in Session 7, unfortunately you can't do everything from a graphical environment such as GNOME or KDE. In such cases, you have to use Linux commands to accomplish specific tasks. Session 7 introduced you to some of the Linux commands you can use from a text terminal to manipulate files and directories. This session introduces you to the Bash shell — the default command interpreter in Linux. Here you learn some important features of how the shell executes commands.

Getting Started with the Bash Shell

If you have used MS-DOS, you may be familiar with the DOS command interpreter. That program (named COMMAND.COM) displays the infamous C:\> prompt. (In Windows, you can see this prompt in an MS-DOS command window.) Linux provides a command interpreter that resembles the DOS command interpreter, but, as you might expect, it has a lot more capabilities than the DOS command interpreter. The Linux command interpreter is referred to as a *shell*.

The default Linux shell is called *bash*, and its program is named /bin/bash (found in the /bin directory). When you open a terminal window from the GNOME or KDE desktop or log in at a text console, the bash shell prompts you for commands. When you type a command, the shell executes that command.

In addition to the standard Linux commands, bash can execute any program stored in an executable file. bash can also execute a shell script, which is a text file that contains one or more commands.

In the minutes ahead, you can try out various features of the bash shell, ranging from the general command syntax to the basics of shell programming. If you haven't already done so, go ahead and open a terminal window so you can use the shell.

Using the Bash Shell

Because a shell interprets what you type, it is important to know how the shell processes the text you enter. All shell commands have this general format:

```
command option1 option2 ... optionN
```

A single line of command is commonly referred to as a *command line*. On a command line, you enter a command followed by one or more options (or *arguments*) known as *command-line options* (or *command-line arguments*).

One basic rule is that you have to use a space or a tab to separate the command from the options. You also must separate options with a space or a tab. If you want to use an option that contains embedded spaces, you have to put that option inside quotation marks. For example, to search for my name in the password file, I enter the following grep command (grep searches for text in files):

```
grep "Naba Barkakati" /etc/passwd
```

When grep prints the line with my name, it looks like this:

```
naba:x:500:500:Naba Barkakati:/home/naba:/bin/bash
```

If you create a user account in your name, go ahead and type the grep command with your name as an argument.

In the output from the grep command, you can see the name of the shell (/bin/bash) following the last colon (:).

The number and the format of the command-line options, of course, depend on the actual command. When you learn more about the commands, you see that the command-line options controlling the behavior of a command usually take the form -*X*, in which *X* is a single character.

Because various GNU tools and utilities implement most Linux commands, you should know that GNU command-line options begin with two dashes followed by a descriptive word. Thus, the GNU options take the form --xxxx, in which xxxx is a word denoting the option. For example, the GNU ls --all **command shows all directory entries, including those that begin with a period (.). This is the same as the** ls -a **command in all UNIX systems.**

If a command is too long to fit on a single line, you can press the backslash (\) key, followed by Enter. Then, continue entering the command on the next line. For example, type the following command (press Enter after each line):

```
cat \
/etc/passwd
```

The cat command then displays the contents of the /etc/passwd file.

You can concatenate several shorter commands on a single line; just use the semicolon (;) as a separator between the commands. For example, the following command

```
cd; ls -F
```

changes the current directory to your home directory and then lists the contents of that directory.

Combining commands

Linux follows the UNIX philosophy of giving the user a toolbox of many simple commands. You can, however, combine these simple commands to create more sophisticated commands. Suppose you want to find out whether a device file named sbpcd resides in your system's /dev directory because some documentation tells you that for a Sound Blaster Pro CD-ROM drive, you need that device file. You can use the command ls /dev to get a directory listing of the /dev directory and to see whether anything that contains sbpcd appears in the listing. Unfortunately, the /dev directory has a great many entries, and it may be difficult to locate any item that has sbpcd in its name. You can, however, combine the ls command with grep and come up with a command that does exactly what you want:

```
ls /dev | grep sbpcd
```

The shell sends the output of the ls command (the directory listing) to the grep command, which searches for the string sbpcd. That vertical bar (|) is known as a *pipe* because it acts as a conduit between the two programs; the output of the first command becomes the input of the second one.

 Most Linux commands are designed in a way that enables the output of one command to feed into the input of another. To do this, simply concatenate the commands, placing pipes between them.

Redirecting command input and output

**20 Min.
To Go**

Linux commands designed to work together have a common feature — they always read from the *standard input* (usually the keyboard) and write to the *standard output* (usually the screen). Error messages are sent to the *standard error* (usually the screen). These three devices often are referred to as *stdin*, *stdout*, and *stderr*, respectively.

If you want a command to read from a file, you can redirect the standard input to come from that file. Similarly, to save the output of a command in a file, redirect the standard output to a file. These features of the shell are called *input* and *output redirection,* or *I/O redirection*.

For example, type cd to change to your home directory, and then type the following command:

```
grep typedef /usr/include/* > typedef.out
```

This command searches through all files in the /usr/include directory for the occurrence of the string typedef and then saves the output in a file called type-def.out. As this command shows, the greater than sign (>) redirects stdout to a file.

This command also illustrates another feature of bash. When you use an asterisk (*), bash replaces the asterisk with a list of all the filenames in the specified directory. Thus, /usr/include/* means all the files in the /usr/include directory.

You can also redirect stdin so that a command reads from a file instead of the keyboard. For example, type the following command:

```
sort < /etc/passwd
```

This should display a sorted list of the lines in the /etc/passwd file. In this case, the less than sign (<) redirects stdin so the sort command reads its input from the /etc/passwd file.

Letting bash complete your commands

Many commands take a filename as an argument. To browse through a file named /etc/X11/XF86Config, for example, type the following command:

```
more /etc/X11/XF86Config
```

This command displays the file /etc/X11/XF86Config one screen at a time. For the commands that take a filename as an argument, bash includes a feature that enables you to type short filenames. All you have to type is the bare minimum — just the first few characters — to identify the file uniquely in its directory.

To see an example, type more /etc/X11/XF, but don't press Enter; press Tab instead. bash automatically completes the filename so that the command becomes more /etc/X11/XF86Config. Now press Enter to run the command.

Using wildcard characters

Another way to avoid typing too many filenames is to use *wildcards* — special characters, such as the asterisk (*) and question mark (?), that match zero or more characters in a string. If you are familiar with MS-DOS, you may use commands such as COPY *.* A: to copy all files from the current directory to the A: drive. Bash accepts similar wildcards in filenames. In fact, bash provides many more wildcard options than MS-DOS does.

Bash supports three types of wildcards:

- The asterisk (*) character matches zero or more characters in a filename. Therefore, * denotes all files in a directory.

- The question mark (?) matches any single character.

- A set of characters in brackets matches any single character from that set. The string [xX]*, for example, matches any filename that starts with x or X.

Wildcards are handy when you want to perform a task on a group of files. To copy all the files from a directory named /mnt/cdrom to the current directory, for example, type the following:

```
cp /mnt/cdrom/* .
```

Bash replaces the wildcard character * with the names of all the files in the /mnt/cdrom directory. The period at the end of the command represents the current directory.

You can use the asterisk with other parts of a filename to select a more specific group of files. Suppose you want to use the grep command to search for the string typedef struct in all files of the /usr/include directory that meet the following criteria:

- The filename starts with s.
- The filename ends with .h.

The wildcard specification s*.h denotes all filenames that meet these criteria. Thus, you can perform the search with the following command:

```
grep "typedef struct" /usr/include/s*.h
```

The string contains a space you want the grep command to find, so you have to enclose that string in quotation marks. This method ensures that Bash does not try to interpret each word in the string as a separate command-line argument.

Although the asterisk (*) matches any number of characters, the question mark (?) matches only a single character. Suppose you have four files — image1.pcx, image2.pcx, image3.pcx, and image4.pcx — in the current directory. To copy these files to the /mnt/floppy directory, use the following command:

```
cp image?.pcx /mnt/floppy
```

Bash replaces the single question mark with any single character and copies the four files to /mnt.

The third wildcard format — [...] — matches a single character from a specific set. You may want to combine this format with other wildcards to narrow down the matching filenames to a smaller set. To see a list of all filenames in the /etc/X11/xdm directory that start with x or X, type the following command:

```
ls /etc/X11/xdm/[xX]*
```

 If bash does not find any filenames matching the [...] wildcard format when expanding it, bash leaves the wildcard specification intact.

Looking at the command history

To make it easy for you to repeat long commands, bash stores up to 500 old commands. Essentially, bash maintains a *command history* (a list of old commands). To see the command history, type history. Bash displays a numbered list of the old commands, including those that you entered during previous logins. That list may resemble the following:

```
1  cd
2  ls -a
3  more /etc/X11/XF86Config
4  history
```

If the command list is too long, you may choose to see only the last few commands. To see the last 10 commands only, type this command:

```
history 10
```

To repeat a command from the list that the `history` command shows, simply type an exclamation point (!), followed by that command's number. To repeat command number 3, type !3.

You also can repeat an old command without knowing its command number. Suppose you typed `more /usr/lib/X11/xdm/xdm-config` a while ago, and now you want to look at that file again. To repeat the previous `more` command, type the following:

```
!more
```

Often, you may want to repeat the last command you typed — perhaps with a slight change. For example, perhaps you displayed the contents of the directory by using the `ls -l` command. To repeat that command, type two exclamation points as follows:

```
!!
```

Sometimes, you may want to repeat the previous command but add extra arguments to it. Suppose that `ls -l` shows too many files. Simply repeat that command, but pipe the output through the `more` command as follows:

```
!! | more
```

Bash replaces the two exclamation points with the previous command and then appends | more to that command.

An easy way to recall previous commands is to press the up arrow key, which causes bash to go backward in the list of commands. To move forward in the command history, press the down arrow key.

Using aliases for commands

To see the benefit of aliases, type the following command:

```
alias goboot='cd /usr/src/linux/arch/i386/boot'
```

This defines goboot as an *alias* — another name — for the text that appears within the single quotes. That text is a command to change the current directory to /usr/src/linux/arch/i386/boot.

Now that you've defined the alias, type the following at the bash prompt:

```
goboot
```

Now type pwd to confirm that the current directory is indeed /usr/src/linux/arch/i386/boot.

As you can see, an alias simply is an alternative (and usually shorter) name for a lengthy command. bash replaces the alias with its definition and performs the equivalent command.

If you no longer need an alias, use the unalias command to remove the alias. For example, if you no longer want to use the goboot alias, type:

```
unalias goboot
```

After this step, typing goboot causes you to get an error message like this:

```
bash: goboot: command not found
```

Many users use the alias feature to give more familiar names to common commands. If you are a DOS user and you use the md command to create a directory, you can simply define md as an alias for mkdir (the Linux command that creates a new directory). You do this as follows:

```
alias md=mkdir
```

Now, you can type **md *dirname*** to create a new directory named *dirname*.

Another good use of an alias is to redefine a dangerous command, such as rm, to make it safer. By default, the rm command deletes one or more specified files. If you type rm * by mistake, rm deletes all files in your current directory. I learned this the hard way one day when I wanted to delete all files that ended with .xwd. (These files contained old screen images I no longer needed.) I intended to type rm *.xwd, but somehow I ended up typing rm * .xwd. I got the following message:

```
rm: .xwd: No such file or directory
```

At first, I was puzzled by the message, so I typed ls to see the directory's contents again. When the listing showed nothing, I realized that I had an extra space between the * and .xwd. All the files in that directory, of course, were gone forever.

The rm **command provides the** -i **option, which asks for confirmation before deleting a file. To make that option a default, add the following** alias **definition to the** .bash_profile **file in your home directory:**

```
alias rm='rm -i'
```

From now on, when you use rm **to delete a file, the command first asks for confirmation as follows:**

```
rm .bash_profile
rm: remove `.bash_profile'? n
```

Press y to delete the file; otherwise, press n.

Running commands in the background

**10 Min.
To Go**

When you use MS-DOS, you have no choice but to wait for each command to complete before you enter the next command. (You can type ahead a bit, but the MS-DOS system can hold only a few characters in its internal buffer.) Linux, however, can handle multiple tasks simultaneously. The only problem you may have is that the terminal or console is tied up until a command completes.

If you work in a terminal window and a command takes too long to complete, you can open another terminal window and continue to enter other commands. If you work in text mode, however, and a command seems to take too long, you need some other way to access your system.

You can start a lengthy command *in the background*, which means that the shell starts the process corresponding to a command and immediately returns to accept more commands. The shell does not wait for the command to complete; the command runs as a distinct process in the background. To start a process in the background, you simply place an ampersand (&) at the end of a command line.

For example, when I want to search the entire file system for a file by using the find command, I typically run that command in the background and send the output to a file. To try out the find command in the background, type cd to change to your home directory, and then type the following command:

```
find / -name "README*.*" -print > all.readme &
```

You should immediately get a bash prompt. You can now go on with other commands. When the find command finishes, the search results should appear in the file all.readme in your home directory.

If a command (that you did not run in the background) seems to be taking a long time, press Ctrl+Z to stop it. Then type bg **to put that process in the background.**

Using virtual consoles

Linux comes with a number of *virtual consoles*. Even though your Linux system only has one physical terminal or console (the combination of monitor and keyboard is called the *terminal* or *console*), it gives you the appearance of having multiple consoles. From the graphical X screen (the GNOME or KDE desktop), press Ctrl+Alt+F1 to get to the first virtual console; press Ctrl+Alt+F2 for the second one, and so on. Each of these virtual consoles is a text screen where you can log in and type Linux commands to perform various tasks.

Go ahead and press Ctrl+Alt+F2 to switch to the second virtual console. Then log in and try some Linux commands. You can log out by typing **exit** at the bash prompt. To get back to the graphical X display, press Ctrl+Alt+F7.

Done!

REVIEW

In this session, you tried out many key features of the bash shell — the Linux command interpreter. Among other things, you learned the syntax of commands, how you can combine commands, how to run commands in the background, and how to use aliases.

QUIZ YOURSELF

1. What is the shell, and what does it do? (See "Using the Bash Shell.")

2. How would you continue a long command on multiple lines? (See "Combining Commands.")

3. How do you save the output of a Linux command in a file? (See "Redirecting Command Input and Output.")

4. What are aliases, and why would you use them? (See "Using Aliases for Commands.")

5. What keys would you press to get the second virtual console? (See "Using Virtual Consoles.")

Linux Commands

Session Checklist

✔ Reviewing commands you've learned thus far

✔ Exploring several categories of Linux commands: managing processes, setting date and time, processing files, and maintaining the file system

**30 Min.
To Go**

I n this session, you review the commands you already learned about in previous sessions, and you also learn about several new categories of Linux commands. However, because of the large number of Linux commands, you cannot really explore each and every command in a half-hour session. You try out more commands in later sessions. To begin this session, log in at the graphical login screen, and open a terminal window. You can then type the commands in that login screen.

Reviewing Commands You've Learned Thus Far

You already tried quite a few Linux commands in previous sessions. Take a look at Table 9-1, and browse through the list. These are the commands you used in the previous sessions. To refresh your memory about what a command does, follow the instructions shown in the Description column of Table 9-1 to try out that command. For your convenience, I organize the commands in categories.

Table 9-1
Linux Commands You've Learned in Previous Sessions

Command Name	Description
Getting Online Help	
man	Displays online help information. Type man ls for help with the ls command.
Making Commands Easier	
Alias	Defines an abbreviation (shortcut) for a long command. Type alias alone to view all currently defined aliases. Type alias topdir='cd' and then type topdir to change the directory to the root directory (/).
unalias	Deletes an abbreviation defined by using alias. Type unalias topdir to undefine the topdir abbreviation.
Managing Files and Directories	
cd	Changes the current directory. Type cd /usr to change to the /usr directory.
chmod	Changes file permissions. Type chmod +x filename to make that file executable (replace *filename* with the name of an existing file).
chown	Changes the owner of a file. Type chown ownername filename to make the owner of the file. (Replace ownername and filename with the name of a person and file, respectively.)
cp	Copies files. Type cd to change the directory to your home directory. Then type cp /etc/X11/ XF86Config . to copy a file to your home directory.
ls	Displays the contents of a directory. Type ls -F to see the contents of the current directory.

Command Name	Description
mkdir	Creates a directory. Type cd to change to your home directory, and then type mkdir temp to create a directory named temp.
mv	Renames file as well as moves a file from one directory to another. Type mv filename1 filename2 to change a file's name (use an existing file's name for *filename1*).
rm	Deletes files. The syntax is rm *filename*. (Use with caution because the file gets deleted without a prompt for confirmation.)
Rmdir	Deletes directories. Type rmdir ~/temp to remove the directory named temp in your home directory (see the mkdir command).
Pwd	Displays the current directory. Type pwd to see the current directory name.
Finding Files	
Find	Finds files based on specified criteria such as name, size, and so on. Type find /usr -name "README*" -print to try this command.
Processing Files	
cat	Displays a file on standard output (can concatenate several files into one big file). Type cd to go to your home directory, and then type cat .bash_profile to see the contents of that file.
Grep	Searches for regular expressions within a text file. Type cd to go to your home directory, and then type grep BASH .b* to see the result of searching for the string BASH in some files.
more	Displays a text file one page at a time. Type more /etc/inittab to see the contents one page at a time. (Press the Spacebar to advance or type q to quit.)
Managing Processes	
Printenv	Displays the current environment variables. Type printenv to see the list of environment variables.

Continued

Table 9-1   *Continued*

Command Name	Description
ps	Checks for running processes. You can see programs that are running, resources the programs are using, and who is running them. Type ps lau to see a long listing showing all users and their names.
Managing Users	
adduser	Use this command to add a user to the system. Type adduser -d home_dir to add a user and a home directory. (The default is to name the home directory the same as the login name.) There are many options for this command. Type man adduser for more details.
passwd	Changes the password. Type passwd, and follow the prompts to change your password.
su	Becomes another user or root (when invoked without any argument). Type su, and enter the root password when prompted. Be careful what you do because now you are the super user. Type exit to return to normal user.

The following sections cover new commands (by category) not covered in the earlier sessions.

Commands for Managing Processes

**20 Min.
To Go**

Every time the shell acts on a command you type, it starts a *process*. The shell itself is a process, as are any scripts or programs the shell executes. You can use the ps command to see a list of processes. When you type ps x, for example, Bash shows you the current set of processes. Following is a partial output from the ps x command. (I also include the --cols 132 option to ensure that you can see each command in its entirety):

```
  PID TTY   STAT TIME COMMAND
    1 ?     S    0:05 init [5]
  325 ?     S    0:00 syslogd -m 0
  335 ?     S    0:00 klogd
```

```
480 ?    S    0:00 crond
511 ?    S    0:00 xinetd -reuse -pidfile /var/run/xinetd.pid
580 ?    S    0:00 sendmail: accepting connections
596 ?    S    0:00 gpm -t imps2
849 ?    S    0:01 /usr/bin/gnome-session
893 ?    S    0:00 gnome-smproxy --sm-client-id default0
901 ?    S    0:02 sawfish --sm-client-id=default2
967 ?    S    8:36 magicdev --sm-client-id=default12
985 ?    S    0:00 gnome-name-service
994 ?    S    0:01 panel --sm-client-id default7
1001 ?   S    0:00 gmc --nowindows --sm-client-id default8
21437 ?  S    0:00 gnome-terminal --use-factory --start-factory-server
21443?     S  0:00 gnome-pty-helper
21444 pts/1 S  0:00 bash
21455 pts/0 R  0:00 ps x --cols 132
```

In the output, the COMMAND column shows the commands that create the processes. This list shows the bash shell and the ps command as processes. Other processes include all the programs the shell starts when you log in at the graphical login screen and start a GNOME session. In particular, the list includes the sawfish (window manager) process and the gnome-terminal (terminal window) process.

The default ps x command does not provide all the processes running on a Linux system. What ps x shows are the commands you start either directly or indirectly through shell scripts that run automatically when you log in. To see the full complement of processes, use the a option of the ps command together with the x option as follows:

```
ps ax
```

If you study the output of the ps **command, you find that the first column has the heading PID and that it shows a number for each process.** *PID* **stands for** *process ID* **(identification), which is a sequential number the Linux kernel assigns. If you look through the output of the** ps ax **command, you should see that the** init **command is the first process; it has a PID or process number of 1. That's why** init **is referred to as the** *mother of all processes.*

Date and Time Commands

You can use the date command to display the current date and time or to set a new date and time. Type date at the shell prompt, and you get a result similar to the following:

```
Wed Aug 16 18:34:10 EDT 2000
```

You can also format the way you want the date or time to appear. For example, to view the date alone (without the current time), try the following command:

```
date +"%A %B %d %Y"
```

The result of this command will be similar to the following:

```
Wednesday August 16 2000
```

The format specification is in the form of a text string containing single letters with the percentage sign (%) prefix — similar to the way formats are specified in the C and C++ programming languages. In this example, the format characters mean the following:

%A   Displays the full name of the weekday

%B   Displays the full name of the month

%d   Displays the day of the month

%Y   Displays the year by using all four digits

To set the date, log in as root, and then use date -s followed by the date and time in the MMDDhhmmYYYY format in which each character is a digit. For example, to set the date and time to December 31, 2001 at 10:30 p.m., type:

```
date -s 123122302001
```

As you can see, the date and time specification has the following meaning:

MM   A two-digit number for the month (01 through 12)

DD   A two-digit number for the day of the month (01 through 31)

hh   A two-digit hour in 24-hour format (00 is midnight and 23 is 11:00 p.m.)

mm   A two-digit number for the minutes (00 through 59)

YYYY The 4-digit year (such as 2001)

The other interesting date-related command is cal. If you type cal without any options, it prints a calendar for the current month. If you type cal followed by a number, cal treats the number as the year and prints the calendar for that year. To view the calendar for a specific month in a specific year, provide the month number (1 = January, 2 = February, and so on) followed by the year. Thus, to view the calendar for January 2001, type cal 1 2001 to get the following:

```
      January 2001
Su Mo Tu We Th Fr Sa
       1  2  3  4  5  6
 7  8  9 10 11 12 13
14 15 16 17 18 19 20
21 22 23 24 25 26 27
28 29 30 31
```

**10 Min.
To Go**

Commands for Processing Files

You've already seen how to search through a text file with the grep command and how to view a text file one screen at a time with the more command. Linux includes many more utilities that work on files — mostly on text files, but some commands work on any file.

Counting characters, words, and lines in a text file

For example, you can use the wc command to display the character, word, and line count of a text file. Try the following:

wc /etc/inittab

This gives you this result:

```
    57      244     1756 /etc/inittab
```

which is the number of lines (57), words (244), and characters (1756) in the /etc/inittab file. If you simply want to see the number of lines in a file, use the -1 option like this:

wc -1 /etc/inittab

You will see this result:

```
    57 /etc/inittab
```

In this case, wc simply displays the line count.

If you don't specify a filename, the wc command expects input from the standard input. You can use the pipe feature of the shell to feed the output of another command to wc. This is handy sometimes. Suppose you want a rough count of the processes running on your system. You can get a list of all processes with the ps ax command; but instead of manually counting the lines, just pipe the output of ps to wc to get a rough count as follows:

```
ps ax | wc -l
```

This command returns:

```
61
```

This means the ps command produces 61 lines of output. Because the first line simply shows the headings for the tabular columns, you can estimate that there are about 60 processes running on your system. (Of course, this count probably includes the processes used to run the ps and wc commands, but who's counting?)

Sorting text files

You can sort the lines in a text file by using the sort command. To see how the sort command works, first type more /etc/passwd to see the current contents of the /etc/passwd file. Now type sort /etc/passwd to see the lines sorted alphabetically. If you want to sort a file and save the sorted version in another file, you have to use the bash shell's output redirection feature like this:

```
sort /etc/passwd > ~/sorted.text
```

This command sorts the lines in the /etc/passwd file and saves the output in a file named sorted.text in your home directory.

Splitting any file into several smaller files

The split command is handy when you want to copy a file to a floppy disk but the file is too large to fit on a single floppy. You can then use the split command to break the file into smaller files, each of which can fit on a floppy.

By default, split puts 1,000 lines into each file. The files are named by groups of letters such as aa, ab, ac, and so on. You can specify a prefix for the filenames. For example, to split a large file called hugefile.tar into smaller files that fit onto several high-density 3.5-inch floppy disks, use split as follows:

```
split -b 1440k hugefile.tar part.
```

This command splits the hugefile.tar file into 1440K chunks so that each can fit onto a floppy disk. The command creates files named part.aa, part.ab, part.ac, and so on.

To combine the split files back into a single file, use the `cat` command as follows:

```
cat part.?? > hugefile.tar
```

In this command line, each question mark matches a single character. Thus, the bash shell expands `part.??` to file names such as `part.aa`, `part.ab`, `part.ac`, and so on.

Commands for Maintaining the File System

Suppose you want to access the files on this book's companion CD-ROMs. To do so, you first have to mount the CD-ROM drive's file system on a specific directory in the Linux file system. To try the `mount` command, log in as root, insert a CD-ROM in the CD-ROM drive, and then type the following command:

```
mount /dev/cdrom /mnt/cdrom
```

You will see the following result:

```
mount: block device /dev/cdrom is write-protected, mounting read-only
```

This command mounts the file system on the device named `/dev/cdrom` (the CD-ROM) in the `/mnt/cdrom` directory (also called the *mount point*) in the Linux file system. The response from the `mount` command indicates that the CD-ROM is mounted as a read-only file system. After the `mount` command successfully completes its task, you can access the files in the CD-ROM by referring to the `/mnt/cdrom` directory as the top-level directory of the CD-ROM. In other words, to see the contents of the `RedHat` directory on the CD-ROM, type:

```
ls -F /mnt/cdrom/RedHat
```

You will see this result:

```
RPMS/   TRANS.TBL  base/
```

You can actually mount a device on any directory on the Linux file system. Essentially, the mount point does not have to be `/mnt/cdrom`; it can be any empty directory. For example, if you like to refer to the CD-ROM drive as `/cd`, first create the `/cd` directory with the `mkdir /cd` command, and then use the following `mount` command:

```
mount /dev/cdrom /cd
```

Before you try this command, you have to "unmount" the CD-ROM with the following umount command:

```
umount /dev/cdrom
```

Only then can you mount the CD-ROM again on another directory in the Linux file system.

I have shown you the longer syntax for the mount command in which you explicitly specify the device name and the mount point, but Linux contains a line in the /etc/fstab file that enables you to mount the CD-ROM through one of the following commands:

```
mount /mnt/cdrom
mount /dev/cdrom
```

It is customary to mount devices on directories in the /mnt directory. Linux comes with two predefined directories: /mnt/cdrom for mounting the CD-ROM and /mnt/floppy for mounting the floppy.

In addition to mount and umount, you should know two more commands — df and du — that enable you to check the disk space usage. These commands are simple to use. The df command shows you a summary of disk space usage for all mounted devices, as shown in this example:

```
Filesystem            1k-blocks       Used Available Use% Mounted on
/dev/hda2              2000236     1103852    794776  59% /
/dev/hda1              2096160     1833600    262560  88% /dosc
/dev/hdc                656560      656560         0 100% /mnt/cdrom
```

The output is a table that shows the device, the total kilobytes of storage, how much is being used, how much is available, the percentage being used, and the mount point. For example, on my system, the /dev/hda2 device (a disk partition) is mounted on the Linux file system's root directory (/). It has about 2GB of space, of which 1.1GB (or 59 percent) are used and 794MB are available. Similarly, you can see from the last line that the CD-ROM has about 656MB of storage in use.

The du command is useful for finding out how much space a directory takes up. For example, type the following command:

```
du /var/log
```

to view the contents of all the directories in the /var/log directory (containing various error logs):

```
4        /var/log/httpd
4        /var/log/news/OLD
```

```
8        /var/log/news
4        /var/log/vbox
4        /var/log/samba
4        /var/log/sa
120      /var/log
```

A number precedes each directory name — this number denotes the number of kilobytes of disk space the directory uses. Thus, the /var/log directory as a whole uses 120K disk space, whereas the /var/log/httpd subdirectory uses 4K. If you simply want the total disk space a directory uses (including all the files and subdirectories contained in that directory), use the -s option as follows:

```
du -s /var/log
```

You will get a result similar to this:

```
120      /var/log
```

Notice that the -s option causes du to print just the summary information for the /var/log directory.

Done!

REVIEW

You began this session by reviewing the Linux commands you encountered in previous sessions. Then you tried out a number of Linux commands in several important categories — managing processes, date and time, and file system maintenance.

QUIZ YOURSELF

1. How do you see a list of all currently defined aliases or shortcuts? (See "Reviewing Commands You've Learned Thus Far.")

2. How do you find the process ID (PID) of a process? (See "Commands for Managing Processes.")

3. What command do you use to print the calendar for the month of August 2001? (See "Date and Time Commands.")

4. How do you find out how many processes are currently running on your Linux system? (See "Counting Characters, Words, and Lines in a Text File.")

5. What do you have to do to access the files on this book's companion CD-ROMs? (See "Commands for Maintaining the File System.")

Linux Text Editors

Session Checklist

✔ Using the GUI text editors in GNOME and KDE

✔ Using the ed and vi text-mode text editors

30 Min.
_To Go_

I n this session, you learn to use text editors — the GUI editors and the ed and vi text-mode editors. Text editing is an important part of all operating systems because many system configuration files are text files. In Linux, you may have to create and edit a variety of text files, such as: system configuration files, including `/etc/fstab`, `/etc/hosts`, `/etc/inittab`, and `/etc/X11/XF86Config`; user files, such as `.newsrc` and `.bash_profile`; mail messages and news articles; shell script files; Perl and Tcl/Tk scripts; and C or C++ programs.

Using GUI Text Editors for Text Editing

Both of the Linux graphical desktops — GNOME and KDE — come with _GUI text editors_ (text editors that have graphical user interfaces).

To try the GNOME text editor, gEdit, select Main Menu ⇨ Programs ⇨ Applications ⇨ gEdit from the GNOME desktop. You can open a file by clicking the

Open button on the toolbar. This brings up the Open File dialog box. You can then change directories and select the file to edit by clicking the OK button.

The gEdit editor then loads the file in its window. You can open more than one file and move among them as you edit the files. Figure 10-1 shows a typical editing session with gEdit.

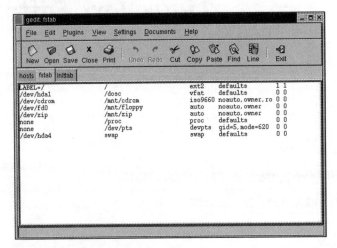

Figure 10-1
Editing several text files with gEdit

In this case, the editor has three files — hosts, fstab, and innittab (all from the /etc directory) — open for editing. The filenames appear as tabs below the toolbar of the editor's window. You can switch among the files by clicking the tabs with the filenames.

The rest of the text-editing steps are intuitive. To enter new text, click to position the cursor and begin typing. You can select text and then copy, cut, and paste it using the buttons on the toolbar above the text-editing area.

From the KDE desktop, you can start KEdit (the KDE text editor) by selecting K ⇨ Applications ⇨ Text Editor. To open a text file, select File ⇨ Open from the menu. A dialog box appears. From this dialog box, you can go to the appropriate directory, select the file to open, and click the OK button. The KDE text editor then opens the /etc/fstab file and displays its contents in the window.

Using ed and vi for Text Editing

All Linux systems come with two text-mode text editors:

- ed, a line-oriented text editor
- vi, a full-screen text editor that supports the command set of an earlier editor named ex

Although the graphical text editors are easy to use, ed and vi may be more cryptic than other — more graphical — text editors. You should learn the basic editing commands of ed and vi because sometimes these two may be the only editors available. When you run into a system problem and Linux refuses to boot from the hard disk, for example, you may have to boot from a floppy. In this case, you have to edit system files with the ed editor because that editor is small enough to fit on the floppy. As the next two sections demonstrate, learning the basic text-editing commands of ed and vi isn't hard.

Using ed

The ed text editor works with a *buffer* — an in-memory storage area where the actual text resides until you explicitly store the text in a file. Typically, you have to use ed only when you boot a minimal version of Linux (for example, from a boot floppy) and the system does not support full-screen mode. In all other situations, you can use the vi editor that works in a text-mode full-screen.

As you see in the following examples using the ed editor, you work in either command mode or text-input mode:

- *Command mode* is what you get by default. In this mode, anything you type is interpreted as a command. The ed text editor has a simple command set wherein each command consists of one or more characters.

- *Text-input mode* enables you to enter text into the buffer. You can enter input mode with the commands a (append), c (change), or i (insert). After entering lines of text, you can leave input mode by entering a period (.) on a blank line.

To practice editing a file, copy the /etc/fstab file to your home directory by using the following commands:

```
cd
cp /etc/fstab .
```

Now you should have a file named fstab in your home directory. Type the following command to begin editing a file in ed:

```
ed -p: fstab
```

You'll see a result like this:

```
608
:
```

This example uses the -p option to set the prompt to the colon character (:) and opens the fstab file (in the current directory, which should be your home directory) for editing. The ed editor opens the file, reports the number of characters in the file (608), displays the prompt (:), and waits for a command.

 When editing with ed, you may find it helpful to turn on a prompt character by using the -p option. Without the prompt, it's difficult to tell whether ed is in input mode or command mode.

After ed opens a file for editing, the current line is the last line of the file. To see the current line number (the *current line* is the line to which ed applies your command), use the .= command as follows:

```
:.=
```

to see a result similar to this:

```
8
```

This output tells you that the fstab file has eight lines. (Your system's /etc/fstab file may have a different number of lines, in which case you see a different number.)

You can use the 1,$p command to see all lines in a file, as the following example shows:

```
LABEL=/              /                  ext2     defaults            1 1
/dev/hda1            /dosc              vfat     defaults            0 0
/dev/cdrom           /mnt/cdrom         iso9660  noauto,owner,ro 0 0
/dev/fd0             /mnt/floppy        auto     noauto,owner        0 0
/dev/zip             /mnt/zip           auto     noauto,owner        0 0
none                 /proc              proc     defaults            0 0
none                 /dev/pts           devpts   gid=5,mode=620  0 0
/dev/hda4            swap               swap     defaults            0 0
:
```

To go to a specific line, type the line number:

```
:8
```

The editor responds by displaying a line such as this:

```
/dev/hda4            swap               swap     defaults            0 0
:
```

Suppose you want to delete the line that contains cdrom. To search for a string, type a slash (/) followed by the string you want to locate:

```
:/cdrom
```

The editor locates the line that contains the string and then displays it as follows. That line becomes the current line.

```
/dev/cdrom              /mnt/cdrom                iso9660 noauto.owner.ro 0 0
:
```

To delete the current line, use the d command as follows:

```
:d
:
```

To replace a string with another, use the s command. To replace cdrom with the string cd, for example, use this command:

```
:s/cdrom/cd/
:
```

To insert a line in front of the current line, use the i command:

```
:i
   (type the line you want to insert)
.  (type a single period to indicate you're done)
:
```

You can enter as many lines as you want. After the last line, enter a period (.) on a blank line. The period marks the end of text-input mode, and the editor switches to command mode. In this case, you can tell that ed has switched to command mode because you see the prompt (:).

When you are happy with the changes, you can write them to the file by using the w command. If you want to save the changes and exit, type wq to perform both steps at the same time:

```
:wq
```

The ed editor saves the changes in the file, displays the number of saved characters, and then exits.

```
632
```

If you want to quit the editor without saving any changes, use the Q command.

The sample session gives you an idea of how to use ed commands to perform the basic tasks of editing a text file. Table 10-1 lists some commonly used ed commands.

Table 10-1
Commonly Used ed Commands

Command	Meaning
!command	Executes a shell command (for example, !pwd shows the current directory)
$	Goes to last line in the buffer
%	Applies a command to all following lines in the buffer (for example, %p prints all lines)
+	Goes to next line
+n	Goes to n-th next line (n is a number)
,	Applies a command to all following lines in the buffer (for example, ,p prints all lines); similar to %
-	Goes to preceding line
-n	Goes to nth previous line (n is a number)
.	Refers to the current line in the buffer
/text/	Searches forward for the specified text
;	Refers to a range of line: current through last line in the buffer
=	Prints line number
?text?	Searches backward for the specified text
^	Goes to the preceding line; also see the - command
^n	Goes to nth previous line (where n is a number); also see the -n command
a	Appends after current line
c	Changes specified lines
d	Deletes specified lines
i	Inserts text before current line

Continued

Command	Meaning
n	Goes to line number *n*
newline	Displays next line and makes that line current
q	Quits editor
Q	Quits editor without saving changes
r *file*	Reads and inserts contents of file after the current line
s/*old*/*new*/	Replaces *old* string with *new*
u	Undoes the last command
W *file*	Appends contents of buffer to the end of the specified *file*
w *file*	Saves buffer in the specified *file* (if no file is named, saves in the default file — the file whose contents ed is editing)

Using vi

**20 Min.
To Go**

The vi editor is a full-screen text editor that enables you to view a file several lines at a time. Most UNIX systems, including Linux, come with vi. Therefore, if you learn the basic features of vi, you can edit text files on almost any UNIX system.

Like the ed editor, vi works with a buffer. When vi edits a file, it reads the file into a buffer — a block of memory — and enables you to change the text in the buffer. The vi editor also uses temporary files during editing, but the original file is not altered until you save the changes with a specific vi command.

Before you start a full-screen text editor such as vi, you have to set the TERM environment variable to the terminal type (such as vt100 or xterm). For example, type export TERM=vt100 to set the terminal type to VT100. The vi editor uses the terminal type to control the terminal in full-screen mode.

When you run X and a graphical user interface such as GNOME or KDE, you can use vi in a terminal window. The terminal window's terminal type is xterm. (To verify this, type echo $TERM at the command prompt.) When you start the terminal window, it automatically sets the TERM environment variable to xterm. Therefore, you should be able to use vi in an xterm window without explicitly setting the TERM variable.

To start the editor, use the vi name followed by an optional filename. You can provide other arguments besides the filename. However, most of the time vi starts with a filename as the only argument, as shown here:

```
vi /etc/hosts
```

Another common way to start vi is to jump to a specific line number right at startup. To begin editing at line 296 of the file /etc/X11/XF86Config, for example, use this command:

```
vi +296 /etc/X11/XF86Config
```

This way of starting vi is useful when you edit a source file after the compiler reports an error at a specific line number.

When you edit a file with vi, the editor loads the file into a buffer, displays the first few lines of the file in a full-screen window, and positions the cursor on the first line. When you type the command vi /etc/fstab in a terminal window, for example, you get a full-screen text window.

The last line shows information about the file, including the number of lines and the number of characters in the file. Later, this area functions as a command-entry area. The rest of the lines display the file. If the file contains fewer lines than the window, vi displays the empty lines with a tilde (~) in the first column.

The current line is marked by the cursor, which appears as a small black rectangle. The cursor appears on top of a character.

In vi, you work in one of three modes:

- *Visual command mode* is what you get by default. In this mode, anything you type is interpreted as a command that applies to the line containing the cursor. The vi commands are similar to the ed commands.

- *Colon command mode* enables you to read or write files, set vi options, and quit. All colon commands start with a colon (:). When you enter the colon, vi positions the cursor at the last line and enables you to type a command. The command takes effect when you press Enter.

- *Text input mode* enables you to enter text into the buffer. You can enter input mode with the command a (insert after cursor), A (append at end of line), or i (insert after cursor). After entering lines of text, you have to press Esc to leave input mode and re-enter visual command mode.

One problem with all these modes is that you cannot easily tell vi's current mode. It is frustrating to begin typing, only to realize that vi is not in input mode. The converse situation also occurs commonly — you may be typing text when you want to enter a command. If you want to make sure vi is in command mode, just press Esc a few times. (Pressing Esc more than once doesn't hurt.)

To view online help in vi, type :help **while in command mode. Type** :q **to exit the help screen and to return to the file you are editing.**

The vi editor initially positions the cursor on the first character. One of the first things you need to learn is to move the cursor around. Try the following commands. Just type the letter, and vi responds.

j   Moves the cursor one line down

k   Moves the cursor one line up

h   Moves the cursor one character to the left

l   Moves the cursor one character to the right

w   Moves the cursor one word forward

b   Moves the cursor one word backward

Ctrl+d   Moves down half a screen

Ctrl+u   Scrolls up half a screen

Luckily, you can also move the cursor by using the arrow keys. If you cannot remember the meaning of the jkhl **characters, just use the arrow keys to move around the file.**

You can go to a specific line number at any time. This is when a colon command comes in. To go to line 1, for example, type the following and then press Enter:

    :1

When you type the colon, vi displays the colon on the last line of the screen. From then on, vi uses the text you type as a command. You have to press Enter to submit the command to vi. In colon command mode, vi accepts all the commands that the ed editor accepts — and then some.

To search for a string, first type a slash (/). The vi editor displays the slash on the last line of the screen. Type the search string and then press Enter. The vi editor locates the string and positions the cursor at the beginning of that string. Thus, to locate the string cdrom in the file /etc/fstab, type:

    /cdrom

To delete the line that contains the cursor, type dd (two lowercase *d*s). The vi editor deletes that line of text and makes the next line the current one.

To begin entering text in front of the cursor, type i (a lowercase *i* all by itself). The vi editor switches to text input mode. Now you can enter text. When you finish entering text, press Esc to return to visual command mode.

After you finish editing the file, you can save the changes in the file by using the :w command. To quit the editor without saving any changes, use the :q! command. If you want to save the changes and exit, you can type :wq to perform both steps at the same time. The vi editor saves the changes in the file and exits. You can also save the changes and exit the editor by pressing Shift+zz (hold the Shift key down and press z twice).

In addition to the few commands illustrated in the sample session, vi accepts a large number of commands. Table 10-2 lists some commonly used vi commands, organized by task. To try these commands, copy a file such as /etc/X11/XF86Config to your home directory, and use vi to edit that file with the following commands:

**10 Min.
To Go**

```
cd
cp /etc/X11/XF86Config .
vi XF86Config
```

As you edit the file, try the commands shown in Table 10-2. Because good vi skills are useful in all UNIX systems you should spend a few minutes familiarizing yourself with some of the commands in Table 10-2.

Table 10-2
Commonly Used vi Commands

Command	Meaning
Insert text	
a	Inserts text after the cursor
A	Inserts text at the end of the current line
I	Inserts text at the beginning of the current line
i	Inserts text before the cursor
Delete text	
D	Deletes up to the end of the current line
dd	Deletes the current line
dw	Deletes from the cursor to the end of the following word
x	Deletes the character on which the cursor rests
Change text	
C	Changes up to the end of the current line

Command	Meaning
cc	Changes the current line
J	Joins the current line with the next one
r*x*	Replaces the character under the cursor with *x* (*x* is any character)
Move cursor	
h	Moves one character to the left
j	Moves one line down
k	Moves one line up
L	Moves cursor to the end of the screen
l	Moves one character to the right
w	Moves to the beginning of the following word
Scroll text	
Ctrl-d	Scrolls forward by half a screen
Ctrl-u	Scrolls backward by half a screen
Refresh screen	
Ctrl-l	Redraws screen
Cut and paste text	
P	Puts yanked line above the current line
p	Puts yanked line below the current line
Yy	Yanks (copies) current line into an unnamed buffer
Colon commands	
:!*command*	Executes shell *command*
:q	Quits editor
:q!	Quits without saving changes
:r *filename*	Reads file and inserts after current line
:w *filename*	Writes buffer to file
:wq	Saves changes and exits

Continued

Done!

Table 10-2 *Continued*

Command	Meaning
Search text	
/string	Searches forward for *string*
?string	Searches backward for *string*
Miscellaneous	
U	Undoes last command
Esc	Ends input mode and enters visual command mode
u	Undoes recent changes to current line

REVIEW

This session showed you how to use the graphical text editors in GNOME and KDE to edit files. The graphical text editors are intuitive to use, but sometimes you may have to edit text files without the benefit of a graphical login. For those situations, you practiced editing text files with the text-mode editors: ed and vi.

QUIZ YOURSELF

1. How do you start the GNOME text editor? (See "Using GUI Text Editors for Text Editing.")

2. When editing with the ed editor, how do you view all lines of a file? (See "Using ed.")

3. When editing a file with the ed editor, what command do you use to locate a line containing the string monitor? (See "Using ed.")

4. What are the three modes of the vi editor? (See "Using vi.")

5. How do you exit the vi editor without saving any changes? (See "Using vi.")

PART

II

Saturday Morning

1. Briefly explain the X client/server architecture. What does the X server do?

2. What is the configuration file that configures the X server in Linux? How do you create a new X configuration file?

3. Suppose your system is set up for graphical login and X does not seem to start up properly. What steps do you take to recover from this situation?

4. To be able to print successfully, the printer must understand the data sent to it by the operating system. How is data sent to the printer so that the printer is able to print as intended? What are the most common print languages?

5. What is stair-stepping and how can it be corrected?

6. What is the Linux file system? Can you have parts of the file system stored on different hard drives or different partitions?

7. What Linux command do you use to change the current directory to your home directory and then list detailed information about all files, including the ones with names that begin with a period?

8. What Linux command do you use to locate all files in the /usr/doc directory tree with names that begin with README?

9. How do you type several Linux commands on a single line? What is the syntax for continuing a command on multiple lines?

10. Show an example that uses the output of one command as the input to another.

11. What is the "I/O redirection" feature of the shell?

12. What is an alias, and how do you define an alias? How do you get a list of all currently defined aliases? Define the alias docdir to change the directory to /home/httpd/html. How do you undefine the docdir alias?

13. Suppose your system's date and time is wrong. Show the command line you use to set the date and time to December 31, 2001 10:30 PM.

14. Show the Linux command line you use to find all processes with gnome in their names.

15. Suppose you want to kill the gpm process. Explain the steps you follow to perform this task.

16. Suppose you want to split a 4MB file into four equal parts so that you can copy them on to four floppy disks. What command do you use to perform this task? How do you recombine the parts again?

17. Why is it important to learn to edit text files in Linux? What text editor do you use when you are working from a text console?

18. Suppose you are using the ed text editor to edit the /etc/inittab file. Show the command to start the editing session with the colon (:) as the command prompt. Explain how you enter a line of text in front of line number 16 and then save the file and exit.

19. Explain how you edit the /etc/inittab file with the vi editor. What keys do you press to go to line number 16 and enter a new line of text? How do you save the file and exit?

20. How do you cut a line of text in vi? What vi command do you use to paste the cut text below the current line?

PART

III

Saturday
Afternoon

Configuring a Modem

Session Checklist

**30 Min.
To Go**

✔ Connecting a modem to the PC

✔ Dialing out with Minicom

The Saturday afternoon sessions focus on data communications that use a modem or an Ethernet local area network (LAN). This first session introduces you to serial ports through which you can connect modems to a Linux system. If you're using Linux at home or in your office, you probably want to use a modem for one or more of the following reasons: to dial out to another computer (such as a bulletin-board system) or another UNIX system; to enable other people to dial in and use your Linux system; or to use dial-up networking with Point-to-Point Protocol (PPP) to connect to the Internet through an Internet Service Provider (ISP). This session covers the first use of a modem: to dial out from your Linux PC.

Session 12 covers dial-up networking with PPP.

Connecting a Modem to the PC

When you install Red Hat Linux from this book's companion CD-ROMs, you automatically install tools you can use to dial out from your Linux system with a modem. Other distributions also include tools you can use for dialing out. Before you can dial out, however, you have to make sure that you have a modem properly connected to one of the serial ports of your PC and that the Linux devices for the serial ports are set up correctly. Make sure that your modem is properly connected to the power supply and that the modem is also connected to the telephone line.

If you have an external modem, buy the right type of cable to connect the modem to the PC. You need a straight-through serial cable to connect the modem to the PC. The connectors at the ends of the cable depend on the type of serial connector on your PC. The modem end of the cable needs a male 25-pin connector. The PC end of the cable often is a female 9-pin connector. You can buy modem cables at most computer stores. The 9-pin female — 25-pin male modem cables are often sold under the label "AT Modem Cable."

 If your PC has an internal modem, all you have to do is connect the phone line to a phone jack at the back of the internal-modem card. (There are some modems that will only work with Microsoft Windows. The Linux community calls these modems winmodems, and if you have one of these winmodems, the instructions in this section will not make it work.)

Learning the serial-port device names

The PC typically has two serial ports, called COM1 and COM2 in MS-DOS parlance. (Most new PCs with a Universal Serial Bus have only one serial port.) The PC can support two more serial ports: COM3 and COM4. Because of these port names, the serial ports are often referred to as *COM ports*.

Like other devices, the serial ports need interrupt request (IRQ) numbers and I/O port addresses. Two IRQs — 3 and 4 — are shared among the four COM ports. Table 11-1 lists the IRQs and I/O port addresses assigned to the four serial ports. Like other devices in Linux, device files in the /dev directory represent the serial port devices. Table 11-1 shows the serial device names corresponding to the PC's COM ports.

Table 11-1
Device Names for Serial Ports

COM Port	Device Name	IRQ	I/O Address
COM1	/dev/ttyS0	4	0x3f8
COM2	/dev/ttyS1	3	0x2f8
COM3	/dev/ttyS2	4	0x3e8
COM4	/dev/ttyS3	3	0x2e8

If you install Red Hat Linux from this book's companion CD-ROMs, all these devices should already be in your system. Other distributions also install these devices. If you check the /dev directory, you should find the /dev/ttyS* devices in which * is 0, 1, 2, and 3. From a terminal window, type ls -l /dev/ttyS* to see a listing of these device files.

Checking if Linux detects the serial devices

When you install Linux, the necessary Linux serial devices are automatically created for you. You should have the /dev/ttyS* devices for dialing in and out through the modem.

To verify that Linux detects the serial port correctly, check the boot messages with the dmesg command:

```
dmesg | grep ttyS*
```

If you see a message such as the following, Linux detects a serial port in your PC:

```
ttyS01 at 0x02f8 (irq = 3) is a 16550A
```

In this case, the message indicates that Linux detects the second serial port (COM2). It shows the I/O address (0x2f8) and IRQ (3). The last part of the message — 16550A — refers to the identifying number of the *universal asynchronous receiver/transmitter (UART)* chip, which is at the heart of all serial communications hardware. (The UART converts each byte to a stream of ones and zeros and then back to bytes when needed.)

The boot messages are also stored in the /var/log/messages file. Therefore, you can search for the serial port's name in the /var/log/messages file with the grep command, as follows:

```
grep ttyS /var/log/messages
```

You can also check for the serial ports with the setserial command. Type the following command to see detailed information about the serial ports:

```
setserial -g /dev/ttyS*
```

A telltale sign of a problem is a message from setserial that shows the UART as unknown (as shown in the following example):

```
/dev/ttyS0, UART: unknown, Port: 0x03f8, IRQ: 4
```

If the UART shows up as unknown, Linux does not detect the serial port.

Red Hat Linux not detecting the serial port usually occurs because your PC's BIOS is set up to expect a Plug and Play (PnP) operating system. Reboot your PC, and, as it powers up, press a key (typically a function key, such as F2, but the exact key depends on your PC's BIOS) to enter BIOS setup. In the setup screen, locate the option for PnP operating system (often labeled "Plug & Play O/S"), and turn off that option. Then save the BIOS settings and exit. This causes the PC to reboot. This time, when Red Hat Linux boots, the kernel should be able to detect the PC's serial port correctly.

Dialing Out with Minicom

**20 Min.
To Go**

After you complete the physical installation of the modem and verify that the necessary Linux device files exist, you can try to dial out through the modem. The best approach is to use the Minicom serial communications program included in the Red Hat Linux distribution on this book's CD-ROMs and installed in the /usr/bin directory. The Minicom program is a serial communications program with a text-based interface that emulates a VT102 terminal. Minicom is similar to other communications software such as Procomm or Crosstalk, which you may have used under MS-DOS or Windows. Minicom may also be included with other Linux distributions. Check the documentation from your version to see whether it is included.

Running Minicom as the root user

To run Minicom, type minicom at the shell prompt in the terminal window or in a virtual console. If you run Minicom as a normal user (not root), Minicom displays the following error message and exits (unless the system manager has already set up Minicom for use by normal users):

```
minicom: there is no global configuration file /etc/minirc.dfl
Ask your sysadm to create one (with minicom -s).
```

Log in as root and then type

```
minicom -s
```

You may have to type the full path: /sbin/minicom.

Minicom starts and displays a dialog box (see Figure 11-1) with a setup menu that enables you to configure various aspects of Minicom, including the serial port and the modem and dialing commands. To enter the modem initialization commands, use the arrow key to highlight the Modem and dialing item (as shown in Figure 11-1).

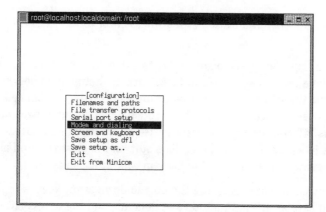

Figure 11-1
Minicom's setup menu

With the Modem and dialing entry highlighted, press Enter. Minicom displays another menu (see Figure 11-2) with a list of settings you can change. Minicom places the cursor on the first line, as shown in Figure 11-2. Press A to change the modem initialization string.

```
root@localhost.localdomain: /root                              _ □ ×
            ┌─[Modem and dialing parameter setup]─┐
    A - Init string ........ ~^M^AT S7=45 S0=0 L1 V1 X4 &c1 E1 Q0^M█
    B - Reset string ........ ^M^ATZ^M^
    C - Dialing prefix #1.... ATDT
    D - Dialing suffix #1.... ^M
    E - Dialing prefix #2.... ATDP
    F - Dialing suffix #2.... ^M
    G - Dialing prefix #3.... ATX1DT
    H - Dialing suffix #3.... ;X4D^M
    I - Connect string ...... CONNECT
    J - No connect strings .. NO CARRIER        BUSY
                             NO DIALTONE        VOICE
    K - Hang-up string ...... ~~+++~~ATH^M
    L - Dial cancel string .. ^M

    M - Dial time .......... 45    Q - Auto bps detect ..... No
    N - Delay before redial . 2    R - Modem has DCD line .. Yes
    O - Number of tries ..... 10   S - Status line shows ... DTE speed
    P - DTR drop time (0=no). 1    T - Multi-line untag .... No

    Change which setting?    (Return or Esc to exit)
```

Figure 11-2
Setting up modem and dialing parameters in Minicom

You can then use the Backspace key to edit that line and type the AT command you need to initialize the modem. For example, I have a 56K modem I initialize by using the following AT command:

```
AT &F1 E1 V1
```

After you enter the modem initialization string, press Enter to return to the top-level menu.

By the way, the AT **commands refer to commands you can use to control a modem and perform tasks such as dialing a number, turning the modem's speaker on or off, and setting the modem to answer an incoming call. These commands start with two characters:** AT **(for attention). You can use** AT **commands for situations in which the communications software is primitive and all the software does is send the modem whatever you type.**

If you have no more changes to make, use the up and down arrow keys to highlight the item labeled Save as dfl (meaning save as default), and then press Enter. Minicom saves the settings in the /etc/minirc.dfl file — the default configuration file for Minicom. After that, you can exit Minicom by selecting Exit from Minicom and pressing Enter.

Running Minicom as an ordinary user

**10 Min.
To Go**

You need to do the following before any user can run Minicom:

- Open the text file /etc/minicom.users in a text editor, and verify that it has a line with the word ALL. (This enables all users to access Minicom's default configuration file.) If not, add a line with the word ALL.

- Assuming that you want all users to be able to dial out using the modem, enable any user to read from and write to the serial port where the modem is connected. For example, if the modem is on COM1 (/dev/ttyS0), type chmod o+rw /dev/ttyS0 to give everyone write permission for that device.

- Establish a link between the /dev/modem and the serial port device to which the modem is connected. If the modem is on COM1 (/dev/ttyS0), type the following command:

  ```
  ln -s /dev/ttyS0 /dev/modem
  ```

After that, you can run Minicom as an ordinary user. When Minicom first runs, it resets the modem. Figure 11-3 shows the result of running Minicom in a terminal window.

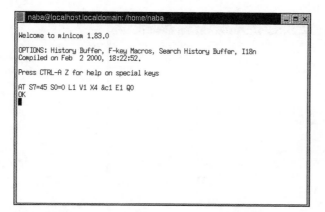

Figure 11-3
The initial Minicom screen in a terminal window

Press Ctrl+A to get the attention of the Minicom program. Then if you press Z, a help screen appears in the form of a text window (as shown in Figure 11-4).

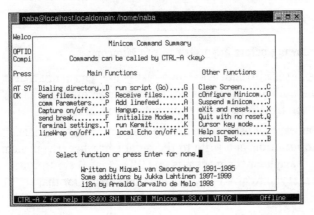

Figure 11-4
The Minicom help screen

In the help screen, you can get information about other Minicom commands. From the help screen, press Enter to return to online mode. In online mode, you can use the modem's AT commands to dial out. In particular, you can use the ATDT command to dial the phone number of another modem (for example, your Internet Service Provider's computer or a system at your office), as shown in Figure 11-5. Once you get the login prompt, you can log in as usual and use the remote system.

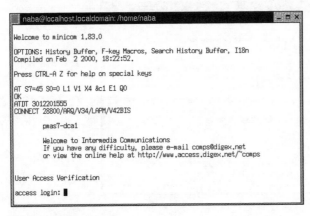

Figure 11-5
Dialing a remote system using Minicom

When you log out of the other system and want to exit Minicom, press Ctrl+A, and then type X to exit the program. Press Enter again in response to the Minicom prompt.

Done!

REVIEW

You started the session by learning the device names for serial ports in Linux. You used the Minicom serial communications program to dial out with a modem. In the course of dialing out, you learned several AT commands used to control the modem.

QUIZ YOURSELF

1. What is the device name for the second serial port (COM2)? (See "Learning the Serial-Port Device Names.")

2. How can you check to see if Linux detects any serial ports in your PC? (See "Checking if Linux Detects the Serial Devices.")

3. What program can you use to dial out through the modem? (See "Dialing out with Minicom.")

4. What AT command do you use to make the modem dial a phone number? (See "Running Minicom as an Ordinary User.")

5. What do you have to do to establish a link between the /dev/modem and the serial port device to which the modem is connected? (See "Running Minicom as an Ordinary User.")

Connecting to the Internet

✔ Learning the basics of dial-up networking

✔ Connecting to the Internet using PPP

✔ Using IP masquerading to share an Internet connection

*30 Min.
To Go*

After installing Linux, you may want to connect your Linux PC (and perhaps your own LAN) to the Internet. You have the following popular options for connecting a small office or home office to the Internet: Digital Subscriber Line (DSL), cable modem, and dial-up networking. The DSL and cable modem options essentially involve connecting a special modem to an Ethernet card on your Linux system. In these cases, the setup procedures are the same as the ones discussed in Session 14.

This session focuses on dial-up networking, which involves setting up a PPP connection from your Linux PC to your ISP's system. You also learn to use IP masquerading to share a Linux system's Internet connection with other systems on a LAN.

Learning the Basics of Dial-up Networking

Dial-up networking refers to the connection of a PC to a remote network (such as the Internet) through a dial-up modem. In this case, the maximum data transfer rate is 56Kbps. A significant difference exists between dial-up networking and plain old serial communication. Both approaches use a modem to dial up another computer and establish a communications path, but the serial communication software (such as Minicom in Session 11) makes your computer act like a terminal connected to the remote computer. The serial communications software exclusively uses dial-up connection. For example, you cannot run another copy of the communications software and use the same modem connection.

In dial-up networking, you run TCP/IP or other network-protocol software on your PC as well as on the remote system with which your PC has a dial-up communications path. The communications path simply provides the physical data transport. The network protocols exchange data packets over the dial-up connection. You can use any number of network applications simultaneously to communicate over the single dial-up connection. With dial-up networking, your PC truly becomes part of the network to which the remote computer belongs. (If the remote computer is not on a network, the dial-up networking creates a network that consists of the remote computer and your PC.) Thus, you can have any number of network applications (ranging from a Web browser to a TELNET session) running at the same time, with all applications sharing the physical data-transport capabilities of the dial-up connection.

Dial-up networking involves TCP/IP data transfers over a dial-up connection. Like TCP/IP networking over an Ethernet, TCP/IP networking over a dial-up link is a matter of specifying the *protocol* — the convention — for packaging a network packet over the communications link. There are two popular protocols for TCP/IP networking over point-to-point (PPP) serial communications links:

- Serial Line Internet Protocol (SLIP) is a simple protocol that specifies how to frame an IP packet on a serial line.

- Point-to-Point Protocol (PPP) is a more advanced protocol for establishing a TCP/IP connection over any point-to-point link, including dial-up serial links.

PPP is the most popular method of TCP/IP networking over a dial-up connection and has, for all intents and purposes, replaced SLIP. Therefore, I show you in the next section how to use PPP to set up a network connection to a remote system.

Connecting to the Internet Using PPP

Many Internet Service Providers (ISPs) provide PPP access to the Internet through one or more systems that the ISP maintains. If you sign up for such a service, the ISP should provide you the information you need to make a PPP connection to the remote system. Typically, this information includes the following:

- The phone number to connect to the remote system
- The user name and password you must use to log into the remote system
- The IP addresses of the ISP's Domain Name Servers (DNS). Typically, the ISP gives you two IP addresses — one for the primary DNS and one for the secondary DNS.
- The IP address for your side of the connection. (This IP address is associated with your PC's PPP interface — the serial port.) Usually, this IP address is assigned dynamically (meaning the IP address may change every time your system establishes a connection).

Most ISPs also provide the IP addresses of the mail and news servers. These addresses, however, are not important for the mechanics of setting up a PPP connection.

Before you set up a PPP connection, you must have an internal or external modem installed on your system. The modem should be connected to a phone line. You can use Minicom, as described in Session 11, to dial your ISP's phone number and to make sure the modem successfully establishes a connection. After you see a login prompt, you can hang up the modem and proceed to set up PPP.

To set up a PPP connection by using Red Hat's graphical Dialup Configuration tool, log in as root and select Main Menu ⇨ Programs ⇨ Internet ⇨ Dialup Configuration Tool from the GNOME desktop. The Dialup Configuration tool displays the Add New Internet Connection dialog box, as shown in Figure 12-1.

Click the Next button. The dialog box then guides you through steps where you select a modem and provide information such as the phone number of the ISP, your user name, and password (for your account on the ISP's system). The Dialup Configuration Tool saves the configuration information in the `/etc/sysconfig/network-script/ifcfg-ppp0` file.

Figure 12-1
Creating a new Internet connection with Red Hat's Dialup Configuration Tool

To establish a PPP connection, select Main Menu ⇨ Programs ⇨ Internet ⇨ RH PPP Dialer from the GNOME desktop. A dialog box appears with a list of the interfaces you can use to make a connection. Select the interface you have defined with the Dialup Configuration Tool, and click the OK button to start the connection.

To set up a PPP connection by using the KDE gui, which is the default for the Caldera and Suse distributions, click the K icon, and then choose Internet ⇨ KPPP. In the dialog box shown in Figure 12-2, choose Setup to open the KPPP Configuration dialog box, which is shown in Figure 12-3.

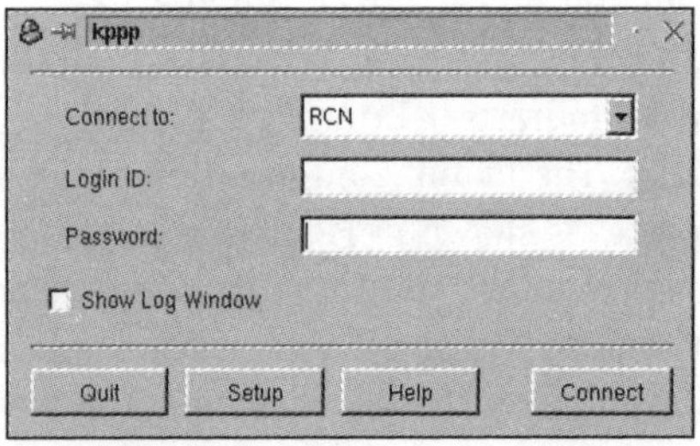

Figure 12-2
You can choose an account, enter a password and user name in, connect from, and access the KPPP Configuration dialog box from the KPPP dialog box.

Let's start by setting up a new account by clicking the New button to open the New Account dialog box shown in Figure 12-4.

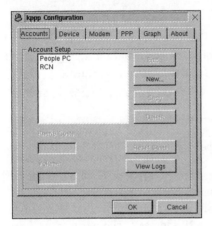

Figure 12-3
You can configure all KPPP options in the KPPP Configuration dialog box.

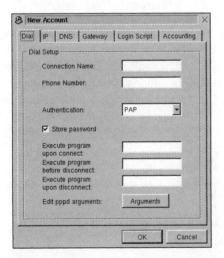

Figure 12-4
Enter information about your ISP account in the New Account dialog box.

The Dial tab is very important. Be sure to fill in the following fields:

- Connection Name — Enter a name for this connection, such as the name of your ISP.
- Phone Number — Enter the number to dial to connect to the ISP.

- Authentication — In this drop-down list, choose the security type your ISP uses. Check with your ISP to get this information. (Most ISPs use PAP.)

- Execute program upon connect — Enter the command for a program, such as a Web browser, that will start after the connection is made.

- Execute program upon disconnect — Enter the command for a program that will start after disconnecting.

- Edit pppd arguments — Click the Arguments button to change pppd parameters. These usually don't need to be changed.

On the IP tab, you can choose either a static or dynamic IP address. The default is Dynamic and usually doesn't need to be changed.

The DNS tab defines name resolution after the connection is made. You need to enter the domain name of your ISP and the IP address of the name server.

The Gateway tab defines the route to the outside network. The default is to use a static gateway, and it is usually not necessary to change this setting.

The last two tabs, Login Script and Accounting, do not require any changes, so you can click OK to return to the KPPP Configuration dialog box.

Next, you need to configure the modem by clicking the Device tab and then choosing the correct port. (See Figure 12-5.) Refer to Session 11 to review the appropriate COM port-to-device relationships. After entering the correct device for the modem, click OK to return to the main KPPP window. To connect, choose the name of the connection you just created, enter the appropriate login ID and password, and click Connect.

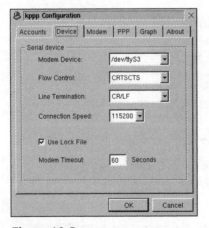

Figure 12-5
You can enter the device name for the modem on the Device tab of the KPPP Configuration dialog box.

Verifying the PPP connection is up

After you connect, you can verify that the PPP connection is up by typing the `/sbin/ifconfig` command, which shows a listing such as this:

```
eth0      Link encap:Ethernet  HWaddr 02:60:8C:8E:C6:A9
          inet addr:192.168.1.200  Bcast:192.168.1.255  Mask:255.255.255.0
          UP BROADCAST RUNNING MULTICAST  MTU:1500  Metric:1
          RX packets:4363 errors:0 dropped:0 overruns:0 frame:0
          TX packets:2111 errors:0 dropped:0 overruns:0 carrier:0
          collisions:0 txqueuelen:100
          Interrupt:5 Base address:0x300

lo        Link encap:Local Loopback
          inet addr:127.0.0.1  Mask:255.0.0.0
          UP LOOPBACK RUNNING  MTU:3924  Metric:1
          RX packets:50 errors:0 dropped:0 overruns:0 frame:0
          TX packets:50 errors:0 dropped:0 overruns:0 carrier:0
          collisions:0 txqueuelen:0

ppp0      Link encap:Point-to-Point Protocol
          inet addr:209.100.18.220  P-t-P:209.100.18.4  Mask:255.255.255.255
          UP POINTOPOINT RUNNING NOARP MULTICAST  MTU:1500  Metric:1
          RX packets:132 errors:2 dropped:0 overruns:0 frame:2
          TX packets:146 errors:0 dropped:0 overruns:0 carrier:0
          collisions:0 txqueuelen:10
```

Find the ppp0 device listed in the output. The ifconfig output also shows the IP addresses of the local and remote ends of the PPP connection. This output confirms that the PPP device is up and running.

Verifying that the routing table is set up correctly

To verify that the routing table is set up correctly, type the `/sbin/route` command without any arguments to see the following:

```
Kernel IP routing table
Destination     Gateway         Genmask         Flags Metric Ref  Use Iface
209.100.18.4    *               255.255.255.255 UH    0      0      0 ppp0
192.168.1.200   *               255.255.255.255 UH    0      0      0 eth0
192.168.1.0     *               255.255.255.0   U     0      0      0 eth0
127.0.0.0       *               255.0.0.0       U     0      0      0 lo
default         209.100.18.4    0.0.0.0         UG    0      0      0 ppp0
```

In the routing table, the first line shows a route to the remote end of the PPP connection, which should be set to the ppp0 device. Also, the default route should be set up so the remote end of the PPP connection serves as the gateway for your system (as the last line of the routing table shows).

Verifying that Internet hosts can be reached

After checking the interface configuration (with the `ifconfig` command) and the routing table (with the `route` command), verify that you can reach some well-known host. If your ISP gives you the IP address of a name server or a mail server, you can try to ping those addresses. Otherwise, try to ping the IP address of a system at your workplace or your university.

The following example shows you what you see if you try the ping command (for example, `ping 140.90.23.100`):

```
PING 140.90.23.100 (140.90.23.100): 56 data bytes
64 bytes from 140.90.23.100: icmp_seq=0 ttl=243 time=143.2 ms
64 bytes from 140.90.23.100: icmp_seq=1 ttl=243 time=220.2 ms
64 bytes from 140.90.23.100: icmp_seq=2 ttl=243 time=140.2 ms
64 bytes from 140.90.23.100: icmp_seq=3 ttl=243 time=130.3 ms

--- 140.90.23.100 ping statistics ---
4 packets transmitted, 4 packets received, 0% packet loss
round-trip min/avg/max = 130.3/158.4/220.2 ms
```

The end of each line shows the round-trip time for a packet originating at your system to reach the designated IP address (140.90.23.100, in this case) and to return to your system. For a PPP connection over dial-up lines, you can see times in hundreds of milliseconds.

Incidentally, you do not have to have an account on a system to ping its IP address. Although a system may disable the automatic response to ping messages (ping uses Internet Control Message Protocol or ICMP messages), most systems respond to ping.

To see your connection speed, type `tail -100 /var/log/mes-sages | grep V42BIS`**. This shows lines such as the following, with connection speed as reported by the modem:**

```
Mar 19 17:31:27 lnbp200 chat[1533]:   42666/ARQ/V90/LAPM/V42BIS^M
Mar 19 17:32:24 lnbp200 chat[1579]:
33333/ARQ/V90/LAPM/V42BIS^M
```

Turning the PPP connection on or off

You can also enter console commands to turn the PPP connection on or off. After you configure the ppp0 interface, you can simply type the following command to initiate the PPP connection:

```
/sbin/ifup ppp0
```

When you no longer need the PPP connection, you can disconnect by logging in as root and typing the following command:

```
/sbin/ifdown/ppp0
```

Using IP Masquerading to Share an Internet Connection

**10 Min.
To Go**

Linux supports a feature called *IP masquerading* that enables you to connect an Ethernet LAN with a private IP address to the Internet. This occurs through a Linux PC (with an officially assigned IP address) that has a connection to the Internet. The Linux PC may be connected to the Internet by dial-up PPP or some other connection, such as DSL or cable modem.

With IP masquerading enabled, your PC acts as a stand-in for any of the other systems on the Ethernet LAN. As with the router setup, the Linux PC is designated as the gateway for the Ethernet LAN. However, masquerading involves more than simply forwarding IP packets back and forth between the LAN and the Internet.

When the Linux PC masquerades as another system on the LAN, it modifies outgoing packets so that they always appear to originate from the Linux PC. When a response to one of the outgoing packets is received, the Linux PC performs the reverse task — it modifies the packets so that they appear to come from the Internet directly to the system that sends the outgoing packet. The end result is that each system on the Ethernet LAN appears to have full access to the Internet, even though the Ethernet LAN uses a non-unique private IP address.

To enable and use IP masquerading, perform the following steps:

1. Make sure the Linux kernel — the core operating system — supports IP firewall chains. This should be true for the version of Red Hat Linux you install from the companion CD-ROMs. Other distributions of Linux usually also support IP chains. If the file /proc/net/ip_fwchains exists, the kernel supports IP firewall chains. (Type ls /proc/net/ip_fwchains to verify that the file exists.)

2. Make sure the Linux PC has an Internet connection and a network connection to your LAN. Typically, the Linux PC has two network interfaces — an Ethernet card for the LAN and a dial-up PPP connection to the Internet (through an ISP).

3. Make sure all other systems on your LAN use the Linux PC as the default gateway for TCP/IP networking. Use the same ISP-provided DNS addresses on all systems.

4. Enable IP forwarding in the kernel by typing the following command:

```
echo "1" > /proc/sys/net/ipv4/ip_forward
```

This is necessary because IP forwarding is disabled by default. To ensure that IP forwarding is enabled when you reboot your system, place this command in the /etc/rc.d/rc.local file. In Linux, you can achieve the same result by changing the line FORWARD_IPV4=false to FORWARD_IPV4=true in the /etc/sysconfig/network file.

5. Run /sbin/ipchains — the IPCHAINS firewall administration program — to set up the rules that enable the Linux PC to masquerade for your LAN. For example, to enable masquerading for a LAN via the Linux PC's ppp0 network interface, you can use the following commands:

```
/sbin/ipchains -P forward DENY
/sbin/ipchains -A forward -i ppp0 -j MASQ
```

If you want the IP masquerading set up at system startup, you should place these commands in the /etc/rc.d/rc.local file. Be sure to look at the man pages for ipchains to learn about securing your system.

Done!

You may find IP masquerading a convenient way to provide Internet access to a small LAN (for example, a LAN at home or in the office). At home, I use IP masquerading to connect an Ethernet LAN to the Internet through a Linux system. The Linux PC has an Ethernet card for the LAN connection and a modem to connect to the Internet via an ISP. (I have a valid IP address from the ISP.) With IP masquerading on the Linux PC, everyone in your family or small business can access the Internet from any of the other PCs on the LAN.

REVIEW

This session introduced you to dial-up networking — establishing a network connection between your Linux PC and the Internet through a dial-up modem. You learned to use the Red Hat Dialup Configuration Tool to set up a PPP connection. Finally, this session showed you how to share a single Internet connection by using the IP masquerading feature of the IPCHAINS firewall administration program.

QUIZ YOURSELF

1. What are dial-up networking and PPP? (See "Learning the Basics of Dial-up Networking.")

2. What information does an ISP typically provide for you to set up dial-up PPP connections? (See "Connecting to the Internet Using PPP.")

3. What tool do you use to set up a PPP connection? (See "Connecting to the Internet Using PPP.")

4. What commands do you type to turn the PPP connection on and off? (See "Turning the PPP Connection On or Off.")

5. What is IP masquerading? (See "Using IP Masquerading to Share an Internet Connection.")

Setting Up Internet Services

Session Checklist

✔ Understanding Internet services

✔ Using the e-mail server

✔ Setting up the Apache Web server

✔ Setting up the FTP server

**30 Min.
To Go**

Y ou can use the Linux PC as a server if it's connected to the Internet or an *intranet* (a private TCP/IP network). Both internal and external networks rely on Internet services. Each Internet service involves configuring and running one or more servers on the Linux system. This session introduces you to the commonly used Internet services. It then focuses on the servers that implement the mail, Web, and information retrieval Internet services: the e-mail server, the Apache Web server, and the FTP server (which enable anyone to download files from your system in a reasonably secure manner).

 You learn about securing your Linux system in Session 29.

Understanding Internet Services

The term *Internet service* refers to a number of network applications that employ a client/server architecture to perform specific tasks. (In the client/server architecture, two separate programs — a server that provides information and one or more clients that request information — implement a service.)

Many Internet services are specifically designed to deliver information from one system to another. The information may be in the form of mail messages, news items, or data files. As a user, you expect to access these common Internet services from a typical Internet host:

- *Electronic mail (e-mail)*. From an Internet host, you can send e-mail to any other user on the Internet by using addresses such as `president@whitehouse.gov`.

- *World Wide Web*. You can use a Web browser to download and view Web pages by using a Uniform Resource Locator (URL) address such as `http://www.whitehouse.gov`. The Web pages are usually documents formatted in Hypertext Markup Language (HTML).

- *Newsgroups*. You can read newsgroups and post news items to newsgroups by using names such as `comp.os.linux.networking` or `comp.os.linux.setup`.

- *Information retrieval*. You can search for information by using tools such as the World Wide Web browser. You also can download files by using File Transfer Protocol (FTP). Reciprocally, users on other systems also can download files from your system — typically through a feature known as anonymous FTP.

- *Remote access*. You can use TELNET to log in to another computer (the remote computer) on the Internet, assuming you have a user name and password to access the remote computer.

All Internet services rely on client and server software. For example, an e-mail server takes care of transferring mail from one system to another while you read e-mail by using e-mail client software. Similarly, you use a Web browser client to download and view Web pages from a Web server.

The clients and servers that implement Internet services employ TCP/IP protocols to communicate with one another. You're already familiar with the IP address that identifies a host in a TCP/IP network. The IP address alone, however, cannot sufficiently distinguish among many services running on the same system. The concept of a port number (or, simply, *port*) is used to enable various Internet servers to communicate with clients. The port is not a physical entity — it's simply a number between 1 and 65,535 that uniquely identifies each end point of a TCP/IP communications link between two processes (typically, a server and a client).

All well-known Internet services have preassigned port numbers. For example, here are some commonly used Internet protocols and their assigned port numbers:

- *FTP (File Transfer Protocol)* allows transfer of files among computers on the Internet. FTP uses two ports — data is transferred on port 20, while control information is exchanged on port 21. FTP is the underlying protocol for file transfers.

- *HTTP (Hypertext Transfer Protocol)* is a recent protocol for sending HTML documents from one system to another. HTTP is the underlying protocol of the Web. By default, the Web server and client communicate on port 80.

- *SMTP (Simple Mail Transfer Protocol)* exchanges e-mail messages among systems. SMTP uses port 25 for information exchange. SMTP is the underlying protocol for the e-mail service.

- *NNTP (Network News Transfer Protocol)* distributes news articles in a store-and-forward fashion across the Internet. NNTP uses port 119. NNTP is the underlying protocol for the newsgroups service.

- *TELNET* enables a user on one system to log into another system on the Internet. (The user must provide a valid user ID and password to log into the remote system successfully.) TELNET uses port 23 by default. However, the TELNET client can connect to any specified port. TELNET is the underlying protocol for remote access.

- *NFS (Network File System)* shares files among computers. NFS uses Sun's *Remote Procedure Call (RPC)* facility, which exchanges information through port 111.

A text configuration file — /etc/services — stores the association between an Internet service and a port number (as well as the underlying data communications protocol). To see the contents of this file, use the more command as follows:

```
more /etc/services
```

The following is a small subset of entries in the /etc/services file of a Linux system:

```
ftp-data     20/tcp
ftp          21/tcp
fsp          21/udp      fspd
ssh          22/tcp                  # SSH Remote Login Protocol
ssh          22/udp                  # SSH Remote Login Protocol
```

```
telnet          23/tcp
# 24 - private
smtp            25/tcp          mail
# 26 - unassigned
time            37/tcp          timserver
time            37/udp          timserver
rlp             39/udp          resource        # resource location
nameserver      42/tcp          name            # IEN 116
whois           43/tcp          nicname
```

Each line starts with the name of a service followed by a port number and a data communications protocol (tcp or udp). The rest of the line shows another name for the service, if any. Anything following the pound sign (#) is taken as a comment.

Browsing the entries in the /etc/services file is instructive because they show the breadth of networking services available under TCP/IP.

During Red Hat Linux installation from this book's companion CD-ROMs, you can opt to install the necessary packages for mail, Web, and news. Other distributions provide the same options during installation. All you need to do is select the Mail/WWW/News Tools package group from the installation screen that shows the package groups. *Mail* refers to the e-mail Internet service; *WWW* refers to the World Wide Web Internet service; *News* refers to the newsgroups Internet service.

If you install the mail and news software during Linux installation, you do not have to do much more to begin using the mail, Web, and news services. Otherwise, you can use the Red Hat Package Manager (RPM) to install individual packages. Other Linux distributions, not just the Red Hat Distribution, use the RPM file format.

Session 23 describes how to use the rpm program to install new software.

Using the E-mail Server

Electronic mail — e-mail — is one of the most popular services on the Internet. E-mail started as a simple mechanism in which messages were copied to a user's mailbox file. That simple mechanism remains in use. In Linux, your mail messages are stored in the /var/spool/mail directory in a text file that has the same name as your user name.

Messages still are addressed to a user name. That means if John Doe logs in with the user name jdoe, e-mail addressed to him is addressed to jdoe. The only other piece of information needed to identify the recipient is the fully qualified domain name of the recipient's system. Thus, if John Doe's system is named `someplace.net`, his complete e-mail address is `jdoe@someplace.net`. Given that address, anyone on the Internet can send e-mail to John Doe.

To set up and use e-mail on your Linux PC, you need two types of mail software:

- *Mail-user agent* software enables you to read your mail messages, write replies, and compose new messages. Typically, the mail-user agent retrieves messages from the mail server by using POP3 or IMAP4 protocol. POP3 is the Post Office Protocol version 3, and IMAP4 is the Internet Message Access Protocol version 4. This book's Red Hat Linux CD-ROMs include several popular mail-user agents such as `pine` and `elm`.

- *Mail-transport agent* software actually sends and receives mail-message text. The exact method used for mail transport depends on the underlying network. In TCP/IP networks, the mail-transport agent delivers mail by using the Simple Mail Transfer Protocol (SMTP). This book's Red Hat Linux CD-ROMs include `sendmail`, a powerful and popular mail-transport agent for TCP/IP networks.

Most mail-transport agents run as *daemons* — background processes that run as long as your system is up. Because you or another user on the system can send mail at any time, the transport agent has to be there to deliver the mail to its destination. The mail-user agent runs only when the user wants to check mail.

 Typically, a mail-transport agent starts after the system boots. The system startup files for Linux are set up so that the `sendmail` **mail-transport agent starts when the Linux system is in multiuser mode. The shell script file** `/etc/rc.d/init.d/sendmail` **starts** `sendmail`**.**

Because the system is already set up to start `sendmail` at boot time, all you have to do is use an appropriate `sendmail` configuration file to get e-mail going on your Linux system.

You cannot send or receive e-mail until the `sendmail` mail-transport agent is configured properly. The `sendmail` transport agent has the reputation of being a complex, but complete, mail-delivery system. If you take a quick look at `sendmail`'s configuration file, `/etc/sendmail.cf`, you can see that `sendmail` is indeed complex. Luckily, you do not have to be an expert on the `sendmail` configuration file. All you need is the predefined configuration files from this book's companion CD-ROMs. A good source for Sendmail information is the Sendmail Web site, `www.sendmail.org`. This site contains the latest version of Sendmail and information about security patches and bug fixes.

If you install the Mail/WWW/News Tools component during Linux installation (see Session 3), your system should have a working `sendmail` configuration file — `/etc/sendmail.cf`. The default file assumes an Internet connection and a name server. Provided you have an Internet connection, you should be able to send and receive e-mail from your Linux PC once you connect it to the Internet. Then you can use a mail-user agent such as `elm` or `pine` to compose and send mail messages.

Setting Up the Apache Web Server

**20 Min.
To Go**

You probably already know how it feels to use the Web, but you may not know how to set up a Web server so that you, too, can provide information to the world through Web pages. To become an information provider on the Web, you have to run a Web server on your Linux PC on the Internet.

Web servers provide information by using HTTP. Web servers are also known as HTTP daemons (because continuously running server processes are called *daemons* in UNIX) or HTTPD, for short. The Web server program usually is named `httpd`.

Among the freely available Web servers, Apache Web server is the most popular. Apache is freely available over the Internet, and it accompanies Red Hat Linux on this book's companion CD-ROMs.

When you install Red Hat Linux from this book's companion CD-ROMs, you also have the option of installing the Apache Web server. If you install the Mail/WWW/News Tools package during Linux installation, Linux automatically starts the Apache Web server during system boot. Other distributions, such as Caldera and SuSe, also offer the option of installing the Apache Web server and associated tools during their installations. If you choose to install the Web server and associated tools, the Web server will start automatically at system boot.

Perform the following steps to verify that the Apache Web server software is installed and running on your system:

1. Type the following command to check whether the Apache Web server is installed:

   ```
   rpm -q apache
   ```

   If the output shows an `apache` package name such as the following, you have the Apache software installed on your system.

   ```
   apache-1.3.12-21
   ```

2. Type the following command to check whether the `httpd` process (the name of the Apache Web server program is `httpd`) is running:

   ```
   ps ax | grep httpd
   ```

The output should show a number of httpd processes. It is common to run several Web server processes — one parent and several child processes — so that several HTTP requests can be handled efficiently by assigning each request to an httpd process.

3. Use the telnet program on your Linux system, and employ the HTTP HEAD command to query the Web server as follows:

```
telnet localhost 80
Trying 128.0.0.1...
Connected to localhost.
Escape character is '^]'.
HEAD / HTTP/1.0
```

... Press Enter once more to type a blank line

```
HTTP/1.1 200 OK
Date: Sat, 19 Aug 2000 23:57:14 GMT
Server: Apache/1.3.12 (Unix)  (Red Hat/Linux)
Last-Modified: Mon, 07 Aug 2000 10:21:07 GMT
ETag: "328fe-b4a-398e8d93"
Accept-Ranges: bytes
Content-Length: 2890
Connection: close
Content-Type: text/html


Connection closed by foreign host.
```

If you get a response such as the preceding, your system already has the Apache Web server installed and set up correctly. All you have to do is understand the configuration so you can place the HTML documents in the proper directory.

4. Use a Web server to load the home page from your system. Start Netscape Navigator by clicking the big "N" icon on the GNOME Panel; use the URL http://localhost/, and then see what happens. You should see a Web page with the title "Test Page for the Apache Web Server on Red Hat Linux."

The Apache Web server is set up to serve the HTML documents from the /var/.www/html directory. Therefore, you should place your Web pages in the /var/www/html directory. In particular, edit or replace the /var/www/html/index.html file with your own home page.

In addition to the HTML files, the Apache Web server supports *Common Gateway Interface (CGI)* programs — programs the Web server can invoke to access other files and databases. You should place any CGI programs in the /var/www/cgi-bin directory.

Also note the following useful information about the Apache Web server:

- The Apache Web server configuration files are located in the /etc/httpd/conf directory. There are three configuration files: access.conf, httpd.conf, and srm.conf. These configuration files control how the server runs, which documents it serves, and who can access these documents.

- The /var/log/httpd directory is where the Apache Web server's log files (access logs and error logs) are located.

- The /etc/rc.d/init.d/httpd script starts the httpd process as your Linux system boots.

Setting Up the FTP Server

**10 Min.
To Go**

Besides e-mail and Web, *anonymous FTP* is a common service on an Internet host. You may be familiar with FTP, which you can use to transfer files from one system to another on the Internet. When you use FTP to transfer files to or from a remote system, you have to log in to the remote system before you can use FTP.

If you install Red Hat Linux from this book's companion CD-ROMs, you should have anonymous FTP set up on your system and the FTP server configured to run when needed. The default setup also employs the necessary security precautions. Other Linux distributions usually configure anonymous FTP to start by default during their installation.

Anonymous FTP refers to the user name anonymous, which anyone can employ with FTP to transfer files from a system. Anonymous FTP is a common way to share files on the Internet. Many businesses use anonymous FTP to support their customers.

If you have used anonymous FTP to download files from various Internet sites, you already know the convenience of that service. Anonymous FTP enables you to make information available to anyone on the Internet. Even if you haven't used anonymous FTP explicitly, your Web browser often employs anonymous FTP to download files. (You simply click a link; the Web browser does the rest.)

To see anonymous FTP in action, you can try accessing your system by using an FTP client. Here's a sample session that appears when I access my system from another PC on the LAN (my input appears in boldface):

```
ftp lnbp200
Connected to lnbp200
220 lnbp200.lnbsoft.com FTP server (Version wu-2.6.0(1) Fri Feb 4 23:37:48 EST 2
000) ready.
220 lnbp200 FTP server (Version wu-2.6.1(1) Wed Aug 9 05:54:50 EDT 2000) ready.
Name (lnbp200:): anonymous
331 Guest login ok, send your complete e-mail address as password.
Password:
230 Guest login ok, access restrictions apply.
Remote system type is UNIX.
Using binary mode to transfer files.
ftp> bye
221-You have transferred 0 bytes in 0 files.
221-Total traffic for this session was 299 bytes in 0 transfers.
221-Thank you for using the FTP service on lnbp200.
221 Goodbye.
```

When you successfully log in for anonymous FTP, you access the home directory of a user named `ftp` (the default directory is `/var/ftp`). You should place the publicly accessible files in the `/var/ftp/pub` directory.

Done!

REVIEW

This session introduced you to Internet services. You learned to use the mail server (`sendmail`) to exchange e-mail with other systems on the Internet. You also examined the setup of the Apache Web server, as well as where to place the HTML documents and where to look for the log files. Finally, you explored how anonymous FTP is set up on your Linux system.

QUIZ YOURSELF

1. Which configuration file stores the association between Internet services and port numbers? (See "Understanding Internet Services.")
2. What is a mail-transfer agent? (See "Using the E-mail Server.")

3. From which directory does the Apache Web server serve the Web pages (HTML files)? (See "Setting Up the Apache Web Server.")

4. Where are the Web server's configuration files stored? (See "Setting Up the Apache Web Server.")

5. In which directory should you place files you want others to download by using anonymous FTP? (See "Setting Up the FTP Server.")

Networking in Linux

Session Checklist

✔ Setting up an Ethernet LAN

✔ Configuring TCP/IP networking in Linux

✔ Using TCP/IP diagnostic commands in Linux

✔ Examining TCP/IP network configuration files

**30 Min.
To Go**

Linux includes extensive built-in networking capabilities. In particular, Linux supports TCP/IP (Transmission Control Protocol/Internet Protocol) networking over several physical interfaces such as Ethernet cards, serial ports, and parallel ports. (TCP/IP is a suite of networking protocols used for information exchange over the Internet. You do not need to know the details of TCP/IP to set up and use TCP/IP networking on your Linux system.) You typically use an Ethernet network for your local area network (LAN). TCP/IP networking over the serial port enables you to connect to other networks by dialing out over a modem.

This session focuses on Ethernet LANs. You learn to set up, configure, and monitor an Ethernet TCP/IP network. Much of what you learn also applies to TCP/IP networking over a dial-up modem, which is covered in Session 12.

Setting Up an Ethernet LAN

Ethernet is a standard way to move packets of data among two or more computers connected to a single cable. To set up an Ethernet LAN, you need an Ethernet card for each PC. Linux supports a wide variety of Ethernet cards for the PC.

Ethernet is a good choice for the physical data-transport mechanism because it's a proven, low-cost technology that provides good data transfer rates — typically 10 million bits per second (10 Mbps), although there are now 100 Mbps and even Gigabit Ethernet.

In an Ethernet LAN, computers are connected to the network with cables. Nowadays, there are two popular forms of Ethernet cables. The first option is *ThinNet,* or *10Base2*, which uses a thin, flexible coaxial cable. The more recent and more popular alternative is Ethernet over *unshielded twisted pair (UTP)* cable, known as *10BaseT*.

To set up a 10BaseT Ethernet, you need an Ethernet *hub* — a hardware box with RJ-45 jacks. You build the network by running twisted-pair wires (usually, Category 5 or Cat5 cables) from each PC's Ethernet card to this hub. Nowadays, you can get an 8-port 10BaseT hub for about $50 (U.S.). Figure 14-1 shows a typical, small 10BaseT Ethernet LAN you might set up at a small office or your home.

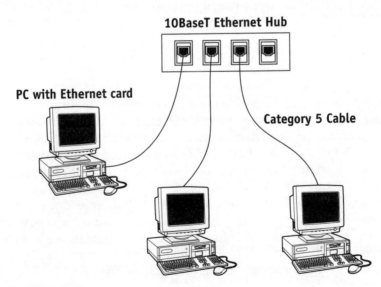

Figure 14-1
A 10BaseT Ethernet LAN with a hub

ThinNet Ethernet does not need a hub, which makes it attractive for small offices or home offices that have more than one PC. You can simply daisy chain the ThinNet cable from one PC to another and construct a small Ethernet LAN, as shown in Figure 14-2.

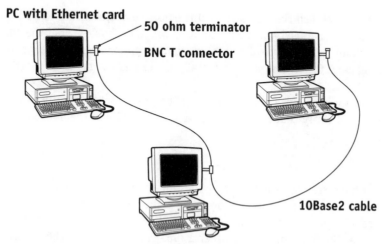

PC with Ethernet card
50 ohm terminator
BNC T connector
10Base2 cable

Figure 14-2
A small ThinNet Ethernet LAN

As Figure 14-2 shows, you need Ethernet cards in the PCs. The cards should have ThinNete connectors, known as *BNC connectors*. You also need segments of ThinNet cable (technically known as RG-58 thin coaxial cables with 50-ohm impedance). For each Ethernet card's BNC connector, you need a BNC *T-connector* (so called because the connector looks like a *T*), and you need two 50-ohm terminators for the two end points of the Ethernet network. Then all you have to do to complete your own Ethernet LAN is connect the parts in the manner shown in Figure 14-2. ThinNet is easy to set up, but it's not convenient to connect a large number of PCs this way. One problem is that any break in the cable causes the entire network to crash.

You can also connect a 10Base2 LAN with a 10BaseT LAN by using a hub that has a 10Base2 port and multiple 10BaseT ports.

On a 10Base2 LAN you can't simply connect the two Ethernet cards with a cable. Remember you have to use the BNC T-connectors and 50-ohm terminators even if you are connecting only two PCs on a 10Base2 LAN.

If you are running a 10BaseT LAN, it is possible to connect two computers together by using a special cable, called a crossover cable, between the Ethernet cards in each computer. This solution works for two computers, but for networks with more than two computers, this is not practical.

When you install Red Hat Linux from this book's companion CD-ROMs on a PC connected to an Ethernet LAN, the installation program should install the appropriate drivers for the card, provided the installation program successfully detects the Ethernet card. Otherwise, you can install Linux in expert mode, as described in Session 4.

Once properly installed, Linux should load the driver for the Ethernet card every time it boots. To verify that the Ethernet driver is loaded, use the dmesg command as follows:

```
dmesg | grep eth0
```

This command searches the boot messages for any line that contains the string eth0. (As discussed later in this session, eth0 is the device name for the first Ethernet card in your Linux system.) On my PC, I have a 3Com 3C503 Ethernet card installed. I get the following output when I type dmesg | grep eth0 on my system:

```
eth0: 3c503 at i/o base 0x300, node  02 60 8c 8e c6 a9, using internal xcvr.
eth0: 3c503-PIO, 16kB RAM, using programmed I/O (REJUMPER for SHARED MEMORY).
```

You should see something similar that shows the name of the Ethernet card and other relevant parameters. If the dmesg command does not show any Ethernet device, type grep eth0 /var/log/messages to look for the eth0 device name in the boot messages stored in the /var/log/messages file.

Configuring TCP/IP Networking

Like almost everything else in Linux, TCP/IP setup is a matter of preparing a bunch of configuration files (text files that you can edit with any text editor). These configuration files reside in the /etc directory and subdirectories of /etc. Most Linux distributions include a network configuration utility that you can use to configure the network. Refer to the documentation or help files for your specific distribution. First, you need to learn how to refer to the network devices.

Learning network-device names

For most devices, Linux uses files in the /dev directory. The networking devices, however, have names defined internally in the kernel; no files for these devices exist in the /dev directory (or, for that matter, in any directory). Following are the common network-device names in Linux:

- lo — the loopback device. This device efficiently handles network packets sent from your system to itself (when, for example, an X client communicates with the X server on the same system).

- eth0 — the first Ethernet card. If you have more Ethernet cards, they get device names eth1, eth2, and so on.

- ppp0 — the first serial port configured for a point-to-point link to another computer, using Point-to-Point Protocol (PPP). If you have more serial ports configured for PPP networking, they are assigned device names ppp1, ppp2, and so on.

- sl0 — the first serial port configured for Serial Line Internet Protocol (SLIP) networking. SLIP establishes a point-to-point link to a TCP/IP network. If you use a second serial port for SLIP, it gets the device name sl1.

You always have a loopback device (lo) regardless of your network. It passes data from one process to another without having to go out to a network. In fact, the loopback device allows network applications to work as long as the communicating processes are on the same system.

If you want to see the names of network devices installed on your system, log in as root, and type the following command:

```
cat /proc/net/dev
```

This command shows the names of currently installed network devices, as well as statistics on the number of packets sent and received for a specific device.

Running Red Hat's network configuration tool

When you set up TCP/IP networking during Red Hat Linux installation, the installation program prepares all appropriate configuration files by using the information you provide. However, Red Hat Linux comes with the netcfg graphical network configuration tool you can use to add a new network interface or to alter information such as name servers and host names. Other distributions also have network configuration tools. Refer to the documentation for your distribution to learn to use these tools.

To start the network configuration tool, log in as root, and type netcfg in a terminal window to start that program. The network configuration tool displays a dialog box, as shown in Figure 14-3.

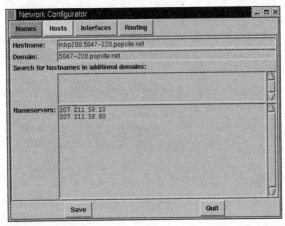

Figure 14-3
Configuring TCP/IP network with the netcfg network configuration tool

You can configure various aspects of your network through the four buttons at the top of the dialog box. Click each button to explore what entries you can add or edit. Specifically, these buttons enable you to do the following:

- *Names.* Enables you to enter the host name for your system and to enter the IP addresses of name servers. The name server addresses are stored in the /etc/resolv.conf file. The host name is stored in a variable in the /etc/sysconfig/network file.

- *Hosts.* Shows you the current contents of the /etc/hosts file and enables you to add, remove, or edit entries. That file contains host names and corresponding IP addresses for each host.

- *Interfaces.* Enables you to add a new network interface, specify the IP address of the interface, and activate the interface. This information gets stored in various files in the /etc/sysconfig directory.

- *Routing.* Enables you to add static routes (each route lists the gateway to use to reach a specified network).

To configure the network interfaces, you need to assign IP addresses to each interface. If you are running a private network, you may use IP addresses in the range 192.168.0.0 to 192.168.255.255. (There are other ranges of addresses reserved for private networks, but this range should suffice for most needs.) For example, I use the 192.168.1.0 address for a small private network.

Using TCP/IP Diagnostic Commands

20 Min. To Go

Assuming the network is configured, you can check to see whether the network is up and running and whether your Linux system is properly configured for TCP/IP networking. You can, of course, use network applications such as TELNET and FTP to verify that the network is up and running, but Linux also includes a number of utility programs that help you monitor and diagnose problems.

Checking the interfaces

Type the /sbin/ifconfig command to view the currently configured network interfaces. The ifconfig command also configures a network interface (associates an IP address with a network device) during system startup. However, if you run ifconfig without any command-line arguments, the command displays information about the current network interfaces. Here is the result of a typical invocation of ifconfig:

```
eth0      Link encap:Ethernet  HWaddr 02:60:8C:8E:C6:A9
          inet addr:192.168.1.200  Bcast:192.168.1.255  Mask:255.255.255.0
          UP BROADCAST RUNNING MULTICAST  MTU:1500  Metric:1
          RX packets:3007 errors:0 dropped:0 overruns:0 frame:0
          TX packets:1140 errors:0 dropped:0 overruns:0 carrier:0
          collisions:0 txqueuelen:100
          Interrupt:5 Base address:0x300

lo        Link encap:Local Loopback
          inet addr:127.0.0.1  Mask:255.0.0.0
          UP LOOPBACK RUNNING  MTU:3924  Metric:1
          RX packets:54 errors:0 dropped:0 overruns:0 frame:0
          TX packets:54 errors:0 dropped:0 overruns:0 carrier:0
          collisions:0 txqueuelen:0
```

This output shows that two interfaces — the loopback interface (lo) and an Ethernet card (eth0) — are currently active on this system. For each interface, you get to see the IP address, as well as statistics on packets delivered and sent. For the Ethernet card, ifconfig also reports the IRQ (shown as Interrupt: 5) and the base I/O port address (0x300). If the Linux system had a dial-up PPP link up and running, you'd also see an item for the ppp0 interface in the output.

Checking the IP routing table

Another network configuration command, /sbin/route, also provides status information when you run it without any command-line argument. If you are having trouble checking a connection to another host (that you specify with an IP address), check the IP routing table to see whether a default gateway is specified. Then check the gateway's routing table to ensure that paths to an outside network appear in that routing table.

A typical output from the /sbin/route command looks like this:

```
Kernel IP routing table
Destination    Gateway      Genmask          Flags Metric Ref    Use Iface
192.168.1.200  *            255.255.255.255  UH    0      0        0 eth0
192.168.1.0    *            255.255.255.0    U     0      0        0 eth0
127.0.0.0      *            255.0.0.0        U     0      0        0 lo
default        192.168.1.1  0.0.0.0          UG    0      0        0 eth0
```

As this routing table shows, the local network uses the eth0 Ethernet interface, and the default gateway is also that Ethernet interface. The *default gateway* is a routing device that handles packets addressed to any network other than the one in which the Linux system resides. In this example, packets addressed to any network address other than addresses that begin with 192.168.1 are sent to the gateway — 192.168.1.1 — and the gateway forwards those packets to other networks (assuming, of course, the gateway is connected to another network).

Checking connectivity to a host

To check for a network path to a specific host, use the ping command. The ping command is a widely used TCP/IP tool that employs a series of *Internet Control Message Protocol* (*ICMP*, often pronounced as *eye-comp*) messages. ICMP provides for an Echo message to which every host responds. Using the ICMP messages and replies, ping can determine whether the other system is alive and then compute the round-trip delay in communicating with that system.

The following example shows how I run ping (`ping 192.168.1.50`) to see whether one of the systems on my network is alive:

```
PING 192.168.1.50 (192.168.1.50): 56 data bytes
64 bytes from 192.168.1.50: icmp_seq=0 ttl=32 time=2.2 ms
64 bytes from 192.168.1.50: icmp_seq=1 ttl=32 time=1.2 ms
64 bytes from 192.168.1.50: icmp_seq=2 ttl=32 time=1.2 ms
64 bytes from 192.168.1.50: icmp_seq=3 ttl=32 time=0.8 ms

--- 192.168.1.50 ping statistics ---
4 packets transmitted, 4 packets received, 0% packet loss
round-trip min/avg/max = 0.8/1.3/2.2 ms
```

In Linux, ping continues to run until you press Ctrl+C to stop it; then it displays summary statistics showing the typical time it takes to send a packet between the two systems. On some systems, ping simply reports that a remote host is alive. However, you can still get the timing information with appropriate command-line arguments.

Examining TCP/IP Configuration Files

**10 Min.
To Go**

Configuring the network during installation or running the network configuration tool may be enough to get TCP/IP configured on your system, but you should also know the configuration files so you can edit them if necessary. For example, you can specify the name servers through the network configuration tool, but suppose you want to add an alternative name server. To do so, you can simply add these names directly to the /etc/resolv.conf file — the configuration file that stores the IP addresses of name servers.

In the remainder of this session, you familiarize yourself with the basic TCP/IP configuration files. Each of these configuration files is a text file you can examine with the cat or more command and edit using any text editor.

/etc/hosts

The /etc/hosts configuration text file contains a list of IP addresses and host names for your local network. In the absence of a name server, any network program on your system consults this file to determine the IP address that corresponds to a host name. Type the cat /etc/hosts command to view the contents of this file.

Following is the /etc/hosts file from my system, showing the IP addresses and names of other hosts on my LAN:

```
127.0.0.1        localhost        localhost.localdomain
# Other hosts on the LAN
192.168.1.100    lnb486
192.168.1.50     lnbp133
192.168.1.200    lnbp200
192.168.1.233    lnbp233
192.168.1.40     lnbp400
192.168.1.60     lnbp600
192.168.1.25     mac        lnbmac
192.168.1.1      lnbp75
```

As the example shows, each line in the file starts with an IP address, followed by the host name for that IP address. You can have more than one host name for a given IP address.

/etc/networks

The /etc/networks configuration file is another text file that contains the names and IP addresses of networks. These network names are commonly used in the routing command (/sbin/route) to specify a network by name instead of by its IP address.

Don't be alarmed if your Linux PC does not have the /etc/ networks **file. Your TCP/IP network works fine without this file. In fact, the Red Hat Linux installation program does not create a** /etc/networks **file.**

/etc/host.conf

The /etc/host.conf configuration text file specifies how Linux obtains the IP address that corresponds to a host name. Type cat /etc/host.conf to view the contents of this file. Typically, this file contains the following lines:

```
order hosts, bind
multi on
```

The entries in the /etc/host.conf file tell the resolver library what services to use, and in which order, to resolve names.

The order option indicates the order of services. The sample entry specifies that the resolver library should first consult the /etc/hosts file and then check the name servers to resolve a name. The name servers are listed in the /etc/resolv.conf file, which you examine next.

The multi on option specifies that hosts listed in the /etc/hosts **file can have multiple IP addresses. Hosts that have more than one IP address are called** *multihomed* **because the presence of multiple IP addresses implies that the host has several network interfaces (in other words, the host "lives" in several networks simultaneously).**

/etc/resolv.conf

The /etc/resolv.conf configuration file is another text file the resolver uses — a library that determines the IP address for a host name. Type cat /etc/resolv. conf to view the contents of this file. Following is a sample /etc/resolv.conf file:

```
search xyz.com
nameserver 164.109.1.3
nameserver 164.109.10.23
```

The search line specifies names of systems where to search for host names. The nameserver line provides the IP addresses of name servers for your domain. If you have multiple name servers, you should list them on separate lines. They are queried in the order they appear in the file. Typically, you list in the /etc/resolv.conf file the name servers your Internet Service Provider provides.

If you do not have a name server for your network, you can safely ignore this file. TCP/IP should still work, even though you can only refer to those hosts listed in the /etc/hosts **file.**

/etc/hosts.allow

This file specifies which hosts are allowed to use the Internet services (such as TELNET and FTP) that may be running on your system. The program that starts Internet services consults the /etc/hosts.allow file before starting. It starts the service only if the entries in the hosts.allow file imply that the requesting host can use the services.

The entries in /etc/hosts.allow are in the form of a *server:IP address* format, in which *server* refers to the name of the program providing a specific Internet service and *IP address* identifies the host allowed to use that service. For example, if you want all hosts in your local network (which has the address 192.168.1.0) to access the FTP service (which the in.ftpd program provides), add the following line in the /etc/hosts.allow file:

```
in.ftpd:192.168.1.
```

If you want to let all local hosts have access to all Internet services, you can use the ALL keyword and rewrite the line as follows:

```
ALL:192.168.1.
```

Finally, to open all Internet services to all hosts, you can replace the IP address with ALL as follows:

```
ALL:ALL
```

You can also use host names in place of IP addresses.

Security experts discourage allowing all hosts access to all services on your system. For a more secure system, you should deny all hosts access and then allow selected hosts access to your system. This means you should explicitly list in /etc/hosts.allow **those hosts that can access your system. Then deny all other hosts access to your system by using the** /etc/hosts.deny **file (which you examine in the next section).**

/etc/hosts.deny

This file is just the opposite of /etc/hosts.allow — whereas hosts.allow specifies which hosts may access Internet services (such as TELNET and FTP) on your system, the hosts.deny file identifies the hosts that must be denied services. The program that starts Internet services consults the /etc/hosts.deny file if it does not find any rules in the /etc/hosts.allow file that apply to the requesting host. The program denies service if it finds a rule in the hosts.deny file that applies to the host.

The entries in the /etc/hosts.deny file follow the same format as those in the /etc/hosts.allow file. They are in the form of a *server:IP address* format, in which *server* refers to the name of the program providing a specific Internet service and *IP address* identifies the host allowed to use that service.

Done!

Tip

Assuming you already set up entries in the `/etc/hosts.allow` **file to allow access to specific hosts, you can place the following line in** `/etc/hosts.deny` **to deny all other hosts access to any service on your system:**

```
ALL:ALL
```

REVIEW

This session showed you how to set up an Ethernet LAN by using 10Base2 or 10BaseT cables. You explored Red Hat's network configuration tool you can use to configure the network interfaces. You used a number of utility programs such as ping, route, and netstat to monitor the status of your TCP/IP network. Finally, you examined several TCP/IP configuration files that specify items such as host name and name servers, as well as which hosts can access services running on your system.

QUIZ YOURSELF

1. What is "ThinWire?" (See "Setting up an Ethernet LAN.")

2. What is the name of the first Ethernet device in a Linux system? (See "Learning Network-Device Names.")

3. How do you start the Red Hat network configuration tool? (See "Running Red Hat's Network Configuration Tool.")

4. What network utility do you use to check the connectivity to another system in the network? (See "Checking Connectivity to a Host.")

5. Which configuration file enables you to deny access to local Internet services? (See "/etc/hosts.deny.")

Setting up a Workgroup Server

Session Checklist

✔ Sharing files with NFS

✔ Setting up your Linux PC as a Windows server with Samba

**30 Min.
To Go**

A low-end Pentium PC (or even a 486) configured with Red Hat Linux (from this book's companion CD-ROMs) makes a very capable workgroup or office server. A *workgroup* is a small local area network (LAN) of perhaps a dozen or so PCs. You can configure the Linux PC to be the file and print server and the other PCs to be the clients. The client PCs can run Windows instead of Linux. This session introduces you to the Samba package, which comes with Linux and provides everything you need to set up your Linux PC as a server in a Windows network. However, first you learn about file sharing through Network File System (NFS), which provides another way of sharing files.

Sharing Files with NFS

The only problem in using NFS for file sharing is that each client system must support NFS. Most PCs do not come with NFS. This means you have to buy NFS software separately if you want to share files by using NFS. Sharing files with NFS is simple; it involves two basic steps:

- On the Linux server, export one or more directories by listing them in the /etc/exports file (thereby making them available to the client system).

- On each client system, mount the directories the Linux server exports by using the mount command.

It makes sense to use NFS if all systems on your LAN run Linux (or other variants of UNIX with built-in NFS support). In this session, I walk you through NFS setup by using an example of two Linux PCs on a LAN.

Exporting a file system with NFS

On the server, you must run the NFS service and designate one or more file systems to export — to make available to the client systems. You can perform both tasks by using the Linuxconf graphical system administration tool.

To start Linuxconf, log in as root, and select Main Menu ⇨ Programs ⇨ System ⇨ Linuxconf from the GNOME desktop. On the Linuxconf Config tab, click the Networking button. This brings up the Network configurator dialog box. Click the Exported file systems (NFS) button on the Server tasks tab of this dialog box. This brings up the Exported file systems dialog box that shows the current contents of the /etc/exports file. If that file is empty, Linuxconf displays the empty Exported file systems dialog box (as shown in Figure 15-1).

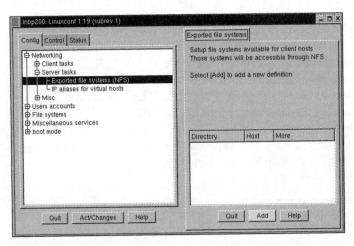

Figure 15-1
The empty Exported file systems dialog box

Click the Add button. This brings up the One exported file system dialog box, where you can specify the details of the exported file system. You specify the file system with a full pathname, as shown in Figure 15-2.

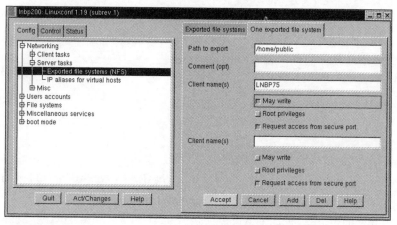

Figure 15-2
Entering information about exported file systems in Linuxconf

In this dialog box, you should also enter the names of client systems that may mount this exported file system. In the example shown in Figure 15-2, the /home/public directory is exported by the server, and the host named LNBP75 can mount this file system for read and write operations. After entering the information, click the Accept button. Linuxconf returns to the dialog box shown in Figure 15-1, where it displays summary information about the exported file system. You can then click the Quit button to finish defining exported file systems.

As a result of this session, Linuxconf adds the following entry to the /etc/exports file:

```
/home/public LNBP75(rw)
```

To verify that the exported directories are listed in the /etc/exports file, type cat /etc/exports in a terminal window. It is also possible to edit the /etc/exports file directly. For information about this file, type man exports in a terminal window.

Now you should turn on the NFS server. To do this, click the Control panel button on Linuxconf's Control tab. The Control panel dialog box appears. Click the Control service activity button in that dialog box. Linuxconf displays the Service control dialog box with a list of all services and their statuses, as shown in Figure 15-3.

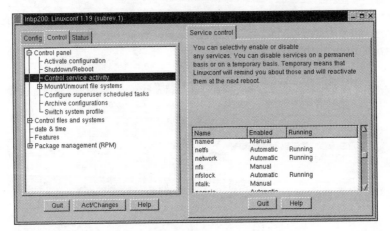

Figure 15-3
Viewing the services and their statuses in the Service control dialog box in Linuxconf

Each line has three fields: one provides the name of a service, another indicates whether it is enabled to run automatically or manually, and the last reveals whether it is already running. Scroll down the list, and locate the entry named nfs — the NFS service. In this case, the NFS service is not running yet. Click that entry. This causes Linuxconf to display the Service nfs tab, as shown in Figure 15-4.

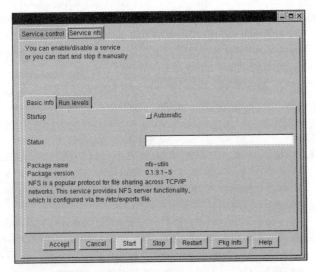

Figure 15-4
Starting the NFS service through the Linuxconf Service nfs tab

The buttons on this tab enable you to start, stop, or restart the service. In this case, click the Start button to start the NFS service. Then click Accept to return to the previous dialog box (Figure 15-3). Now the Service control dialog box should show the status of the `nfs` entry as `Running`. Click Quit to exit this dialog box.

 If you ever make changes to the exported file systems listed in the `/etc/exports` **file, remember to restart the NFS service. Click the Restart button in the dialog box shown in Figure 15-4.**

If you prefer to start the NFS service by using a command, log in as `root` and type the following command in a terminal window:

```
/etc/rc.d/init.d/nfs start
```

This command starts the nfsd server program on the Linux system. Now you can try to mount the exported file system from the client system.

Mounting an NFS file system

You can use Linuxconf on the client system to mount an exported NFS file system. However, the easiest way to perform the mount operation is to log in as `root` and use the `mount` command. For example, to mount the `/home/public` file system from the `lnbp200` system on the `/mnt/lnbp200` directory of the client system, type:

```
mount lnbp200:/home/public /mnt/lnbp200
```

To confirm that the NFS file system is mounted, log in as `root` on the client system, and type `mount` in a terminal window. You should see a line similar to the following regarding the NFS file system:

```
lnbp200:/home/public on /mnt/lnbp200 type nfs (rw,addr=192.168.1.200)
```

Setting Up the Linux PC as a Windows Server with Samba

20 Min. To Go

If your business relies on Windows for file and print sharing, you probably use Windows in your servers and clients. You can move to a Linux PC as your server without losing the Windows file and printer sharing because you can set up a Linux PC as a Windows server. When you install Red Hat Linux from this book's companion CD-ROMs, you also get a chance to install the Samba software package, which performs that task. All you have to do is select the *DOS/Windows Connectivity* package group during installation. Other distributions also offer the opportunity to install Samba during their installation.

After you install and configure Samba on your Linux system, client PCs running Windows 95/98/NT/2000 can access disks and printers on the Linux PC by using the Server Message Block (SMB) protocol, which is the underlying protocol in Windows file and print sharing.

With the Samba package installed, you can make your Linux PC a Windows client. This means the Linux PC can access the disks and printer a Windows server manages. The Samba software package has these major components:

- smbd: the SMB server, which accepts connections from Windows clients and provides file and print sharing services
- nmbd: the NetBIOS name server, which clients use to look up servers (*NetBIOS* stands for *Network Basic Input/Output System* — an interface that applications use to communicate with network transports such as TCP/IP.)
- /etc/samba/smb.conf: the Samba configuration file that the SMB server uses
- testparm: a program that ensures the Samba configuration file is correct
- smbclient: the Windows client, which runs on Linux and allows Linux to access the files and printer on any Windows server
- smbprint: a script, which enables printing on a printer on an SMB server
- smbadduser: a program that adds users to the SMB password file
- smbpasswd: a program that changes the password for an SMB user
- smbstatus: a command that lists the current SMB connections for the local host

The following sections describe how to install Samba from the companion CD-ROMs. They also discuss the process of setting up a printer on the Linux PC to print through Windows.

Checking if Samba is installed and installing Samba

Before installing Samba, check whether Samba is already installed by typing the following command in a terminal window:

```
rpm -q samba
```

If the `rpm` command displays a package name that begins with `samba`, such as

`samba-2.0.7-20`

Samba is already installed on your system, and you should skip the rest of this section. Otherwise, follow these steps to install Samba from this book's companion CD-ROMs:

1. Log in as `root` and make sure the companion CD-ROM is in the drive and mounted. If not, use the `umount /mnt/cdrom` command to dismount the current CD-ROM; replace it with the companion CD-ROM, and then mount it with the `mount /mnt/cdrom` command.

2. Change the directory to the CD-ROM — specifically to the directory where the Red Hat Package Manager (RPM) packages are located — with the following command:

    `cd /mnt/cdrom/RedHat/RPMS`

3. Use the following `rpm` command to install Samba:

    `rpm -ivh samba*`

    If Samba is already installed, this command returns an error message. Otherwise, the `rpm` command installs Samba on your system by copying various files to their appropriate locations.

These steps complete the unpacking and installation of Samba software. Now, to use Samba, simply configure it.

Configuring Samba

To set up the Windows file- and print-sharing services, you have to provide a configuration file named `/etc/samba/smb.conf`. The configuration file is a text file that looks like a Microsoft Windows 3.1 INI file.

Like the Windows INI files, the `/etc/samba/smb.conf` file consists of sections with a list of parameters in each section. Each section of the `smb.conf` file begins with the name of the section in brackets. The section continues until the next one begins or until the file ends.

Each line in a section specifies the value of a parameter by using this syntax:

`name = value`

As in Windows INI files, comment lines begin with a semicolon (`;`). In the `/etc/samba/smb.conf` file, comments may also begin with a hash mark or a number sign (#).

Text Editors are covered in Session 9.

The Samba software comes with a configuration file you can edit to get started. To prepare the configuration file, log in as root and use your favorite text editor to edit the file /etc/samba/smb.conf. Here's a sample configuration file without any comments:

```
[global]
    netbios name = LNBP200
    workgroup = LNB SOFTWARE
    server string = LNB Software-Red Hat Linux-Samba Server
    hosts allow = 192.168.1.   127.
    guest account = naba
    log file = /var/log/samba/log.%m

# Log files can be at most 50KB
    max log size = 50

    security = user
    smb passwd file = /etc/samba/smbpasswd

# Leave the next option as is - they're for performance
    socket options = TCP_NODELAY SO_RCVBUF=8192 SO_SNDBUF=8192

    remote browse sync = 192.168.1.255
    remote announce = 192.168.1.255/LNB SOFTWARE
    local master = yes
    os level = 33

    name resolve order = lmhosts bcast

    dns proxy = no
    unix password sync = no

[homes]
    comment = Home Directories
    browseable = no
    writable = yes
```

```
[printers]
    comment = All Printers
    path = /var/spool/samba
    browseable = no
    guest ok = no
    writable = no
    printable = yes

[tmp]
    comment = Temporary file space
    path = /tmp
    read only = no
    public = yes

[public]
    comment = Public Stuff
    path = /home/samba
    browseable = yes
    public = yes
    guest ok = yes
    writable = yes
    printable = no
    available = yes
    guest only = no
    user = naba
    only user = yes
```

Change the user name from naba to your user name and the server name to your server name. Also make sure all directories mentioned in the configuration file exist. For example, create the /home/samba directory by using the command mkdir /home/samba.

After editing the Samba configuration file, add two users to the Samba password file. First, add your user name. Here's how I add myself:

```
smbadduser naba:naba
- - - - - - - - - - - - - - - - - - - - - - - - - - - - - - - - - - - - - - - - - - - - - - - - - - - -
ENTER password for naba
New SMB password:          type the password
Retype new SMB password:   type password again
Added user naba.
```

Next, add the root user by using the command `smbadduser root:root`, and then provide a password. (This does not change the password of your Linux system's root user.)

After making the changes to the `/etc/samba/smb.conf` file, type `testparm` to verify that the file is OK. The `testparm` command checks the `/etc/samba/smb.conf` file and reports whether the file is OK. After that, restart the SMB services by using the following command:

```
/etc/rc.d/init.d/smb restart
Shutting down SMB services: [  OK  ]
Shutting down NMB services: [  OK  ]
Starting SMB services: [  OK  ]
Starting NMB services: [  OK  ]
```

Using SWAT

**10 Min.
To Go**

Beginning with version 2.0, Samba includes a utility called the Samba Web Administration Tool (SWAT). This tool makes setting up Samba very easy. SWAT allows you to use a Web browser as the interface to `/etc/smb.conf` and makes the necessary modifications to this file. A sample `smb.conf` file is created during installation that can be used for reference. Renaming this file is a good idea because you will be using SWAT to create a new `smb.conf` file, and it will overwrite the original file.

Before you can use SWAT, you need to change two files to enable it. The first file is `/etc/services`. This file is a list of internet services and their port numbers and protocols. You need to add the following line to `/etc/services`:

```
Swat        901/tcp
```

Next, you need to add a line to `/etc/inetd.conf`. The `inetd` daemon runs at system startup and listens for connections at specific ports. The `inetd.conf` file lists the programs that should be run when the `inetd` daemon detects a request at one of the ports. You need to add the following line:

```
swat     stream tcp     nowait.400     root /usr/sbin/swat swat
```

If you're interested in more details about this line, see the `inetd` **man page.**

Finally, you need to restart the `inetd` daemon so it will read the changes you made to `inetd.conf`. To do this type the following at the command prompt:

```
killall -HUP inetd
```

Now you can start a Web browser and get ready to run SWAT. Since most distributions include Netscape, you can use this browser to start SWAT. In the location box, enter the address for `localhost` and the port number for SWAT as `http://localhost:901`. This will open a dialog box that prompts you for a user ID and password. You have to be root to configure Samba, so enter root as the user ID and the password for root. SWAT's main screen, as shown in Figure 15-5, will appear after you enter the user ID and password.

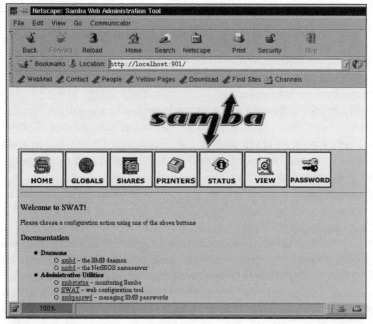

Figure 15-5
The main screen of the SWAT program appears after you enter the login information.

You can begin configuring the [`globals`] section by clicking on the Globals icon. The Globals Variables page appears. The values shown are obtained from the `smb.conf` file, which already exists on the system. As stated earlier, all systems include a default `smb.conf` file that will be used by SWAT. The values shown in your file will be different from those shown here because I have already made configuration changes.

The globals variables page is divided into six sections:

- Base Options
- Security Options
- Logging Options
- Tuning Options
- Browse Options
- WINS Options

After you have entered the appropriate values for your system, click on the Commit Changes button to save them to the file.

Next, you will create shares by clicking on the Shares icon. This will open the Share Parameters page. Enter the appropriate information for the share you want to configure for the computer that is running Windows. The information here is the same as discussed earlier when looking at the smb.conf file. Click on Commit Changes to save them to the smb.conf file.

Now you can set up a printer that the Windows computer can use for printing. Clicking on the Printers icon opens the Printer Parameters page where you can create and modify printer information. This page is similar to the Shares Parameters page except you need to create or select a printer rather than a share. To create a new printer, type the name of the printer and click Create Printer. If you already have a printer configured, it will be marked with an asterisk and can be selected from the drop-down list.

Enter the appropriate information for the [printer] share. The information here is the same as discussed earlier when looking at the [printer] section of the smb.conf file. Pay attention to the "Important Note" at the top of the Printer Parameters page. If you already have a printer configured in Linux, it becomes the default printer for Samba and you cannot delete it from the list. Be sure to click on Commit Changes to save the information to the smb.conf file.

After you create smb.conf, you can run a utility called testparm that checks the file for errors. At a command prompt, type testparm, and if all is well, you should see the sections of the /etc/smb.conf file being processed and an OK status when processing is finished. If you receive an error message, go back to the file and correct the error.

After making changes to the smb.conf file it is necessary to restart Samba services, or start them if they are not running. This can be done through SWAT by clicking the Status icon. The Server Status page shows if the Samba daemons are running. The two daemons are smbd and nmbd, and they can be started or restarted by clicking on the appropriate buttons.

Accessing the Samba server

You can now try to access the Samba server on the Linux system from one of the Windows systems on the LAN. Double-click the Network Neighborhood icon on the Windows desktop. This should open the Network Neighborhood window (see Figure 15-6) that shows with all the other Windows systems on the LAN.

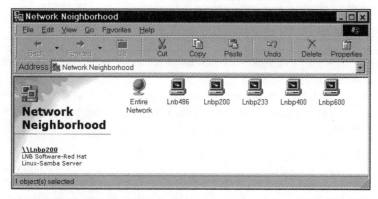

Figure 15-6
Viewing a Linux Samba server in the Windows Network Neighborhood

Click the Linux Samba server's icon to see its server string. Notice from the comment in the lower-left corner of Figure 15-6 that Lnbp200 is actually a Linux system.

If you do not see the Linux Samba server in the Network Neighborhood in Windows, select Start ⇨ Find ⇨ Computer; then type the Linux system's host name (see Figure 15-7), and click the Find Now button. The Linux Samba server should then show up on the screen.

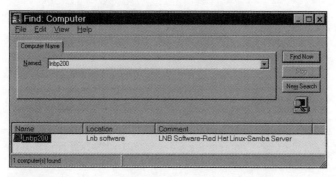

Figure 15-7
Searching for a Linux Samba server from Windows

Once you see the Linux Samba server, you can open it by double-clicking the icon. This should show folders for each shared directory in the Linux Samba server. (For the sample /etc/samba/smb.conf file shown previously, you see two directories: tmp and public). You can then open these folders to explore the contents of the directories further.

Accessing Windows resources with smbclient

You can use the smbclient program to access shared directories and printers on Windows systems on the LAN, as well as to check that your Linux Samba server is working. One quick way to check is to use the smbclient -L command to view the list of services on the Linux Samba server itself.

If you have other Windows servers on the LAN, you can look at their services by using the smbclient program. Here is the smbclient command I use to view the services on my 486 PC running Windows 95:

```
smbclient -L lnb486
```

You can also use smbclient to access a disk on a Windows server, as well as to send a file to a Windows printer. The smbclient program is similar to ftp — you connect to a Windows server and then use commands to exchange and send files to the printer.

The following example shows how I use smbclient to access a disk on my Windows 98 PC and view its directory (I type the command smbclient //lnbp400/c naba naba in a terminal window):

Done!

```
added interface ip=192.168.1.200 bcast=192.168.1.255 nmask=255.255.255.0
Got a positive name query response from 192.168.1.40 ( 192.168.1.40 )
smb: \> dir a*
  ATI                      D        0  Fri Apr 16 21:19:08 1999
  Acrobat3                 D        0  Sat Apr 17 15:14:10 1999
  autoexec.nav             A      230  Sat Apr 17 14:26:08 1999
  AUTOEXEC.BAT             A      321  Mon Apr  3 17:48:54 2000
  AUTOEXEC.BAK             A      272  Sun Apr 18 09:53:04 1999
  ASD.LOG                  HR     362  Tue Feb 29 18:28:06 2000
  ashley                   D        0  Thu Nov 18 21:11:18 1999

                64322 blocks of size 131072. 47399 blocks available
smb: \> quit
```

To see a list of smbclient commands, type help at the smb: \> prompt. To familiarize yourself with smbclient, you may want to try out some of these commands. Note that the smbclient commands are similar to MS-DOS commands.

REVIEW

This session showed you how to use NFS to share files among a Red Hat Linux system and other Linux or UNIX systems. Then you learned to configure your Linux system as a Windows server by using the Samba software package.

QUIZ YOURSELF

1. What are the basic steps in sharing files through NFS? (See "Sharing Files with NFS.")
2. How do you export a file system by using NFS? (See "Exporting a File System with NFS.")
3. How do you check if Samba is installed on your system? (See "Checking if Samba is Installed and Installing Samba.")
4. How do you configure your Linux system to provide Windows file-sharing services? (See "Configuring Samba.")
5. How do you access Windows resources from your Linux system? (See "Accessing Windows Resources with smbclient.")

Accessing Windows and DOS Files

Session Checklist

✔ Mounting and accessing a DOS/Windows partition from Linux

✔ Mounting and accessing a DOS/Windows floppy disk from Linux

✔ Accessing and using DOS floppy disks with the mtools utility program

**30 Min.
To Go**

Typically, you install Linux on a PC that previously had Microsoft Windows installed on it. If you happen to work in Windows as well as in Linux, you probably want to access the DOS/Windows files from Linux. This session shows you how to do this, as well as how to mount and access MS-DOS/Windows floppy disks. You also learn about a package called mtools, which enables you to access locally and use MS-DOS/Windows files on a floppy disk in Linux.

Mounting and Accessing a DOS/Windows File System

Linux has built-in support for MS-DOS files. As Session 7 reveals, Linux has a single file system that starts at the root directory and is denoted by a single slash (/). Even if you have a separate hard disk (or multiple hard disk partitions on a single disk), the contents of those hard disks appear logically somewhere in the Linux file system. *Mounting*, as discussed in Session 9, is the operation you perform to cause a physical storage device (a hard disk partition or a CD-ROM) to appear as part of the Linux file system.

Mounting DOS/Windows file systems during installation

During installation (see Session 2), the Red Hat installation program runs the Disk Druid program. This program finds any DOS/Windows partitions by checking the hard disk drive's partition table. Through the Disk Druid program, you can specify where you want to mount each DOS partition. (Mounting makes the DOS directory hierarchy appear as part of the Linux file system.) For example, you may mount the first DOS partition as /dosc, the second as /dosd, and so on. (You can name these mount points anything you want.) If you specify these mount points, Disk Druid performs the necessary steps to ensure that the DOS partitions are mounted automatically whenever you boot Linux.

To see whether your DOS/Windows hard disk partition is mounted automatically, follow these steps:

1. Use the grep command to look for the string vfat in the file /etc/fstab. Note the result I get by typing grep vfat /etc/fstab on one of my Linux PCs:

   ```
   /dev/hda1  /dosc  vfat   defaults   0 0
   ```

2. If the output shows one or more lines that contain vfat, your Linux system mounts DOS/Windows hard disk drive partitions automatically. In this example, the output shows a matching line whose first field is the partition name /dev/hda1 (the first partition on the first IDE disk); the second field, /dosc, shows where that partition is mounted.

3. If the grep command does not show any lines that contain the string vfat in /etc/fstab, your system does not mount any DOS/Windows hard disk partitions automatically. An explanation, of course, may be that your hard disk does not have any DOS partitions.

 You do not have to be the root user to perform the preceding steps.

Another quick way to find out about the mounted devices is to type mount (without any arguments) at the shell prompt. Following is the output of the mount command on my system:

```
/dev/hda3 on / type ext2 (rw)
none on /proc type proc (rw)
/dev/hda1 on /dosc type vfat (rw)(Windows partition mounted on /dosc)
none on /dev/pts type devpts (rw,mode=0622)
```

If you see any vfat in the output, those lines indicate MS-DOS file systems mounted on Linux. In this case, an MS-DOS partition is mounted on the Linux directory /dosc.

Even if you don't have DOS/Windows partitions on your hard disk, you should learn how to access a DOS/Windows file system from Linux because you may have to access a DOS/Windows floppy disk under Linux. Understanding the concept of mounting is the key to using a DOS file system in Linux.

Mounting a DOS/Windows file system with the mount command

As discussed in Session 9, you can use the mount command to mount a device on the Linux file system manually at a specified directory. That directory is referred to as the *mount point*. You can use any directory as the mount point. However, if you mount a device on a directory containing files, you lose the ability to access the files in that directory until you unmount the device by using the umount command. Therefore, you should always use an empty directory (such as /mnt/cdrom) as the mount point.

If your DOS/Windows partition is the first partition on your IDE drive and you want to mount it on /dosc, use the following mount command:

```
mount -t vfat /dev/hda1 /dosc
```

The -t vfat part of the mount command specifies that the device you mount — /dev/hda1 — has an MS-DOS file system. Linux has built-in support for MS-DOS files. Figure 16-1 illustrates the effect of this mount command.

Figure 16-1 also shows how directories in your DOS partition are mapped to the Linux file system. What once was the C:\DOS directory under DOS is now /dosc/dos under Linux. Similarly, C:\WINDOWS is now /dosc/windows. You probably can see the pattern. To convert a DOS filename to Linux (for this specific case, when you mount the DOS partition on /dosc), perform the following steps:

1. Change the DOS names to lowercase.
2. Change C:\ to /dosc/.
3. Change all backslashes (\) to slashes (/).

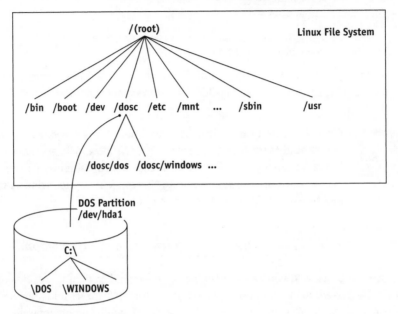

Figure 16-1
Mounting a DOS/Windows partition on the /dosc directory

Mounting and Accessing DOS/Windows Floppy Disks

**20 Min.
To Go**

Just as you can mount a DOS/Windows hard disk partition under Linux, you can mount a DOS/Windows floppy disk. Usually, you have to log in as root to mount a floppy, but you can follow the steps shown in the latter part of this session to set up your system so that any user can mount a DOS/Windows floppy disk. You also need to know the device name for the floppy drive. By default, Linux defines two generic floppy device names:

- /dev/fd0, which is the A: drive (the first floppy drive)
- /dev/fd1, which is the B: drive (the second floppy drive, if you have one)

As for the mount point, an existing directory named /mnt/floppy is specifically for this type of temporary mount operation. Thus, you can mount the DOS floppy disk on the /mnt/floppy directory by using the following command:

```
mount -t vfat /dev/fd0 /mnt/floppy
```

After the floppy is mounted, you can copy files to and from the floppy by using Linux's copy command (cp). To copy the file gnome1.pcx from the current directory to the floppy, type the following:

```
cp gnome1.pcx /mnt/floppy
```

Similarly, to see the contents of the floppy disk, type the following:

```
ls /mnt/floppy
```

When you want to remove the floppy disk from the drive, first dismount the floppy drive. This removes the association between the floppy disk's file system and the mount point on the Linux file system. Use the umount command to dismount a device, as follows:

```
umount /dev/fd0
```

You can set up your Linux system so that any user can mount a DOS floppy. You simply log in as root and add a line in the /etc/fstab file. For example, to enable users to mount a DOS floppy in the A: drive on the /a directory, perform these steps:

1. Log in as root.
2. Create the /a directory by using the following command:

   ```
   mkdir /a
   ```

3. Edit the /etc/fstab file in a text editor (such as vi or Emacs), and insert the following code. Then save the file, and quit the editor.

   ```
   /dev/fd0    /a    vfat    noauto,user    0 0
   ```

   On that line, the user option (which appears next to noauto) enables all users to mount DOS floppy disks. The first field in the line is the device name (/dev/fd0), the second field is the mount directory (/a), and the third field shows the type of file system (vfat).

4. Log out and log in as a normal (not root) user.
5. To test that you can mount a DOS floppy without being root, insert a DOS floppy in the A: drive, and type the following command:

   ```
   mount /a
   ```

   Notice that you use the mount directory as an argument for the mount command. The mount operation should succeed, and you should see a listing of the DOS floppy when you type the command ls /a.

6. To unmount the DOS floppy, type umount /a.

Using mtools to Access DOS/Windows Floppy Disks

So far, you've learned one way to access the MS-DOS file system: mount the DOS hard disk or floppy disk by using the mount command; then use regular Linux commands, such as ls and cp. This approach to mounting a DOS file system is fine for hard disks. Linux can mount the DOS partition automatically at startup, and you can access the DOS directories on the hard disk drive anytime.

If you want to get a quick directory listing of a DOS floppy disk, however, you may find mounting tedious. This is where the mtools package comes to the rescue. The mtools package is a collection of utilities that implements most common DOS commands. The commands have the same names as in DOS, except you add an m prefix to each command. Thus, mdir retrieves a directory listing, and mcopy copies files. The best part of mtools is that you do not have to mount the floppy disk to use the mtools commands.

Because the mtools **commands write to and read from the physical device (floppy disk), you have to log in as** root **to perform these commands. If you want other users to access the** mtools **commands, you have to alter the permission settings for the floppy-drive devices. Use the following command to permit other users to read from and write to the first floppy drive:**

```
chmod o+rw /dev/fd0
```

Verifying if mtools is installed

The mtools package comes with the Red Hat Linux distribution on this book's companion CD-ROMs. When you install Red Hat Linux, mtools is installed automatically as part of the base Linux. The mtools executable files are in the /usr/bin directory. To see whether you have mtools installed, type ls /usr/bin/mdir at the shell prompt. If the ls command shows that this file exists, mtools should be available on your system.

You also can type the following rpm command to verify that mtools is installed on your system:

```
rpm -q mtools
```

If mtools is installed, the output shows the full name of the mtools package.

```
mtools-3.9.7-3
```

This sample output shows that mtools version 3.9.7 is installed on the system. To try mtools, follow these steps:

1. Log in as root, or type su and then enter the root password.
2. Place an MS-DOS floppy disk in your system's A: drive.
3. Type mdir. You should see the directory of the floppy disk (in the standard DOS directory-listing format).

Checking the /etc/mtools.conf file

The mtools package should work with the default setup; but if you get any errors, check the /etc/mtools.conf file. This file contains definitions of the drives (such as A:, B:, and C:) that the mtools utilities see. Following are a few lines from a typical /etc/mtools.conf file:

```
drive a: file="/dev/fd0" exclusive 1.44m
drive b: file="/dev/fd1" exclusive 1.44m

# First SCSI hard disk partition
#drive c: file="/dev/sda1"

# First IDE hard disk partition
drive c: file="/dev/hda1"

# IDE Zip drive
drive X: file="/dev/hdd4" exclusive
```

The pound sign (#) indicates the start of a comment. Each line defines a drive letter, the associated Linux device name, and some keywords that indicate how the device is accessed. In this example, the first two lines define drives A: and B:. The third non-comment line defines drive C: as the first partition on the first IDE drive (/dev/hda1). If you have other DOS drives (D:, for example), you can add another line that defines drive D: as the appropriate disk partition.

If your system's A: drive is a high-density, 3.5-inch drive, you do not have to change anything in the default /etc/mtools.conf file.

Understanding the mtools commands

**10 Min.
To Go**

As I explain previously in this chapter, the mtools package is a collection of utilities. So far, you have seen the command mdir — the mtools counterpart of the DIR command in DOS.

If you know the MS-DOS commands, using the mtools commands is very easy. Type the DOS command in lowercase letters, and add m in front of each command. Because the Linux commands and filenames are case-sensitive, use all lowercase letters when you type the mtools commands.

Table 16-1 summarizes the various mtools utilities and some of their corresponding commands available in mtools version 3.9.6.

Table 16-1
Common mtools Commands

mtools Utility	MS-DOS Command (If Any)	Action
Mattrib	ATTRIB	Changes MS-DOS file-attribute flags
Mcd	CD	Changes an MS-DOS directory
Mcopy	COPY	Copies files between MS-DOS and Linux
Mdel	DEL or ERASE	Deletes an MS-DOS file
Mdeltree	DELTREE	Recursively deletes an MS-DOS directory
Mdir	DIR	Displays an MS-DOS directory listing
Mformat	FORMAT	Places an MS-DOS file system on a low-level formatted floppy disk (use fdformat to low-level format a floppy in Linux)
Mlabel	LABEL	Initializes an MS-DOS volume label
Mmd	MD or MKDIR	Creates an MS-DOS directory

mtools Utility	MS-DOS Command (If Any)	Action
mmove	N/A	Moves or renames an MS-DOS file or subdirectory
mrd	RD or RMDIR	Deletes an MS-DOS directory
mren	REN or RENAME	Renames an existing MS-DOS file
mtype	TYPE	Displays the contents of an MS-DOS file
xcopy	XCOPY	Recursively copies a DOS directory into another

You can use the mtools commands just as you use the corresponding DOS command. For example, the mdir command works like the DIR command in DOS. The same goes for all other mtools commands shown in Table 16-1.

Formatting a DOS/Windows floppy disk

Suppose you have to copy files on an MS-DOS/Windows floppy disk. If you already have a formatted MS-DOS/Windows floppy, you can simply mount that floppy and copy the files to the floppy by using the Linux cp command. What if you do not have a formatted DOS floppy? The mtools package again comes to the rescue.

The mtools package provides the mformat utility, which can format a floppy disk for use under MS-DOS. Unlike the DOS format command that formats a floppy in a single step, the mformat command requires you to follow a two-step process:

1. Use the fdformat Linux command to low-level format a floppy disk. The fdformat command expects the floppy device name to be the argument; the device name includes all parameters necessary for formatting the floppy disk. To format a 3.5-inch high-density floppy disk in your system's A: drive, type fdformat /dev/fd0H1440.

2. Use the mformat command to put an MS-DOS file system on the low-level formatted floppy disk. If the floppy is in drive A:, type the following command:

Done!

```
mformat a:
```

REVIEW

This session showed you how to access and mount the DOS/Windows file systems from Linux and how to mount a DOS/Windows file system by using the mount command. You also learned to use the mtools utility programs to format and access a DOS/Windows floppy disk directly from Red Hat Linux without first having to mount the floppy disk.

QUIZ YOURSELF

1. How do you check if your Linux system is set up to mount any DOS disk partitions automatically? (See "Mounting and Accessing a DOS/Windows File System.")

2. What mount command do you use to mount a DOS partition with the device name /dev/hda1 on the mount point /dosc? (See "Mounting a DOS/Windows File System with the mount Command.")

3. What is mtools? (See "Accessing and Using DOS/Windows Floppy Disks with mtools.")

4. What are some of the mtools commands? (See "Understanding the mtools Commands.")

5. How do you format a DOS/Windows floppy disk in Linux? (See "Formatting a DOS/Windows Floppy Disk.")

PART

III

Saturday Afternoon

1. What are the Linux device names for serial ports COM1 and COM2? What are the IRQ and I/O port address of COM1?

2. Describe how you dial a remote system by using the Minicom program. What must you do before you can run Minicom as an ordinary user?

3. What commands can you use to determine if Linux has detected the serial port in your PC?

4. What is Ethernet? What peripheral do you need to connect to an Ethernet local area network? What do 10Base2 and 10BaseT mean? How do you determine if your Linux system has loaded the Ethernet driver?

5. What are some diagnostic commands for TCP/IP networking in Linux? Which command do you use to check if the network interfaces are up and running? How do you check if your Linux system has a network path to another host?

6. Name a few TCP/IP configuration files in Linux. Which file contains the IP addresses of the name servers?

7. How does a typical home office or small office user connect a Linux system to the Internet? Compare dial-up networking with DSL or cable modem.

8. How does dial-up networking differ from dialing out with a serial communications program such as Minicom?

9. What is PPP? What information do you need from your Internet Service Provider before you can set up dial-up networking with PPP? What programs do you run on your Linux system to set up a PPP connection?

10. Explain how you share a single Internet connection through your Linux system with other systems on the local area network. What software do you have to use to perform this task?

11. What are some common Internet services? What are ports? Which configuration file contains information about services and the corresponding port numbers?

12. What are the two types of software needed to provide the e-mail service? What is the common TCP/IP protocol for transporting e-mail?

13. Where are the Apache Web server's configuration files and log files located by default? Name the script that starts the Apache Web server when your Linux system boots.

14. What is anonymous FTP? Describe the steps involved in downloading a file via anonymous FTP. In which directory of your Linux system should you place files you want to make available for downloading via anonymous FTP?

15. Describe how you can set up a file server with Network File System (NFS). Provide an overview of how you set up the server and what you have to do at a client to access the server's file system.

16. How do you use the Samba software to set up your Linux system as a Windows server? How do you check if Samba is installed? What is the configuration file for Samba? Show the command that enables you to restart the Samba software.

17. Assume your Linux system is on a local area network that includes other PCs running Windows and your Linux system has Samba installed and running. From the Linux system, how do you access the files in a Windows server?

18. Suppose the /dev/hda2 hard disk partition has a DOS file system and you want to mount that file system on your Linux system at the mount point /mnt/dos. Show the command line to perform this task. How do you ensure that Linux mounts the /dev/hda2 partition automatically whenever the system boots?

19. What can you do with the mtools package? How do you check if mtools is installed on your system? What is the mtools configuration file?

20. List a few mtools commands. What are these commands patterned after? How do you copy all the files with the .doc extension from a DOS floppy to the current directory on the hard disk (assume that you are already in that directory when you type the command to perform this task)?

PART

IV

Saturday Evening

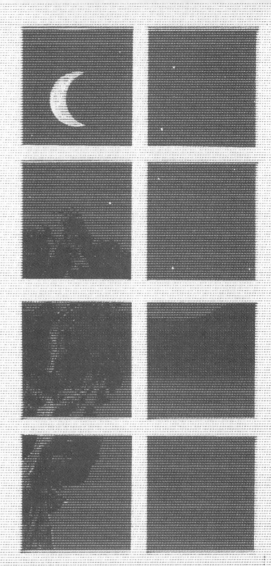

Customizing the GNOME and KDE Desktops

Session Checklist

✔ Customizing the GNOME desktop

✔ Changing the default desktop

✔ Customizing the KDE desktop

**30 Min.
To Go**

This evening, I focus on using the GNOME and KDE graphical desktops, as well as some of the applications and utilities that come bundled with Red Hat Linux. This session shows you how to customize the GNOME and KDE desktops. You also learn how to switch your default desktop from GNOME to KDE and vice versa. The other two major distributions of Linux, Caldera and SuSe, use KDE as their default desktop. My descriptions of KDE in this session are applicable to KDE used in both Caldera and SuSe.

Customizing the GNOME Desktop

As I discuss in Session 4, the default look and feel of the GNOME graphical desktop is similar to that of Windows 95/98/NT/2000, and you do not have to customize anything to begin using it. However, if you want, you can customize the GNOME desktop just as you can customize Windows 95/98/NT/2000. For example, you can select a different background or change the appearance of the window borders.

To try your hands at customizing the GNOME desktop, log in from the graphical login screen. I assume that GNOME is your default desktop environment because that's what you usually get when you install Red Hat Linux. Later in this session, you learn how to switch the default desktop from GNOME to KDE and vice versa.

 If GNOME is not your default desktop, simply select Session ⇨ GNOME from the login window, and then enter your username and password.

You can configure most aspects of the GNOME desktop's look and feel — the appearance and behavior — from a graphical application called the GNOME Control Center. To launch the Control Center, select Main Menu ⇨ Programs ⇨ Settings ⇨ GNOME Control Center, or click the toolbox icon in the GNOME panel.

The GNOME Control Center's window is vertically divided into two parts — a narrower menu area on the left side and a larger workspace on the right side. The left side shows a tree menu of all configuration items (also known as *capplets*). The top-level menu items are organized into several categories, such as Desktop and Multimedia. You can click a category to see its subcategories. To configure an item, locate the item in the tree menu, and click that item. The selected capplet's user interface then appears in the workspace on the right-hand side. The user interface is usually a dialog box with settings you can change.

In the next sections, you try out a few customization steps with the Control Center. After you finish using the Control Center, select File ⇨ Exit to quit.

Changing the background

To try a simple customization, select Desktop ⇨ Background from the tree menu. The GNOME Control Center then runs the background properties capplet that, in turn, displays a window in the workspace (as shown in Figure 17-1).

As you can see, this window looks similar to the Display Properties dialog box in Windows 95/98/NT. It enables you to select a background of solid color or pick the *wallpaper* (an image used as the background). You can select a background of solid color or a color gradient in which the background starts with one color and gradually changes to another color. The gradient can start in the vertical direction (top to bottom) or the horizontal direction (left to right).

Go ahead and click the Gradient button and see what happens. You get to preview the changes in the image of a monitor that appears in the dialog box.

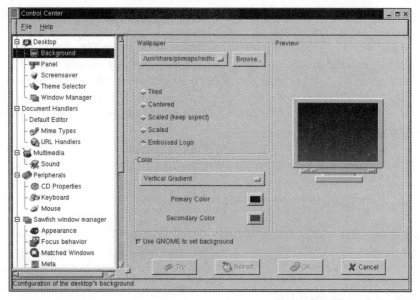

Figure 17-1
Using the GNOME Control Center to customize GNOME desktop's background

To select new colors for Primary Color or Secondary Color (see Figure 17-1), click the button that displays the color (either Primary Color or Secondary Color). This brings up a color selection dialog box from which you can pick a color.

If you want to use an image as the wallpaper, click the Browse button in the Wallpaper section of the dialog box. A Wallpaper selection dialog box displays the contents of the /usr/share/pixmaps/redhat directory — where you can find some background images to select. You can also try the /usr/share/pixmaps/backgrounds directory for more background images. Try, for example, the /usr/share/pixmaps/backgrounds/space directory that has a collection of images of the earth as seen from space. You can select any JPEG or PNG format image file as the wallpaper.

To try out any of these changes on the desktop, click the Try button. You can revert to the original setting by clicking the Revert button. When you are finished making the changes, click the OK button to close the dialog box and apply the changes.

Selecting a theme

Another, more exciting customization is to select a new theme for the entire user interface. A *theme* refers to a consistent collection of appearance and behavior (look and feel) for all the user-interface components such as buttons, check boxes, scroll bars, and so on. To try out some new themes, select Desktop ➪ Theme Selector from the tree menu. From the theme selector dialog box, you can try out different themes and select one you like. When you select a theme, you can see its appearance in the preview area. For example, select the MockMack theme from the list of available themes, and then click the Try button. It causes the look and feel of the GNOME desktop, including the Control Center window, to resemble that of the Apple Macintosh.

If you like a theme, click the OK button to use that theme. Otherwise, click the Revert button to return to the default theme.

Customizing the window manager

**20 Min.
To Go**

GNOME does not depend on any specific window manager. The default window manager is called Sawfish, but you can select another window manager if you want. To choose a window manager, select Desktop ➪ Window Manager from the Control Center tree menu. You should see a list of window managers available on your system, as shown in Figure 17-2.

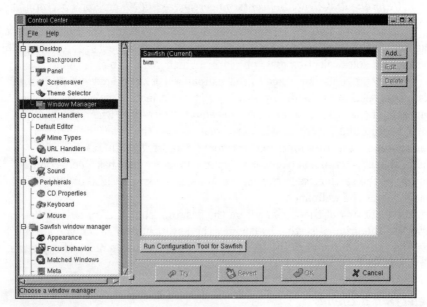

Figure 17-2
Selecting or customizing a window manager

In this case, the list shows two window managers: Sawfish and twm. As you can see, the parenthetical note shows that Sawfish is the current window manager. If you want, you can try out the twm window manager by selecting that window manager and then clicking the Try button. Later on, click Revert to return to the Sawfish window manager.

Like any window manager, Sawfish adds the title bar, frame, and other decorations around each window so users can click and drag to change a window's location or alter its size. (Think for a moment; if there were no frame and title bar, you could not move or resize the window.)

Sawfish includes a configuration tool for changing the look and feel of the window frames and title bars. You can activate the configuration tool by clicking the button labeled Run Configuration Tool for Sawfish (see Figure 17-2). This brings up the Sawfish configurator, which provides a tree menu of configuration options. Through this menu, the Sawfish configurator enables you to change how the Sawfish window manager decorates windows, adds special visual effects and sound, and behaves in response to mouse clicks and keystrokes. You can try out some of the configuration items in the Sawfish configurator.

Changing the Default Desktop

10 Min. To Go

GNOME and KDE are both capable graphical desktop environments. Red Hat Linux comes with both of these GUIs, but you get GNOME as the default desktop. Just before you log in at the graphical login screen, you can always select a specific desktop from the Session menu of the login window. However, Red Hat also includes a Desktop Switcher utility that enables you to switch the default desktop from GNOME to KDE and vice versa. To switch from GNOME to KDE, follow these steps:

1. From your GNOME desktop, select the Main Menu (foot) ⇨ Programs ⇨ System ⇨ Desktop Switching Tool. The Desktop Switcher dialog box appears.

2. In the Desktop Switcher dialog box, click the KDE radio button to select it. Then click the OK button. Another dialog box appears.

3. A message in the new dialog box informs you that the desktop configuration has been changed, but you must restart X. Click the OK button to dismiss the dialog box.

Although the message in Step 3 states that you must restart X, all you need to do is log out of the session and log back in. To log out, select Main Menu ⇨ Log out. When you log in again, you should get the KDE desktop.

To switch the default desktop from KDE to GNOME, log in as root, and select K ⇨ Red Hat ⇨ System ⇨ Desktop Switching Tool from the KDE desktop. In the Desktop Switcher dialog box, select GNOME as the desktop. After you log out of KDE and log back in, GNOME will be your desktop.

Customizing the KDE Desktop

Now that you know how to change your desktop from GNOME to KDE and vice versa, select the KDE desktop, and log in as a user. Like GNOME, KDE also includes a graphical application, called the KDE Control Center. You can use the KDE Control Center to customize various aspects of KDE, including the desktop background, icons, and font. To start the KDE Control Center, select K ⇨ KDE Control Center; or from the panel, click the button with the icon depicting a circuit board and a monitor.

When the KDE Control Center starts, it displays the main window with a tree menu on the left and some summary information about your system in the workspace to the right.

The KDE Control Center's tree menu shows the items you can control with this tool. The tree menu is organized into eleven categories: File Browsing, Look & Feel, Network, Help, Information, Peripherals, Personalization, Power Control, Sound, System, and Web Browsing. Click the plus sign to the left of an item to view the subcategories for that item. To change an item, go through the tree menu to locate the item; then click it. The item's configuration options then appear on a dialog box tab on the right side of the window.

Changing the background and theme

To customize the desktop background, select Look & Feel ⇨ Background on the tree menu. The Background tab appears (see Figure 17-3) with options for customizing the desktop's background.

For the current desktop (labeled One) you can select either a one- or two-color background or wallpaper (an image used as a background). For example, if you want to use wallpaper as your background, click the Browse button. This brings up an Open dialog box showing the JPEG files in the /usr/share/wallpapers directory. You can select one of these images and click OK. Then click the Apply button in the KDE Control Center to apply this wallpaper to the desktop. If you like the appearance, click OK. Otherwise, click Default, and then click Apply again to revert to the original background.

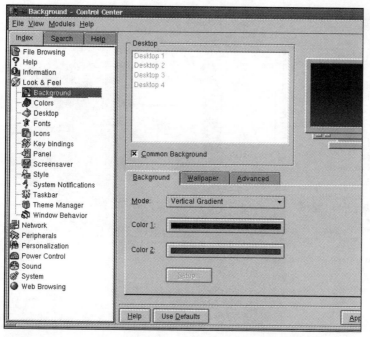

Figure 17-3
Using the KDE Control Center to customize the desktop background

As you can see from the menu items in the Look & Feel category (Figure 17-3), you can customize a number of aspects of the background from borders and colors to language for menus. I won't go through all the items here, but you should experiment with some of these customizations. For example, you can select the Theme Manager to try out one of several themes much like the themes offered in the GNOME Control Center. Figure 17-4 shows the result of selecting and previewing a theme.

Selecting a color scheme

If you want to pick a color scheme for the desktop colors, select Look & Feel ⇨ Colors in the KDE Control Center's tree menu. The Colors tab then appears. You can then scroll down the list of color schemes and select one to preview. When you select a color scheme, the preview area on the tab shows how that color scheme looks. To apply a color scheme to the desktop, click the Apply button. If you don't like the scheme, click Default, and then click Apply again to revert to the default color scheme.

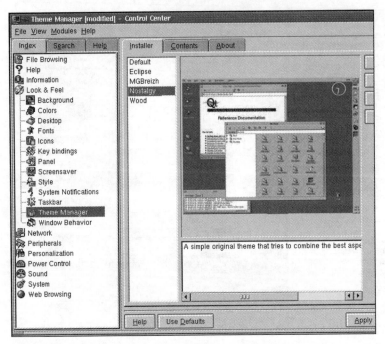

Figure 17-4
Selecting and previewing a theme in the KDE Control Center

Done!

Performing other tasks

In addition to desktop customization, the Information item in the KDE Control Center enables you to perform many more tasks, such as associating sound files with events (such as opening or closing a window), defining keyboard shortcuts, and viewing information about your system. You should take the remaining time in this session to explore the other items in the tree menu of the KDE Control Center.

REVIEW

This session showed you how to customize the GNOME graphical desktop's appearance (look) and behavior (feel). You used the GNOME Control Center to change various aspects of the desktop's look and feel. You learned to change the default desktop from GNOME to the KDE graphical desktop and vice versa. Finally, you also used the KDE Control Center to customize the look and feel of KDE.

QUIZ YOURSELF

1. What graphical application do you use to customize the GNOME desktop? (See "Customizing the GNOME Desktop.")

2. How do you customize the Sawfish window manager? (See "Customizing the Window Manager.")

3. How do you change your default desktop from GNOME to KDE and vice versa? (See "Changing the Default Desktop.")

4. What tool do you use to customize the KDE desktop? (See "Customizing the KDE Desktop.")

5. How do you select a color scheme for the KDE desktop? (See "Customizing the KDE Desktop.")

Screen Savers and Playing Games

Session Checklist

✔ Activating screen savers

✔ Playing games in GNOME

✔ Playing games in KDE

**30 Min.
To Go**

ow that you know how to customize the GNOME and KDE graphical desktops and how to switch from one to the other, you can turn to some fun. Both GNOME and KDE desktops in Linux come with quite a few games and screen savers. In this session, you learn how to set up and activate the screen savers and explore some games.

> **Note**
>
> You should have the games installed on your system, assuming you selected the Games package group when you installed Red Hat Linux from this book's companion CD-ROMs in Session 3. If you did not install the Games package group, go to Session 23 and follow the instructions for installing packages.

Activating Screen Savers

By default, your Linux system uses a randomly selected screen saver. Whenever you do nothing for some time (usually 20 minutes), the screen saver comes on. The screen saver can also act as a screen-locking program — you must type your password to get back to the graphical desktop.

Setting up a screen saver in GNOME

To select and try out a screen saver from the GNOME desktop, start the GNOME Control Center by clicking the toolbox icon on the GNOME panel. Then select Desktop ⇨ Screen Saver from the tree menu in the Control Center. A dialog box, from which you can select a screen saver, appears in the Control Center's workspace. The miniscreen on the upper-right corner of the dialog box shows how the selected screen saver looks, as shown in Figure 18-1.

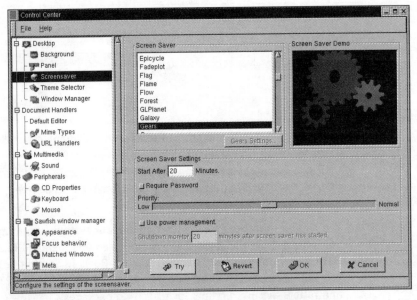

Figure 18-1
Selecting and previewing a screen saver in the GNOME Control Center

From the dialog box shown in Figure 18-1, you can also select several other screen-saver settings. For example, you can set the number of minutes of inactivity after which the screen saver comes on. If you click the Require Password check box and enable it, the screen saver locks the screen and forces you to enter your password before you can return to the desktop.

The scroll bar labeled Priority enables you to specify the priority of the screen saver program. You should leave it at the default setting (which is midway between Low and Normal) or make it low; this ensures that other processes have higher priority. After all, just because there is no mouse or keyboard activity does not mean your Linux system is idle. You may be compiling a huge program when the screen saver activates. In that case, you don't want the screen saver to use up too much of the processor's time.

The check box labeled *Use power management* applies if your PC supports power management features. If you check this check box, the screen saver puts the system and monitor in a "sleep" mode that draws less power than normal operation.

Setting up a screen saver in KDE

If you use the KDE desktop, you can select and test screen savers from the KDE Control Center. Start it by clicking the monitor and circuit board icon on the KDE panel or by selecting K ⇨ KDE Control Center. Then select Look & Feel ⇨ Screensaver from the tree menu in the KDE Control Center. The Screensaver tab, from which you can select and preview screen savers (as shown in Figure 18-2), appears in the Control Center's workspace.

Each screen saver also has its own setup. To set up the selected screen saver, click the Setup button on the KDE Control Center's Screensaver tab. This brings up that screen saver's Setup dialog box, from which you can set up that screen saver's configurable parameters.

You can also easily test a screen saver from the KDE Control Panel's Screensaver tab. Simply click the Test button that appears under the list of screen savers. This causes the screen saver to activate the full screen. You can return to the desktop by pressing a key or moving (or clicking) the mouse. The Test button makes it really easy to test the KDE screen savers.

The KDE Control Center's Screensaver tab also enables you to set other parameters that control the screen saver. Specifically, you can set the number of minutes of inactivity after which the screen saver should start in the Wait for box. You can also click the check box labeled Require password to make the screen saver require a password before returning to the desktop. Additionally, you can set the priority of the screen-saver process.

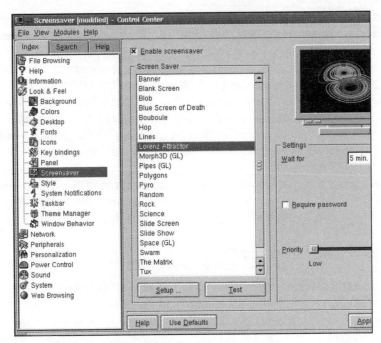

Figure 18-2
Selecting and previewing a screen saver in the KDE Control Center

Playing Games in GNOME

**20 Min.
To Go**

Next, try some games that come with Red Hat Linux. Many of these games also come with the Caldera and SuSe distributions. Check the Games menu in your distribution to see what is available. You can access these games from the GNOME or KDE desktops. First, start with the GNOME games.

Select Main Menu (foot) ⇨ Programs ⇨ Games to view the menu of available games. Figure 18-3 shows a typical Games menu in GNOME. As you can see, the GNOME desktop's Games menu offers over twenty games.

In addition to these games, you can also play all KDE games from the GNOME desktop. Simply select Main Menu (Foot) ⇨ KDE menus ⇨ Games to view the KDE Games menu. The rest of this section describes some of the popular GNOME games.

Card games

If you like card games such as FreeCell or Solitaire, you'll like the AisleRiot game. AisleRiot is a card program that can play 30 different card games, including such well-known games as FreeCell and Klondike.

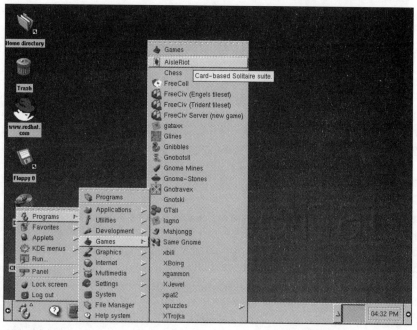

Figure 18-3
The Games menu in GNOME

To start AisleRiot, select Main Menu (Foot) ⇨ Programs ⇨ Games ⇨ AisleRiot. The default game is Klondike, which is what you get when you start AisleRiot.

If you want to play a different card game in AisleRiot, select Games ⇨ New Game from the menu. AisleRiot displays a long list of card games. You can choose another card game from this list. If you need help, select Help ⇨ AisleRiot. This brings up the AisleRiot Help screen in the GNOME Help browser.

GNOME also comes with a stand-alone FreeCell card game. You can play this game by selecting Main Menu ⇨ Programs ⇨ Games ⇨ FreeCell. After the main window appears, click the New button on the toolbar to start a new game. Now you can play the game.

Gnome-Stones

Gnome-Stones is a game in which you run around a cave collecting diamonds and avoiding being crushed by rocks. Select Main Menu ⇨ Programs ⇨ Games ⇨ Gnome-Stones to start the game. You can select Settings ⇨ Preferences to choose the type of cave you want to explore. Then select Game ⇨ New Game to start a game. Use the arrow keys to move the little person around and collect the diamonds.

GNOME Mahjongg

Select Main Menu ⇨ Programs ⇨ Games ⇨ Mahjongg to start the GNOME Mahjongg game. In this version of Mahjongg, your goal is to find and click matching pairs of tiles, which are then removed from the game board.

If you have trouble locating matching tiles, click the Hint button on the toolbar. The game program then flashes two matching tiles for a short time. You can then click those tiles one after another. Of course, the point of the game is for you to figure out which tiles to remove, so you should use the Hint button sparingly.

Chess game

Select Main Menu ⇨ Programs ⇨ Games ⇨ Chess to start a game of chess. By default, the computer plays black and you play white. You get the first move. To make your move, click and drag a white piece to its new position. The chess program checks and stops you from making any illegal moves.

Once you move, the computer responds with its move. Initially, the computer responds promptly, but the moves take longer as the game progresses. A timer counts down the time for whoever has the current turn.

Playing Games in KDE

**10 Min.
To Go**

To try out the games available on the KDE desktop, log in after selecting KDE as the current desktop. (Remember to select Session ⇨ KDE from the login window.) From the KDE desktop, select K ⇨ Games to view the menu of available games. Figure 18-4 shows a typical menu of games in KDE.

As the menu shows, KDE includes more than a dozen games in its game menu. You can try any of these games by selecting one from this menu.

KDE includes its own version of Mahjongg, which is similar to the GNOME version of Mahjongg introduced earlier in this session.

Now that you know where to find and how to start the GNOME games, you can try them out at your leisure. In the remainder of this session, you can play a few KDE games.

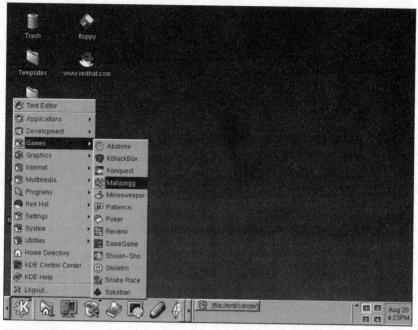

Figure 18-4
The game menu in KDE

Minesweeper

Minesweeper is a popular game you may have played on your PC (because it comes with Microsoft Windows). In Minesweeper, your goal is to locate all the mines in a minefield represented by squares arranged in a grid. You are supposed to uncover all squares that do not contain mines and mark all squares that contain mines.

To run the KDE version of Minesweeper, select K ⇨ Games ⇨ Minesweeper. To play, click squares to clear them. When you uncover a square that does not have adjacent mines, Minesweeper clears out all other neighboring squares that also do not touch squares with mines. The number on an uncovered square tells you how many mines are in the adjacent squares. To mark a square you suspect has a mine, click the right mouse button on that square. When you mark a square by right-clicking, a red flag appears on it.

The Games menu in GNOME also includes a Minesweeper game — it's called GNOME Mines.

Patience

Patience is another Solitaire card game, similar to GNOME's AisleRiot. In Patience, you can play several card games, such as Klondike and FreeCell. To run Patience, select K ⇨ Games ⇨ Patience. By default, Patience starts a Klondike card game. To play another card game, select Game ⇨ Choose New Game, and pick a game from the resulting menu.

Shisen-Sho

Done!

Shisen-Sho is a Mahjongg-like game. To start a game, select K ⇨ Games ⇨ Shisen-Sho. To play the game, you select matching tiles you must connect by horizontal or vertical lines without crossing over any other tile.

REVIEW

In this session, you learned how to select, configure, and preview screen savers in both GNOME and KDE desktops. Then you explored some games in the GNOME desktop. Finally, you spent some time trying out a few games in KDE.

QUIZ YOURSELF

1. How do you select and try out a screen saver in GNOME? (See "Setting up a Screen Saver in GNOME.")

2. How do you configure a screen saver in KDE? (See "Setting up a Screen Saver in KDE.")

3. How can you make sure a GNOME screen saver "locks the screen?" (See "Setting up a Screen Saver in GNOME.")

4. How do you access and start the games available in GNOME? (See "Playing Games in GNOME.")

5. What games are available in KDE, and how do you start them? (See "Playing Games in KDE.")

Multimedia Applications

Session Checklist

✔ Configuring the sound card

✔ Playing audio CDs

✔ Working with graphics and images

**30 Min.
To Go**

L inux comes with quite a few multimedia applications that enable you to play audio CDs and manipulate graphics and images. In this session, you try out several multimedia applications and learn to work with graphics and images. You start the session by configuring your PC's sound card in Red Hat Linux because you need a working sound card to listen to audio CDs.

Configuring the Sound Card

Your PC must have a sound card and speakers to play audio CDs. I assume your PC has a sound card and you have the speakers hooked up according to the instructions from the PC's manufacturer.

Red Hat, and other versions of Linux, requires sound driver software to access and control the sound card. The sound drivers are provided as modules you can load after booting Linux. In Red Hat, you can configure the sound card by running the /usr/sbin/sndconfig utility. This is a text-mode configuration program, so you should run it from a text console by using the following procedure:

1. From the graphics screen, press Ctrl+Alt+F1. This brings you to a text-mode virtual terminal that displays a login prompt. Log in as root.

2. Type /usr/sbin/sndconfig. A message informs you that the utility will probe for sound cards. Press Enter to continue with the probing.

3. The utility displays the result of probing for sound cards. Press Enter to continue the configuration.

4. The utility then displays one or more dialog boxes that indicate existing configuration files will be replaced. Press Enter to continue each step.

5. A dialog box informs you that sndconfig will play a sound sample. Press Enter.

6. If all goes well, you should hear sound. A dialog box asks you if you hear sound. If you hear sound, press Enter to select Yes. Otherwise, press Tab to select No, and then press Enter.

7. If you select No, sndconfig shows a dialog box from which you can manually select the interrupt request number (IRQ), I/O port addresses, and direct memory access (DMA) channels.

8. The utility then plays a *MIDI Musical Instrument Digital Interface* sound sample. You should now hear the MIDI sound sample. You can go through and confirm this part as well.

 You can play audio CDs and other sound files even if you cannot hear the MIDI sample play.

Note

9. After you exit sndconfig, type **exit** to log out. Then press Ctrl+Alt+F7 to return to the graphical user interface.

Once you configure the sound card for Red Hat Linux, you can play audio CDs and other sound files.

The Caldera and SuSe distributions also have programs for configuring sound cards. In Caldera, you need to run the COAS utility and select the Configure Sound Card option. In SuSe, you need to start the YaST2 program and choose the Configure Sound Card option. Both of these utilities probe for a sound card and attempt to configure it. You are then offered the opportunity to test the configuration. If the configuration is correct, you hear a sample sound being played. If there is no sound, you can go back and try different IRQ, DMA, and port addresses for your sound card to try to get it to work. After the sound card is properly configured, you can play audio CDs and other sounds in these distributions.

Playing Audio CDs

You need a special application to play audio CDs in Linux. All Linux distributions come with several CD-player applications such as xplaycd, an X application that provides a graphical control panel for playing audio CDs. Additionally, both GNOME and KDE come with CD players.

 Before using any CD-player program, make sure you dismount any CD-ROM in the drive (use the umount /dev/cdrom **command introduced in Session 8) and place an audio CD in the drive.**

To try out the xplaycd program, type xplaycd in a terminal window from the GNOME or KDE desktop. The graphical user interface of xplaycd is intuitive. Try out the buttons to see how they work. Click the Exit button to quit the program.

If you are using the GNOME desktop, you can play audio CDs by using the CD Player application. To launch the GNOME CD Player, select the Main Menu (Foot) ⇨ Programs ⇨ Multimedia ⇨ CD Player. Figure 19-1 shows this CD player playing a track from an audio CD.

Figure 19-1
The GNOME CD Player playing a track from an audio CD

As you can see, the GNOME CD Player displays the title of the CD and the name of the current track. The GNOME CD Player gets the song titles from CDDB — a CD database on the Internet. This means you need an active Internet connection for the CD Player to download song information from the CD database. Once the CD Player downloads information about a particular CD, it caches that information in a local database for future use. The CD Player's user interface is intuitive, and you can learn it easily. One nice feature is that you have the ability to select a track by title.

To learn more about CDDB, read the Frequently Asked Questions about CDDB at http://www.cddb.com/faq.html.

If you want to log in as a normal user and play audio CDs on the CD-ROM drive, you should first log in as root and set the permissions settings on the CD-ROM device so that everyone can read the CD-ROM device. You have to set the permissions for the actual CD-ROM device, not the generic /dev/cdrom device. To set the permissions settings, follow these steps:

1. Log in as root. If you are already logged in, type the su command, and enter the super user's password to assume the identity of root.

2. Make the CD-ROM device readable by all users by using the chmod command as follows:

   ```
   chmod o+r /dev/cdrom
   ```

Everyone who has access to your Linux PC can now play audio CDs and access the CD-ROM drive.

If you use KDE as your desktop, you can find a similar audio CD player in KDE. Start the KDE CD Player by selecting K ⇨ Multimedia ⇨ CD Player. You can then use it to play a track from an audio CD.

Working with Graphics and Images

The applications in this category enable you to prepare, view, modify, and print graphics and images. In the remainder of this session, you try out a few graphics and image-manipulation applications.

**20 Min.
To Go**

The GIMP

The *GIMP (GNU Image Manipulation Program)* is an image-manipulation program written by Peter Mattis and Spencer Kimball and released under the GNU General Public License (GPL). You install it if you select the Graphics Manipulation package when you install Red Hat Linux from this book's companion CD-ROMs.

To try out the GIMP, select Main Menu ⇨ Programs ⇨ Graphics ⇨ The GIMP from the GNOME desktop (from the KDE desktop, select K ⇨ Graphics ⇨ The GIMP). The

GIMP starts and displays a window containing information about how to complete a personal installation. The message informs you that a personal installation involves creating a directory called .gimp-1.1 in your home directory and placing a number of files in that directory. This directory essentially holds information about any changes to user preferences you might make to the GIMP. Go ahead and click the Continue button at the bottom of the window. The GIMP creates the necessary directories, copies some files to those directories, and guides you through a series of dialog boxes to complete the installation.

After the installation is complete, click the Continue button. From now on, you don't see those two installation windows; you have to deal with them only when you run the GIMP for the first time.

The GIMP then loads any plug-ins — external modules that enhance its functionality. A startup window displays messages about each plug-in as it loads.

After finishing the startup, the GIMP displays a tip of the day in a window. You can browse the tips and then click the Close button to close the tip window. At the same time it displays the tips window, the GIMP displays the toolbox (as shown in Figure 19-2).

Figure 19-2
The GIMP toolbox

Part IV—Saturday Evening
Session 19

The toolbox has three menus on the menu bar: File, Xtns (extensions), and Help. The File menu includes options to create a new image, to open an existing image, and to quit the GIMP. The Xtns menu gives you access to a lot of extensions to the GIMP. The exact content of the Xtns menu depends on which extensions are installed on your system. The Help menu items enable you to get help.

To open an image file in the GIMP, select File ⇨ Open. This brings up the Load Image dialog box that enables you to select an image file. You can change directories and select the image file you want to open. GIMP can read most common image-file formats such as GIF, JPEG, TIFF, PCX, BMP, PNG, and PostScript. After you select the file and click the OK button, the GIMP loads the image into a new window. Figure 19-3 shows an image the GIMP has opened.

Figure 19-3
Displaying an image with the GIMP

The toolbox in Figure 19-2 also has a large number of buttons, each with an icon, that represent the tools you use to edit images and apply special effects. You can get pop-up help on each tool button by placing the mouse pointer on the button. You can select a tool by clicking the tool button; then you can apply that tool's effects on an image.

For your convenience, the GIMP displays a pop-up menu when you right-click your mouse on the image window. The pop-up menu has most of the options from the File and Xtns menus in the toolbox. You also can pick some additional options, such as printing or mailing the image. You can then select specific actions from these pop-up menus.

You can do much more than just load and view images with the GIMP, but you have to spend quite a bit of time learning all of its features. To learn more about GIMP, select Xtns ➪ Web Browser ➪ GIMP.ORG ➪ Documentation. This brings up the Web browser with the online documentation for the GIMP. (You need an Internet connection for this to work.)

Ghostscript

**10 Min.
To Go**

Ghostscript is a utility for previewing and printing PostScript documents. Ghostscript enables you to print PostScript documents on many non-PostScript devices.

At its heart, Ghostscript is a nearly complete implementation of the PostScript language. Ghostscript includes the interpreter that processes PostScript input and generates output on an output device. A Ghostscript device can be a printer (or display screen), as well as an image-file format such as BMP or PCX.

Ghostscript is distributed under the GNU GPL, but Aladdin Enterprises copyrights it and maintains it. Some Ghostscript documentation is installed in the /usr/doc directory. To change to the appropriate directory, type cd /usr/doc/ ghostscript*. (The exact directory name depends on the version of Ghostscript installed on your system.) You can find the latest contact information in the README file in that directory. That directory also contains some other Ghostscript documentation. All of these documentation files are text files you can view by using the more command.

You typically use Ghostscript to load and view a PostScript file. To see how Ghostscript renders a PostScript document, you can use any available PostScript document you have. One good solution is to use one of the sample PostScript files in the `/usr/share/ghostscript/5.50/examples` directory (replace 5.50 with whatever version of Ghostscript is installed on your system) and include it in the `gs` command. Type the following command, for example, in a terminal window:

```
gs /usr/share/ghostscript/5.50/examples/golfer.ps
```

Ghostscript opens that file, processes its contents, and displays the output in another window (as shown in Figure 19-4).

Figure 19-4
Ghostscript displaying a PostScript file

In this case, the output is a picture of a golfer. After displaying the output, Ghostscript produces the following message:

```
>>showpage, press <return> to continue<<
```

Press Enter to continue. For a multiple-page PostScript document, Ghostscript then shows the next page. After all the pages are displayed, you return to the Ghostscript prompt. Type `quit` to exit Ghostscript.

Ghostview

Ghostview is an X-based graphical front end to the Ghostscript interpreter. Ghostview is ideal for viewing and printing PostScript documents. For a long document, you can even print selected pages. You also can view the document at various levels of magnification (zooming in or out).

To run Ghostview, type `ghostview &` in a terminal window. This command causes the Ghostview window to appear. The window is divided into three parts:

- Along the top edge, you see eight buttons. The first six buttons are menu buttons; when you click any of these buttons, a menu appears.

- On the left side, you see several more buttons, text boxes for information display, and scroll bars for scrolling the image.

- The large area occupying most of the Ghostview window is the work area where Ghostview displays the PostScript document.

To load and view a PostScript document in Ghostview, select File ⇨ Open or click the Open button on the left side of the Ghostview window. This action causes Ghostview to display a file-selection dialog box. Use this dialog box to select a PostScript file. You can choose one of the PostScript files that come with Ghostview. For example, select the file `tiger.ps` in the `/usr/share/ghostscript/5.50/examples` directory.

If your system has a version of Ghostscript later than 5.50, you have to use the new version number in place of 5.50.

To open the selected file, click the Open File button in the file-selection dialog box. Ghostview opens the selected file, processes its contents, and displays the output in its window (as shown in Figure 19-5).

In the last two buttons on the upper-right corner of the window, Ghostview displays the current filename and the date the file was created. Ghostview takes this information from the comments in the PostScript file itself, not from the time stamp of the file.

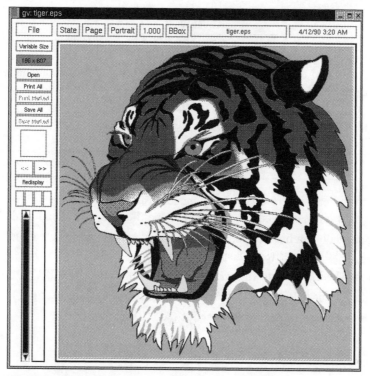

Figure 19-5
Ghostview displaying a PostScript file

As you move the mouse over the image, Ghostview displays the coordinates of the mouse pointer in a button along the upper-left corner of the window.

Done!

Note

Ghostview is useful for viewing documentation that comes in PostScript format. (Files typically have the `.ps` extension in their names.) For example, you can use Ghostview to view the documentation for the CVS program, which comes in several PostScript files you can find in the `/usr/share/doc/cvs*` directory. When viewing such documents in Ghostview, use the magnification button—the button labeled 1.000 in Figure 19-5. If you click that button and hold the mouse down, a menu appears with a number of magnification factors from 0.1 to 10.0. You may have to select a magnification of 2.000 or more to make the document legible onscreen.

REVIEW

This session showed you how to configure the sound card and to use a few CD-player applications to play audio CDs on your Linux system. You also familiarized yourself with several applications — GIMP, Xpaint, Ghostscript, and Ghostview — for working with image files of various formats.

QUIZ YOURSELF

1. How do you employ the /usr/sbin/sndconfig utility to configure the sound card for use in Red Hat Linux? (See "Configuring the Sound Card.")
2. What steps do you have to perform so that any user can play audio CDs on the CD-ROM drive? (See "Playing Audio CDs.")
3. What is "The GIMP," and what can you do with it? (See "The GIMP.")
4. How do you view PostScript files with Ghostscript? (See "Ghostscript.")
5. How is Ghostview related to Ghostscript (See "Ghostview.")

GNOME and KDE Office Tools

Session Checklist

✔ Using the Gnumeric spreadsheet

✔ Using calendars

✔ Using calculators

✔ Using the spelling checker

✔ Learning about commercially available office applications

**30 Min.
To Go**

This session's focus is on office applications — applications you need for day-to-day office work. This book's companion CD-ROMs include all Red Hat Linux office tools I discuss in this session: calendars, calculators, and spelling checkers. These tools are also included with the Caldera and SuSe distributions. I also introduce you to several prominent, commercially available office applications for Linux that are not included on the companion CD-ROMs.

Using the Gnumeric Spreadsheet

The GNOME desktop comes with *Gnumeric* — an X-based graphical spreadsheet program. To try out Gnumeric, select Main Menu ➪ Programs ➪ Applications ➪ Gnumeric spreadsheet from the GNOME panel. The Gnumeric program displays its main window, which looks similar to Windows-based spreadsheets such as Microsoft Excel. (In fact, Gnumeric can read and write Excel 95 spreadsheet files.)

You use Gnumeric the same way you use Microsoft Excel. You can type entries in cells, use formulas, and format the cells (specifying the type of value and the number of digits after the decimal point).

You might want to type data in a sample spreadsheet. Use formulas you normally use in Microsoft Excel. For example, use the formula SUM(D2:D6) to add up the entries from cell D2 to D6. To set cell D2 as the product of the entries A2 and C2, type =A2*C2 in cell D2. To learn more about the functions available in Gnumeric, select Help ⇨ Gnumeric function reference from the menu. This brings up the GNOME Help Browser containing information about the Gnumeric functions. You can browse the list of functions and click one to read more about that function.

When you finish preparing the spreadsheet, select File ⇨ Save As to save it. A dialog box appears from which you can specify the file format, the directory location, and the name of the file. Gnumeric can save the file in a number of formats: XML (eXtensible Markup Language), Excel 95, a simple text file, and Adobe's Portable Document Format (PDF) file. You cannot read the file back into Gnumeric unless you save it as an XML or Excel 95 file. Gnumeric's default file format is XML, which is a text-based format. However, Gnumeric compresses the resulting XML file by using the GNU Zip (gzip) compression program. Gnumeric assigns a .gnumeric extension to files stored in the compressed XML format.

Save the spreadsheet in Excel 95 format. Then transfer that file to a Windows system, and try to open it using Microsoft Excel. Notice that the file loses some of the text styles (such as boldface and justification) in the translation, but the basic elements (the numbers and the formulas) stay intact when you save the spreadsheet in Excel 95 format.

KDE does not come with its own spreadsheet program, but you can run Gnumeric by selecting K ⇨ Programs ⇨ Applications ⇨ Gnumeric from the KDE desktop.

Using Calendars

The companion CD-ROMs contain several calendar programs. The GNOME desktop comes with its own calendar program. Additionally, when you install the X Window System by following the steps outlined in Session 1, you also install ical — an X

Window System–based calendar program. You can start both calendars from the GNOME panel's Main Menu button or from the KDE main menu.

The ical calendar

To start ical, select Main Menu ⇨ Programs ⇨ Applications ⇨ ical from the GNOME desktop. (You can also type ical in a terminal window.) The program displays a full-screen window where you can click a date to view that day's schedule. To add appointments for a specific time, click the time, and type a brief description of the appointment.

You can go to a different month or year by clicking the arrows next to the month and the year. After you finish adding events and appointments, select File ⇨ Save to save the calendar.

The GNOME calendar

GNOME comes with a calendar program. To start the GNOME calendar, select Main Menu ⇨ Programs ⇨ Applications ⇨ Calendar from the GNOME panel. The GNOME calendar's main window appears. The GNOME calendar has a different, but intuitive, user interface from the ical program.

The calendar program has a toolbar that contains a number of buttons for performing common tasks. Underneath the toolbar, a number of tabs display the appointments in four different views: daily, weekly, monthly, and yearly. If you are unsure about what a button does, place the mouse pointer on the button; a small pop-up help message gives you some information.

To add an appointment, double-click the date in the right side of the window; then click the New button on the toolbar. This brings up a dialog box where you can enter information about the appointment. Select File ⇨ Save to store the appointments on the disk.

Using Calculators

You have a choice of three calculators you can use with Red Hat Linux:

- xcalc, the X calculator that comes with the X Window System
- GNOME calculator
- KDE calculator

**20 Min.
To Go**

All of these calculators are scientific calculators capable of performing typical calculations, such as square root and inverse, as well as trigonometric functions, such as sine, cosine, and tangent.

The xcalc calculator

The xcalc calculator is styled after Texas Instrument's TI-30 model. Type xcalc & in a terminal window to use the xcalc calculator. Figure 20-1 shows the resulting calculator. You can use the calculator by clicking the buttons or by entering the numbers on the keyboard.

Figure 20-1
The xcalc TI-30-style calculator

If you prefer the Reverse Polish Notation (RPN) of the Hewlett-Packard calculators, you can get a calculator modeled after the HP-10C by typing the xcalc -rpn & command. In RPN, the operands precede the operation. For example, to add 2.25 to 9.95 on an HP-10C calculator, press the keys in the following order: 2.25 ENTER 9.95 +.

The GNOME calculator

The GNOME calculator is based on xcalc, but has a nicer user interface. To run the GNOME calculator, select Main Menu ➪ Programs ➪ Utilities ➪ Simple Calculator in the GNOME panel. Figure 20-2 shows the resulting display of the GNOME calculator.

If you compare Figure 20-2 with Figure 20-1, you see that both xcalc and the GNOME calculator have the same set of buttons — except the buttons look better in the GNOME calculator.

Figure 20-2
The GNOME calculator

The KDE calculator

KDE also includes a scientific calculator that has more features than xcalc and the
GNOME calculator. For example, it can perform calculations in hexadecimal, decimal, octal, and binary format. From the KDE desktop, you can start the KDE calculator by selecting K ⇨ Utilities ⇨ Calculator (or Main Menu ⇨ KDE menus ⇨
Utilities ⇨ Calculator from the GNOME Panel).

Using the KDE calculator, you can convert a number from one base to another
by choosing the base, entering the number and then clicking to change the desired
base. For example, to convert the hexadecimal value FF to decimal, click the Hex
button, and enter FF. Then click the Dec button to see the answer, which should
be 255.

Using the Spelling Checker

The aspell utility is an interactive spelling checker. When you install Red Hat
Linux from the book's companion CD-ROMs, you have the opportunity to install
ispell.

Using aspell is simple. You use it to check the spelling of words in a text file.
To do so, type aspell check *filename*. To try out aspell, type some notes, and
save them in a text file named notes.txt. To run the spell checker on that file,
type the following command in a terminal window:

```
aspell check notes.txt
```

After aspell runs, it scans the file named notes.txt until it finds a misspelled word (any word that does not appear in aspell's dictionary). As the following output shows, aspell displays the sentence with the misspelled word (*concensus*) and highlights that word by enclosing it in a pair of asterisks.

```
This note describes the *concensus* reached during the August 16
meeting.
1) consensus            6) consensus's
2) con census           7) consensuses
3) con-census           8) consciences
4) condenses            9) condensers
5) concerns             0) consensual
i) Ignore               I) Ignore all
r) Replace              R) Replace all
a) Add                  x) Exit
?
```

Below that sentence, aspell lists possible corrections, numbering them sequentially from 1. In this case, the utility lists *consensus* — the right choice — as the first correction for *concensus*. The list also includes a few items labeled with a letter that represents specific actions, such as ignore the misspelling or accept the targeted word for the rest of the file.

At the end of the list of choices, aspell displays a question mark prompt indicating that you need to select one of the options shown. To choose an option, press one of the numbers or letters from the list shown in aspell's output to indicate what you want aspell to do.

To read the aspell **manual, start the Web browser, and select File ⇨ Open Page; click the Choose File button from the Open Page dialog box. Go to the** /usr/share/doc **directory, and look for a directory name that begins with** aspell **(the complete name depends on the** aspell **version number). From the** man_html **subdirectory of that directory, open the** 1_Introduction.html **file.**

Commercially Available Office Applications

Most businesses need office applications: word processors, spreadsheets, and the like. Initially, Linux lacked in this area; but now, Linux users can choose among several commercial office productivity applications, such as WordPerfect Office

**10 Min.
To Go**

2000 for Linux (http://linux.corel.com/), Applixware Office (http://
www.vistasource.com/), and StarOffice (http://www.sun.com/staroffice/).
These products do cost some money, but the cost is usually less than the cost of
Microsoft Office — the leading office application suite for Windows. (Microsoft
Office is a collection of several applications: Microsoft Word for word processing;
Microsoft Excel for spreadsheets; Microsoft PowerPoint for presentation graphics;
and Microsoft Access for databases, among others.)

**This book's companion CD-ROMs do not include any of these com-
mercial office applications for Linux, but the next few sections
briefly describe these applications. As you read the descriptions,
you can visit each vendor's Web site for the products.**

WordPerfect Office 2000 for Linux

Corel Corporation's WordPerfect Office 2000 for Linux is a complete office-
applications suite that includes WordPerfect 9 for word processing, Quattro Pro 9
for spreadsheets, and Corel Presentations 9 for presentation graphics. The product
comes bundled with many more components, such as Adobe Acrobat Reader (for
PDF files), as well as many clip art images. Corel even bundles a copy of Corel
Linux (based on the Debian distribution), but you can also install and use
WordPerfect Office 2000 on any Linux distribution.

WordPerfect Office can open, edit, and save files in a number of Microsoft Word
and Microsoft Excel formats, as well as WordPerfect formats from other systems.
According to Corel, you need about 140MB of hard disk space for a typical installation of WordPerfect Office 2000; the full installation requires about 450MB.

**You can learn more about the latest release of WordPerfect Office
2000 for Linux by visiting Corel's Web site at** http://linux.
corel.com/. **The links at that Web site also lead you to Corel's
online store, where you can purchase the product.**

Applixware Office

Applixware Office is another prominent office-application suite for all Linux distributions. In April 2000, Applix, Inc. formed a separate group — VistaSource, Inc. —
that focuses solely on Linux applications.

Like other office suites, Applixware Office includes *Words* for word processing,
Spreadsheets for spreadsheets, and *Graphics and Presents* for presentation graphics.

Additionally, it also has *Mail* (an e-mail interface) and *Data* (an interactive relational database browsing tool). Applixware Office can also read and write documents in Microsoft Office and Corel WordPerfect formats, as well as in several other file formats. Although trial versions are not offered, the entire Applixware Office suite is priced below $100 U.S. You can also purchase Words or Spreadsheets separately; each of these costs less than $50 U.S.

You can learn more about Applixware at VistaSource's Web site (http://www.vistasource.com/**).**

StarOffice

StarOffice is another commercial office applications suite, created by StarDivision of Hamburg, Germany and purchased by Sun Microsystems. StarOffice is a cross-platform solution — you can run StarOffice on Linux, Windows 95/98/NT, Sun Solaris SPARC, Sun Solaris x86, and OS/2. Also, StarOffice is available in several languages: English, French, German, Spanish, Italian, Swedish, Dutch, and Portuguese. StarOffice 5.2 for Linux is provided in the form of a large tar file (a form of archive), which you can download for free.

StarOffice is unique in that it combines all of its components into a common desktop from which you can open new documents, drag and drop documents from one application to another, and access the Internet. StarOffice includes the following components:

- *StarOffice Writer* for word processing (Microsoft Word–compatible)
- *StarOffice Calc* for spreadsheets (Microsoft Excel–compatible)
- *StarOffice Impress* for presentations (Microsoft PowerPoint–compatible)
- *StarOffice Draw* for vector graphics drawing
- *StarOffice Base* for data management
- *StarOffice Schedule* for organizing events, tasks, contacts, and projects
- *StarOffice Mail* for electronic mail
- *StarOffice Discussion* for participating in Internet newsgroups

Done!

You can download a copy of StarOffice for free from http://www.sun.com/staroffice/**. You can also find the details of Sun's StarOffice licensing policy at the same URL.**

REVIEW

This session introduced you to office applications for Linux. You tried out a few common office tools — spreadsheets, calendars, calculators, and spelling checkers — that come with Linux. You also learned about several commercially available office-application suites for Linux — WordPerfect Office 2000 for Linux, Applixware Office, and StarOffice. These commercial applications are not part of most Linux distributions, but you learned how to find out more about each product in case you need a Linux office suite for your home or business.

QUIZ YOURSELF

1. What are the default file format and file extension of the Gnumeric spreadsheet? (See "Using the Gnumeric Spreadsheet.")

2. How do you add an appointment in the GNOME Calendar? (See "GNOME Calendar.")

3. What choice of calculators do you have to work with Linux? (See "Using Calculators.")

4. What utility do you use to check the spellings in a text file? (See "Using the Spelling Checker.")

5. What are some commercially available office applications for Linux? (See "Commercially Available Office Applications.")

PART

IV

Saturday Evening

1. Describe how the look and feel of the GNOME desktop is similar to that of Windows 95/98/NT.

2. How do you customize the look and feel of the GNOME desktop? Name some of the features you can customize.

3. What is Sawfish? What role does it play in GNOME? How do you configure Sawfish?

4. Explain how you can change your default desktop from GNOME to KDE and vice versa.

5. Describe how you customize the look and feel of the KDE desktop.

6. Describe how to select and configure a screen saver for the GNOME desktop.

7. What does it mean to "lock the screen?" How do you lock the screen in GNOME?

8. How do you select and configure a screen saver in KDE?

9. What are some of the games available in GNOME? What kind of a game is AisleRiot?

10. Name some of the games that come with the KDE desktop.

11. Describe how you configure the sound card in Linux.

12. What are some of the CD player applications you can use to play audio CDs in Linux? What must you do so that you can play audio CDs as a normal user?

13. The GNOME CD player displays the title of the audio CD and a list of song titles. How does the CD player find this information?

14. Name two image manipulation programs that come with Linux. What can you do with these programs?

15. Suppose you have a PostScript document. Which application do you use to view that document on your Linux system?

16. What are some of the office utilities on this book's Red Hat Linux CD-ROM? Is any complete office productivity suite included?

17. What is the name of the spreadsheet application that comes with the GNOME desktop? What is the default file format of that application? Can you exchange files with Microsoft Excel?

18. Show the command line you type to check the spelling in a text file named `report.txt`.

19. Name a few commercial office application suites — word processor, spreadsheet, presentation graphics, and database — for Linux. How can you find more information about these commercial applications?

20. Which of the office application suites is a cross-platform solution — it works on many different operating systems? Mention the major components of this office application suite.

☑ Friday

☑ Saturday

☑ **Sunday**

PART

V

Sunday Morning

Understanding How Linux Boots

Session Checklist

✔ Understanding the init process

✔ Understanding the Linux startup scripts

**30 Min.
To Go**

Learning the sequence in which Linux starts processes as it boots is important. You can use this knowledge to start and stop services such as the Web server and Network File System (NFS). This session provides you with an overview of how the Red Hat, Caldera, and SuSe distributions of Linux boot and start the initial set of processes. You also become familiar with the shell scripts that start various services.

Understanding the init Process

When Linux boots, it loads and runs the core operating-system program, called the kernel, from the hard disk. The core operating system, however, is designed to run other programs. A process named `init` starts the initial set of processes on your Linux system.

To see the processes currently running on the system, type the command **ps ax |
more**. The first column in the output has the heading PID, and that column shows
a number for each process. *PID* stands for *process ID* (identification), which is a
sequential number the Linux kernel assigns. Right at the beginning of the list of
processes, you notice a process with a process ID (PID) of 1:

```
PID TTY      STAT   TIME COMMAND
  1 ?         S     0:05 init [5]
```

As you can see, init is the first process, and it always has a PID (or process
number) of 1. Also, init starts all other processes in your Linux system. That's
why init is referred to as the *mother of all processes*.

What the init process starts depends on the following:

- The *run level,* which designates a system configuration in which only a
  selected group of processes exists
- The contents of the /etc/inittab file, a text file that specifies the
  processes to start at different run levels
- A number of shell scripts (located in the /etc/rc.d directory and its subdirectories) executed at a specific run level

The current run level, with the contents of the /etc/inittab file, controls
which processes init starts. Linux, for example, has seven run levels: 0, 1, 2, 3, 4,
5, and 6. By convention, some of these levels indicate specific processes that run
at that level. Run level 1, for example, denotes a single-user, stand-alone system.
Run level 0 means the system is halted, and run level 6 means the system is being
rebooted. Run levels 2 through 5 are multiuser modes that have various levels of
capabilities. It is possible to change from one run level to another by typing init
followed by the run level you want. See the section, "Trying out a new run level
with the init command" later in this session.

The initial default run level is 3 for text-mode login screens and 5 for the
graphical login screen. As the following section explains, you can change the
default run level by editing a line in the /etc/inittab file.

To check the current run level, type the following command:

```
/sbin/runlevel
```

This command prints two alphanumeric characters as output.

```
N 5
```

The first character of the output shows the previous run level (N means there was
no previous run level), and the second character shows the current run level (5).

Examining the /etc/inittab file

The /etc/inittab file is the key to understanding the processes that init starts at various run levels. You can look at the contents of the file by using the more command as follows:

```
more /etc/inittab
```

When looking at the contents of the /etc/inittab **file with the** more **command, you do not have to log in as** root.

The following is a listing of the /etc/inittab file on my Caldera Linux system that is set up for a graphical login screen:

```
#
# inittab       This file describes how the INIT process should set up
#               the system in a certain run-level.
#
# Author:       Miquel van Smoorenburg, <miquels@drinkel.nl.mugnet.org>
#               Modified for RHS Linux by Marc Ewing and Donnie Barnes
#

# Default runlevel. The runlevels used by RHS are:
#   0 - halt (Do NOT set initdefault to this)
#   1 - Single user mode
#   2 - Multiuser, without NFS (The same as 3, if you do not have networking)
#   3 - Full multiuser mode
#   4 - unused
#   5 - X11
#   6 - reboot (Do NOT set initdefault to this)
#
id:5:initdefault:

# System initialization.
si::sysinit:/etc/rc.d/rc.sysinit

l0:0:wait:/etc/rc.d/rc 0
l1:1:wait:/etc/rc.d/rc 1
l2:2:wait:/etc/rc.d/rc 2
l3:3:wait:/etc/rc.d/rc 3
l4:4:wait:/etc/rc.d/rc 4
l5:5:wait:/etc/rc.d/rc 5
l6:6:wait:/etc/rc.d/rc 6

# Things to run in every runlevel.
ud::once:/sbin/update

# Trap CTRL-ALT-DELETE
ca::ctrlaltdel:/sbin/shutdown -t3 -r now
```

```
# When our UPS tells us power has failed, assume we have a few minutes
# of power left.  Schedule a shutdown for 2 minutes from now.
# This does, of course, assume you have powerd installed and your
# UPS connected and working correctly.
pf::powerfail:/sbin/shutdown -f -h +2 "Power Failure; System Shutting Down"

# If power was restored before the shutdown kicked in, cancel it.
pr:12345:powerokwait:/sbin/shutdown -c "Power Restored; Shutdown Cancelled"

# Run gettys in standard runlevels
1:2345:respawn:/sbin/mingetty tty1
2:2345:respawn:/sbin/mingetty tty2
3:2345:respawn:/sbin/mingetty tty3
4:2345:respawn:/sbin/mingetty tty4
5:2345:respawn:/sbin/mingetty tty5
6:2345:respawn:/sbin/mingetty tty6

# Run xdm in runlevel 5
# xdm is now a separate service
x:5:respawn:/etc/X11/prefdm -nodaemon
```

Lines that start with a hash mark (#) are comments. The first non-comment line in the /etc/inittab file specifies the default run level as follows:

```
id:5:initdefault:
```

Even though you do not know the syntax of the /etc/inittab file (and you really do not have to learn the syntax), you probably can guess that the 5 in that line denotes the default run level for the graphical login screen. Thus, if you want your system to run at level 3 after startup (for a plain text-mode login screen), all you have to do is change 5 to 3.

Type man inittab **to see the detailed syntax of the entries in the** inittab **file.**

**20 Min.
To Go**

In regard to the file format of the /etc/inittab file, each entry in the /etc/inittab file specifies a process that init should start at one or more specified run levels. Simply list all the run levels at which the process should run. Each entry in the inittab file has four fields — separated by colons — in the following format:

```
id:runlevels:action:process
```

The fields have the following meanings:

- The *id* field is a unique, one- or two-character identifier. The init process uses this field internally. You can use any identifier you want as long as you do not use the same identifier on more than one line. For example, si, x, and 1 are all valid identifiers.

- The *runlevels* field is a sequence of zero or more characters, each denoting a run level. The line with the identifier 1, for example, applies to run levels 1 through 5, so the *runlevels* field for this entry is 12345. This field is ignored if the action field is set to sysinit, boot, or bootwait.

- The *action* field tells the init process what to do with the specific entry. If this field is initdefault, for example, init interprets the *runlevels* field as the default run level. If this field is set to wait, init starts the process specified in the *process* field and waits until that process exits. Table 21-1 summarizes the valid action values you can use in the *action* field.

- The *process* field specifies the process that init has to start. Of course, some settings of the *action* field require no process field. (When *action* is set to initdefault, for example, no need exists for a *process* field.)

Table 21-1
Valid Actions in /etc/inittab

Action	Description
Respawn	Restarts the process whenever it terminates.
Wait	Restarts the process once at the specified run level; init waits until that process exits.
Once	Executes the process once at the specified run level.
Boot	Executes the process as the system boots, regardless of the run level (the *runlevels* field is ignored).
Bootwait	Executes the process as the system boots; init waits for the process to exit (the *runlevels* field is ignored).
Off	Nothing happens for this action.
Ondemand	Executes the process at the specified run level, which must be of a, b, or c.

Continued

Table 21-1 *Continued*

Action	Description
Initdefault	Starts the system at this run level after it boots. The *process* field is ignored for this action.
Sysinit	Executes the process as the system boots, before any entries with the boot or bootwait actions (the *runlevels* field is ignored).
Powerwait	Executes the process when init receives the SIGPWR signal indicating something is wrong with the power. Then init waits until the process exits.
Powerfail	Similar to powerwait except that init does not wait for the process to exit.
Powerokwait	Executes the process when init receives the SIGPWR signal and the /etc/powerstatus file contains the word OK (indicating the power is back on).
Ctrlaltdel	Executes the process when init receives the SIGINT signal, which occurs when you press Ctrl+Alt+Del. Typically, the *process* field should specify the /sbin/shutdown command and the -r option to reboot the PC.
Kbdrequest	Executes the process when init receives a signal from the keyboard driver that a special key combination has been pressed. The key combination should be mapped to KeyboardSignal in the keymap file.

The *process* field is typically specified in terms of a shell script, which, in turn, can start several processes. The 15 entry, for example, is specified as follows:

```
l5:5:wait:/etc/rc.d/rc 5
```

This entry specifies that init should execute the file /etc/rc.d/rc with 5 as an argument. If you look at the file /etc/.rc.d/rc, you notice it is a shell script file. You can study the file /etc/rc.d/rc to see how it starts various processes for run levels 1 through 5.

Getting back to the graphical login screen, the last line of the /etc/inittab file, which follows, starts the graphical login process.

```
x:5:respawn:/etc/X11/prefdm -nodaemon
```

This command runs /etc/X11/prefdm, which is a symbolic link to a specific display manager. For the GNOME graphical desktop (the default in Red Hat Linux), /etc/X11/prefdm is a symbolic link to /usr/bin/gdm—the GNOME display manager. If you use the KDE desktop as your default desktop (the default in the Caldera and SuSe distributions), /etc/X11/prefdm is a symbolic link to /usr/bin/kdm—the KDE display manager. This means that regardless of your choice of GUI, init starts a display manager at run level 5. The display manager, in turn, displays the graphical login dialog box and enables you to log into the system.

If you do not enable the graphical login screen during Linux installation (covered in Sessions 1 through 3), you can do so by editing the /etc/inittab **file. Locate the line containing** initdefault, **and make sure it reads as follows (the run level appearing between two colons should be 5):**

```
id:5:initdefault:
```

Before you edit the /etc/inittab file, you should know that any errors in this file may prevent Linux from starting up to a point at which you can log in. If you cannot log in, you cannot use your system. As I explain next, you can always try out a specific run level by using the init command before you actually change the default run level in the /etc/inittab file.

Trying out a new run level with the init command

To try a new run level, you do not have to change the default run level in the /etc/inittab file. If you log in as root, you can change the run level (and, consequently, the set of processes that run in Linux) with the init command. The init command has the following format:

```
init runlevel
```

Here, runlevel must be a single character denoting the run level you want. To put the system in single-user mode, for example, type the following:

```
init 1
```

Thus, if you want to try run level 5 (assuming your system is not set up for a graphical login screen yet) without changing the /etc/inittab file, enter the following command at the shell prompt:

```
init 5
```

The system should end all current processes and enter run level 5. By default, the `init` command waits 20 seconds before stopping all current processes and starting the new processes for run level 5.

 To switch to run level 5 immediately, type the command `init -t0 5`. **The number after the** `-t` **option indicates the number of seconds that** `init` **waits before changing the run level.**

You can also use the `telinit` command, a symbolic link to `init`. If you make changes to the `/etc/inittab` file and want `init` to reload its configuration file, use the command `telinit q`.

**10 Min.
To Go**

Understanding the Linux Startup Scripts

The `init` process runs a number of scripts at system startup. Notice the following lines that appear near the beginning of the `/etc/inittab` file:

```
# System initialization.
si::sysinit:/etc/rc.d/rc.sysinit
```

As the comment on the first line indicates, the second line causes `init` to run the `/etc/rc.d/rc.sysinit` script — the first Red Hat Linux startup script that `init` runs. The `rc.sysinit` script performs many initialization tasks, such as mounting the file systems, setting the clock, configuring the keyboard layout, starting the network, and loading many other driver modules. The `rc.sysinit` script performs these initialization tasks by calling many other scripts and reading configuration files located in the `/etc/sysconfig` directory.

After executing the `/etc/rc.d/rc.sysinit` script, the `init` process runs the `/etc/rc.d/rc` script with the run level as its argument. For example, for run level 5, the following line in `/etc/inittab` specifies what `init` has to execute:

```
l5:5:wait:/etc/rc.d/rc 5
```

This says that `init` should execute the command `/etc/rc.d/rc 5` and should wait until that command completes.

The `/etc/rc.d/rc` script is somewhat complicated. Here is how it works:

- It changes to the directory corresponding to the run level. For example, to change to run level 5, the script changes to the `/etc/rc.d/rc5.d` directory.

- In the directory that corresponds with the run level, it looks for all files that begin with a K and executes each of them with an argument of stop. This kills currently running processes. Then it locates all files that begin with an S and executes each file with an argument of start. This starts the processes needed for the specified run level.

To see what executes at run level 5, type the following command:

```
ls -l /etc/rc.d/rc5.d
```

This command provides the following output:

```
total 0
lrwxrwxrwx   1 root    root     15 Aug 14 16:24 K01pppoe -> ../init.d/pppoe
lrwxrwxrwx   1 root    root     14 Aug 14 16:08 K05innd -> ../init.d/innd
lrwxrwxrwx   1 root    root     13 Aug 19 22:18 K20nfs -> ../init.d/nfs
lrwxrwxrwx   1 root    root     16 Aug 14 16:24 K20rstatd -> ../init.d/rstatd
lrwxrwxrwx   1 root    root     17 Aug 14 16:24 K20rusersd -> ../init.d/rusersd
lrwxrwxrwx   1 root    root     16 Aug 14 16:24 K20rwalld -> ../init.d/rwalld
lrwxrwxrwx   1 root    root     15 Aug 14 16:24 K20rwhod -> ../init.d/rwhod
lrwxrwxrwx   1 root    root     19 Aug 14 16:34 K34yppasswdd -> ../init.d/yppasswdd
lrwxrwxrwx   1 root    root     13 Aug 14 16:25 K35smb -> ../init.d/smb
lrwxrwxrwx   1 root    root     18 Aug 14 15:56 K45arpwatch -> ../init.d/arpwatch
lrwxrwxrwx   1 root    root     15 Aug 14 15:57 K45named -> ../init.d/named
lrwxrwxrwx   1 root    root     15 Aug 14 16:31 K50snmpd -> ../init.d/snmpd
lrwxrwxrwx   1 root    root     18 Aug 14 16:17 K60mars-nwe -> ../init.d/mars-nwe
lrwxrwxrwx   1 root    root     16 Aug 14 16:34 K84ypserv -> ../init.d/ypserv
lrwxrwxrwx   1 root    root     15 Aug 14 16:14 S05kudzu -> ../init.d/kudzu
lrwxrwxrwx   1 root    root     18 Aug 14 16:08 S08ipchains -> ../init.d/ipchains
lrwxrwxrwx   1 root    root     17 Aug 14 15:56 S10network -> ../init.d/network
lrwxrwxrwx   1 root    root     16 Aug 14 15:56 S12syslog -> ../init.d/syslog
lrwxrwxrwx   1 root    root     17 Aug 14 16:21 S13portmap -> ../init.d/portmap
lrwxrwxrwx   1 root    root     17 Aug 14 16:19 S14nfslock -> ../init.d/nfslock
lrwxrwxrwx   1 root    root     14 Aug 14 15:56 S16apmd -> ../init.d/apmd
lrwxrwxrwx   1 root    root     16 Aug 14 15:56 S20random -> ../init.d/random
lrwxrwxrwx   1 root    root     15 Aug 14 15:56 S25netfs -> ../init.d/netfs
lrwxrwxrwx   1 root    root     16 Aug 14 16:20 S35identd -> ../init.d/identd
lrwxrwxrwx   1 root    root     13 Aug 14 15:56 S40atd -> ../init.d/atd
lrwxrwxrwx   1 root    root     15 Aug 14 15:56 S40crond -> ../init.d/crond
lrwxrwxrwx   1 root    root     16 Aug 14 16:12 S45pcmcia -> ../init.d/pcmcia
lrwxrwxrwx   1 root    root     16 Aug 14 16:33 S50xinetd -> ../init.d/xinetd
lrwxrwxrwx   1 root    root     20 Aug 14 15:56 S56rawdevices ->
../init.d/rawdevices
lrwxrwxrwx   1 root    root     13 Aug 14 16:16 S60lpd -> ../init.d/lpd
lrwxrwxrwx   1 root    root     18 Aug 14 15:58 S75keytable -> ../init.d/keytable
lrwxrwxrwx   1 root    root     14 Aug 14 16:09 S80isdn -> ../init.d/isdn
lrwxrwxrwx   1 root    root     18 Aug 14 16:26 S80sendmail -> ../init.d/sendmail
lrwxrwxrwx   1 root    root     13 Aug 14 16:07 S85gpm -> ../init.d/gpm
lrwxrwxrwx   1 root    root     15 Aug 14 15:56 S85httpd -> ../init.d/httpd
lrwxrwxrwx   1 root    root     13 Aug 14 15:58 S90xfs -> ../init.d/xfs
lrwxrwxrwx   1 root    root     17 Aug 14 15:55 S95anacron -> ../init.d/anacron
lrwxrwxrwx   1 root    root     19 Aug 14 16:16 S99linuxconf -> ../init.d/linuxconf
lrwxrwxrwx   1 root    root     11 Aug 14 15:56 S99local -> ../rc.local
```

As the output shows, all files with names starting with K and S are symbolic links to scripts that reside in the /etc/rc.d and /etc/rc.d/init.d directories. In fact, the /etc/rec.d/rc script executes these files exactly in the order they appear in the directory listing.

Note that the last file in the directory listing is a symbolic link to the ../rc.local script. This means that /etc/rc.d/rc.local is executed after all other scripts. So you can place any command in that script you want executed whenever your Linux system boots.

Most of the startup scripts reside in the /etc/rc.d/init.d directory. You can manually invoke scripts in this directory to start, stop, or restart specific processes — usually servers. For example, to stop the Web server, type the following command:

/etc/rc.d/init.d/httpd stop

The following response displays:

Shutting down http: [OK]

You can enhance your system administration skills by familiarizing yourself with the scripts in the /etc/rc.d/init.d directory. To see the following listing, type the **ls /etc/rc.d/init.d** command:

```
anacron    halt       keytable   netfs      pppoe       sendmail  ypbind
apmd       httpd      killall    network    random      single    yppasswdd
arpwatch   identd     kudzu      nfs        rawdevices  smb       ypserv
atd        innd       linuxconf  nfslock    rstatd      snmpd
crond      ipchains   lpd        pcmcia     rusersd     syslog
functions  isdn       mars-nwe   portmap    rwalld      xfs
gpm        kdcrotate  named      postgresql rwhod       xinetd
```

Done!

The script names give you some clue about what server the script can start and stop. For example, the nfs script starts and stops the processes required for NFS (Network File System) services. At your leisure, you may want to study some of these scripts to see what each script does. You don't have to understand all the shell programming; the comments should help you learn the purpose of each script.

REVIEW

This session provided an overview of how the `init` process starts an initial set of processes. You learned about the `/etc/inittab` file that controls what `init` does. You also learned about the Red Hat Linux startup scripts in the `/etc/rc.d` directory and its subdirectories.

QUIZ YOURSELF

1. Why is `init` referred to as the "mother of all processes?" (See "Understanding the init Process.")

2. How can you determine the current run level of your Linux system? (See "Understanding the init Process.")

3. What can you do to make your Linux system start at run level 3 when you reboot the system? (See "Examining the /etc/inittab File.")

4. How do you figure out which scripts `init` executes for run level 5? (See "Understanding the Red Hat Linux Startup Scripts.")

5. In which script do you place commands you want executed every time your Linux system boots? (See "Understanding the Red Hat Linux Startup Scripts.")

Building Software Packages from Source Files

Session Checklist

30 Min. To Go

✔ Downloading and unpacking software

✔ Building and installing software from source files

I n Session 23, you will learn how to install software packages distributed in the Red Hat Package Manager (RPM) format. All major distributions of Linux, such as Caldera Open Linux and SuSe, use this format. RPM files bundle every-thing — all the executable binary files and configuration files — needed to install a software package. However, many open source software packages are distributed in source code form without executable binaries. Before you can use such software, you have to build the executable binary files; then you have to follow some instructions to install the package. This session shows you how to download and unpack source files. It then shows you how to build software packages from source files and install them.

Downloading and Unpacking the Software

Open source software source files are typically distributed in compressed `tar` archives. As you will learn in Session 26, the `tar` program creates these archives, and the `gzip` program compresses them. The distribution is in the form of a single, large file that has the `.tar.gz` or `.tar.Z` extension — often referred to as a *compressed tarball*. If you want the software, you have to download the compressed tarball and unpack it.

Download the compressed `tar` file by using anonymous FTP or the Web browser. Typically, this involves no more effort on your part than clicking a link and saving the file in an appropriate directory on your system.

To try your hand at downloading and building a software package, you can practice on the *X Multimedia System (XMMS)* — a graphical X application for playing MP3 files and other multimedia files. XMMS is bundled with Linux and is installed on your system when you select the Multimedia Support package group during the Red Hat Linux installation you did in Session 3. However, there is no harm in downloading and rebuilding the XMMS package again.

You can access source files for XMMS from `http://www.xmms.org/download.html` in the form of a compressed `tar` archive. You can also download files from the `xmms/1.0` directory of the anonymous FTP server (`ftp.xmms.org`). You should try downloading from the anonymous FTP server so you can learn to download files manually.

Before attempting to download a file from an FTP server, make sure your Linux system is connected to the Internet. You should also change the directory to the location where you want to store the downloaded file (although you can always move the file after downloading). I typically log in as `root` and change the directory to `/usr/local` before typing the `ftp` command. If you use the GNOME or KDE desktop, type these commands from a terminal window.

Downloading the software

Here is a sample session you can use as a guideline when you download the compressed `tar` file for XMMS from the anonymous FTP server. The lines I type appear in boldface.

```
ftp ftp.xmms.org
Connected to ftp.xmms.org.
220 ProFTPD 1.2.0pre10 Server (FTP server for awpti.org) [awpti.org]
Name (ftp.xmms.org:naba): anonymous
331 Anonymous login ok, send your complete e-mail address as password.
Password:   (Type your e-mail address and press Enter)
230 Anonymous access granted, restrictions apply.
Remote system type is UNIX.
Using binary mode to transfer files.
ftp> cd xmms/1.0
250 CWD command successful.
ftp> ls
200 PORT command successful.
```

```
150 Opening ASCII mode data connection for file list.
drwxr-xr-x    6 xmms      xmms        4096 Jan 30 15:20 rpm
-rw-r--r--    1 xmms      xmms      700909 Jan 30 15:22 xmms-1.0.0.tar.gz
-rw-r--r--    1 xmms      xmms      715574 Jan 30 15:15 xmms-1.0.1.tar.gz
226 Transfer complete.
ftp> binary
200 Type set to I.
ftp> get xmms-1.0.1.tar.gz
200 PORT command successful.
150 Opening BINARY mode data connection for xmms-1.0.1.tar.gz (715574 bytes).
226 Transfer complete.
715574 bytes received in 383 secs (1.8 Kbytes/sec)
ftp> bye
```

**20 Min.
To Go**

Notice that you have to log in using the user name anonymous — that's why the FTP server is called the anonymous FTP server. For the password, you should type your e-mail address; then press Enter. To change the directory, use the cd command. For a directory listing, use the ls command.

You need to type the binary command to make sure the data transfer occurs in binary mode (because the .tar.gz file is a binary file). Then you can use the get command to download the file — in this case, xmms-1.0.1.tar.gz. As I mention previously, the .tar.gz extension tells you this is a compressed tar archive. After the download is complete, type bye to end the anonymous FTP session.

After downloading the compressed tar file, you should first examine the contents :

```
xmms-1.0.1/
xmms-1.0.1/Makefile.in
xmms-1.0.1/README
xmms-1.0.1/stamp-h.in
xmms-1.0.1/AUTHORS
xmms-1.0.1/COPYING
xmms-1.0.1/ChangeLog
xmms-1.0.1/INSTALL
xmms-1.0.1/Makefile.am
xmms-1.0.1/NEWS
xmms-1.0.1/TODO
xmms-1.0.1/acconfig.h
xmms-1.0.1/acinclude.m4
xmms-1.0.1/aclocal.m4
xmms-1.0.1/config.guess
xmms-1.0.1/config.h.in
xmms-1.0.1/config.sub
xmms-1.0.1/configure
... rest of the output not shown ...
```

The output of this command shows you the contents of the archive and gives you an idea of the directories created once you unpack the archive. In this case, a directory named xmms-1.0.1 is created in the current directory (which, in my case, is /usr/local). From the listing, you also learn the programming language used to write the package. If you see .c and .h files, that means source files are in the C programming language used to write many open source software packages.

Unpacking the software

To extract (or unpack) the contents of the tar archive, type the following tar command:

```
tar zxvf xmms*.gz
```

You again see the long list of files as they are extracted from the archive and copied to the appropriate directories on your hard disk. Now you are ready to build the software.

Building the Software from Source Files and Installing It

After you unpack the compressed tar archive, all source files are in a directory whose name is usually the name of the software package and a version number suffix. For example, the XMMS version 1.0.1 source files are extracted in the xmms-1.0.1 directory. To start the process of building the software, change the directory by using this command:

```
cd xmms*
```

You don't have to type the entire name. The shell can expand the directory name and change it to the xmms-1.0.1 **directory.**

Nearly all software packages come with some sort of README or INSTALL files — text files with instructions on what to do to build and install the packages. XMMS is no exception; it comes with a README file you can read by typing more README. There is also an INSTALL file that contains instructions for building and installing XMMS.

Most open source software packages, including XMMS, also come with a file named COPYING. This file contains the full text of the GNU *General Public License (GPL)*, which spells out the conditions under which you can use and redistribute the software. If you are not familiar with the GNU GPL, you should read this file and show the license to your legal counsel for a full interpretation and assessment of its applicability to your business.

For the XMMS package, the README file lists some of the prerequisites — such as libraries you need — and then tells you what commands you should type to build and install the package. In the case of XMMS, the instructions direct you to use the following commands:

1. Type ./configure to run a shell script that checks your system configuration and creates a *Makefile*, a file that the make command uses to build and install the package. The configure shell script guesses system-dependent variables and creates a Makefile that contains commands needed to build and install the software.

2. Type make to build the software. This step compiles source files in all subdirectories.

3. Type make install to install the software. This step copies libraries and executable binary files to appropriate directories on your system.

Although these steps are specific to XMMS, most other packages follow this procedure — configure, make, and install.

Usually, you do not have to do anything but type the commands to build the software; however, you must install software development tools on your system. This means you must install the Development package when you install Linux. Because XMMS is an X application, you must also install the X Window System package to build and run XMMS.

Building the software

10 Min. To Go

To begin building XMMS, type the following command to run the configure script (while in the xmms-1.0.1 directory):

```
./configure
```

The `configure` script starts running and prints lots of messages as it checks various features of your system, from the existence of the C compiler to various libraries needed to build XMMS. Finally, the `configure` script creates a Makefile you can use to build software.

If the `configure` **script displays error messages and fails, read the** `INSTALL` **and** `README` **files again to find any clues in solving the problem. You may be able to circumvent the problem by providing information through command-line arguments to the** `configure` **script.**

After the `configure` script finishes, build the software by typing the following command:

```
make
```

This command runs the GNU `make` utility (which takes 10 to 15 minutes to complete) that reads the Makefile and starts compiling the source files according to information specified in the Makefile. The `make` command goes through source directories, compiles source files, and creates executable files and libraries needed to run XMMS. You see a lot of messages scroll by as each file is compiled. These messages show the command used to compile and link the files.

Installing the software

After the `make` command finishes, you can install the XMMS software by using the following command:

```
make install
```

This command also runs GNU `make`, but the install argument instructs GNU `make` to perform a specific set of commands from the Makefile. These instructions essentially search the subdirectories and copy various files to their final locations. For example, the binary executable files `xmms`, `gnomexmms`, `wmxmms`, and `xmms-config` are copied to the `/usr/bin` directory.

Running the software

Now that you have installed XMMS, try running it by typing `xmms` in a terminal window from the GNOME or KDE desktop. From the XMMS window, you can open an MP3 file and try playing it. Note that your PC must have a sound card and you must have it configured correctly. (Session 19 discusses sound-card configuration.) Figure 22-1 shows a typical view of XMMS playing an MP3 music clip.

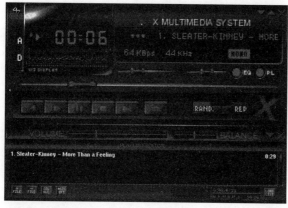

Figure 22-1
Playing MP3 music with XMMS

An overview of the basic building steps

Now you know how to download, unpack, build, and install a typical software package. Here's an overview of the steps you follow:

1. Download the source code, usually in the form of a `.tar.gz` file, from the anonymous FTP site or Web site. Use the Web browser, or download the source code manually from the anonymous FTP server.

2. Unpack the file with a `tar zxvf filename` command.

3. Use a command such as the following to change the directory to the new subdirectory where the software is unpacked:

   `cd software_dir`

4. Read any `README` or `INSTALL` files to learn any specific instructions you must follow to build and install software.

5. The details of building software may differ slightly from one software package to another, but typically you type the following commands to build and install the software:

   `./configure`

   `make`

   `make install`

Done!

6. Read any other documentation that comes with the software to learn to use the software and to determine whether you must configure the software further before using it.

REVIEW

This session showed you how to download and unpack open source software distributed in compressed `tar` archives. Using the X Multimedia System (XMMS) package as an example, you learned to build and install software.

QUIZ YOURSELF

1. What is a *compressed tarball*? (See "Downloading and Unpacking the Software.")

2. What command do you use to unpack a compressed tarball? (See "Downloading and Unpacking the Software.")

3. What are some typical files that provide information on building and installing the software package? (See "Building the Software from Source Files and Installing It.")

4. What is the name of the file that usually contains the full text of the GNU General Public License? (See "Building the Software from Source Files and Installing It.")

5. What are the three commands you have to type to build and install the XMMS package? (See "Building the Software from Source Files and Installing It.")

Installing Software Packages

Session Checklist

✔ Using Gnome RPM to install and remove packages

✔ Using the RPM commands to install and remove packages

**30 Min.
To Go**

As a system administrator of your Linux system, you should know how to install and remove software packages distributed in the form of Red Hat Package Manager (RPM) files. Most distributions use RPM files as an easy way to install software. In this session, you learn to install and remove RPMs by using the Gnome RPM graphical tool and the RPM commands.

Using Gnome RPM to Install and Remove Packages

A significant innovation of Red Hat is the *Red Hat Package Manager (RPM)* — a system for packaging all necessary files for a software product in a single file (referred to as an RPM file, or simply an RPM). Most Linux distributions are in the form of a large number of RPMs. If you install Red Hat Linux from the companion CD-ROMs, all of the RPM files (packages) are located in the /mnt/cdrom/RedHat/RPMS directory (assuming you have mounted the CD-ROM on the /mnt/cdrom directory).

Gnome RPM is a graphical front utility for installing and uninstalling RPMs. The operations you can perform with Gnome RPM are similar to what you can do with the rpm command from the command line. You learn the rpm command later in this session.

To start Gnome RPM, log in as root; then select Main Menu ⇨ Programs ⇨ System ⇨ GnoRPM. Figure 23-1 shows the initial Gnome RPM window. Gnome RPM has a standard GNOME user interface with a menu bar and a toolbar. The toolbar has buttons for common RPM operations: Install a New Package, Query a Package, or Uninstall a Package. The tree menu on the left of the window shows the currently installed packages organized in a hierarchy of package groups. (A *package group* contains a number of packages or RPMs.) You can click the plus signs to view the hierarchy. If you click a specific package group, Gnome RPM displays all packages in that group in the area to the right of the tree menu. For example, Figure 23-1 shows the packages in the package group named Desktops, which contains the packages that make up the GNOME and KDE desktops.

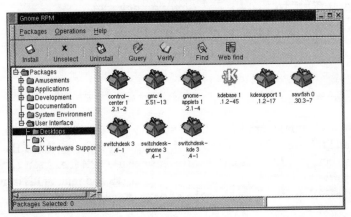

Figure 23-1
Gnome RPM displaying the contents of the Desktops package group

You typically select one or more packages and then perform tasks such as uninstalling the package, querying the package (to see when it was installed and the files it contains), or verifying the package (to check that none of the files have changed). To perform these operations, open the package group, and select the package by clicking the package icon. Then click the Uninstall, Query, or Verify button to initiate the operation. Each of these operations brings up a window in which Gnome RPM displays relevant information and provides buttons through which you can initiate further action. For example, when you query a package, Gnome RPM displays the information about that package in a window. From the information, you can see when the package was installed, when it was built, its size in bytes, a brief description of the package, and what files make up the package (including the full pathname of each file). There is even a URL where you can find more information about the package. Gnome RPM displays the URL as a link you can click to view that Web page in the Web browser. You can learn a lot about a package by browsing the information in the query results.

To uninstall or remove a package, select the package from the Gnome RPM window, and click the Uninstall button on the tool bar (see Figure 23-1). Gnome RPM then displays a dialog box asking you to confirm if you really want to remove the package. Click the Yes button to remove the package.

To install a new package from any one of this book's companion CD-ROMs, mount the CD-ROM (type mount /mnt/cdrom), and click the Install button on the Gnome RPM toolbar. An empty Install dialog box appears. Click the Add button on the Install dialog box. Gnome RPM displays an Add Packages dialog box that contains the contents of the /mnt/cdrom/RedHat/RPMS directory in which all of the RPM files (packages) are located, as shown in Figure 23-2.

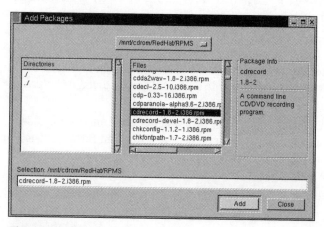

Figure 23-2
Adding a package to the list of packages to be installed

From the Add Packages dialog box, you can select packages one by one and click the Add button to add these to the list of packages to be installed. Each time you click the Add button, the selected package is added to the list in the Install dialog box. When you finish selecting packages, click Close to get rid of the Add Packages dialog box. The selected packages appear in the Install dialog box.

To finish installing the selected packages, click the Install button in the Install dialog box. Gnome RPM installs the packages and displays any errors it encounters. For example, if the packages are already installed, Gnome RPM displays a message that says so.

Gnome RPM is a handy utility for installing, removing, and upgrading various software packages for Linux. If you want to learn more about Gnome RPM, read the online help text by selecting the appropriate item from Gnome RPM's Help menu.

Using the rpm Command to Install and Remove Packages

**20 Min.
To Go**

When you install Red Hat Linux from the companion CD-ROM, or install other distributions, the installation program uses the rpm command to unpack the packages (RPM files) and to copy the contents to appropriate locations on the disk.

Although you do not need to understand the internal structure of an RPM file, you should know how to use the rpm command to work with RPM files. Specifically, you may want to perform one or more of the following tasks with RPMs:

- Find the version numbers and other information about RPMs installed on your system.
- Install a new software package from an RPM. For example, you can install a package you skipped during the initial installation. In particular, you have to install the source files for the Linux kernel before you can rebuild the kernel.
- Remove (uninstall) unneeded software you installed from an RPM. You can uninstall a package to reclaim the disk space if you find you never use the package.
- Upgrade an older version of an RPM with a newer one. You can upgrade after you download a new version of a package from Red Hat's, Caldera's or SuSe's FTP server. Often, you must upgrade an RPM to benefit from the fixes in the new version.
- Verify that an RPM is in working order. You can verify a package to check if all necessary files are in their correct locations.

You can perform all of these tasks with the rpm command — simply by using different options. The next few sections briefly introduce you to the rpm command.

If you ever forget the rpm options, type the following command to see a list of its command-line options:

```
rpm --help | more
```

The number of options rpm has will amaze you!

Understanding RPM filenames

An RPM contains a number of files, but it appears as a single file on your Linux system. By convention, the RPM filenames have a specific structure. To see the names of RPM files on the companion CD-ROM, use the following steps:

1. Place the CD-ROM in the CD-ROM drive, and mount it by using the following command (you must be logged in as root):

   ```
   mount /mnt/cdrom
   ```

   This mount command works because an entry for this mount point is in the /etc/fstab file.

2. Go to the directory in which the RPMs are located, and type the following:

   ```
   cd /mnt/cdrom/RedHat/RPMS
   ls *.rpm | more
   ```

   to view a listing such as this:

   ```
   ElectricFence-2.2.2-4.i386.rpm
   ImageMagick-5.2.2-5.i386.rpm
   ImageMagick-devel-5.2.2-5.i386.rpm
   Inti-0.2preview-1.i386.rpm
   Inti-devel-0.2preview-1.i386.rpm
   LPRng-3.6.22-3.i386.rpm
   (some lines deleted)
   XFree86-100dpi-fonts-4.0.1-0.43.i386.rpm
   XFree86-3DLabs-3.3.6-32.i386.rpm
   XFree86-4.0.1-0.43.i386.rpm
   (rest of the listing deleted)
   ```

As you can guess from the listing, all RPM files end with an .rpm_extension. To understand the various parts of the filename, consider the following RPM:

```
XFree86-4.0.1-0.43.i386.rpm
```

This filename has the following parts separated by dashes (-):

Package name	XFree86
Version number	4.0.1
Release number	0.43 (a Red Hat-assigned release number)
Architecture	i386 (for Intel 80386-compatible processors)

Usually, the package name is descriptive enough for you to guess the contents of the RPM. The version number is the same as that of the software package's current version number (even when it is distributed in some other form, such as a tar file). Red Hat assigns the release number to keep track of changes. The architecture should be i386 or noarch for the RPMs you want to install on a PC with an Intel x86-compatible processor.

Querying RPMs

As it installs packages, the rpm command builds a database of installed RPMs. You can use the rpm -q command to query this database to find information about packages installed on your system. For example, to find the version number (such as the following) of the Linux kernel installed on your system, type the **rpm -q kernel** command:

```
kernel-2.2.16-21
```

The response is the name of the RPM for the kernel (the executable version of the kernel, not the source files). The name is the same as the RPM filename except that the last part — .i386.rpm — does not appear. In this case, the version part of the RPM tells you the kernel is 2.2.16.

You can see a list of all installed RPMs by typing the following command:

```
rpm -qa | more
```

If you want to search for a specific package, feed the output of rpm -qa to the grep command. For example, to see all packages that have kernel in their names, type:

```
rpm -qa | grep kernel
```

to see a result such as this:

```
kernel-pcmcia-cs-2.2.16-21
kernel-headers-2.4.0-0.20
kernel-2.2.16-21
kernel-source-2.2.16-21
kernelcfg-0.5-9
kernel-utils-2.2.16-21
```

You can query much more than a package's version number by using the rpm -q command. By adding single-letter options, you can find other useful information about a package. For example, try the following command:

```
rpm -ql kernel
```

to see the files in the kernel package.

```
/boot/System.map-2.2.16-21
/boot/module-info-2.2.16-21
/boot/vmlinux-2.2.16-21
/boot/vmlinuz-2.2.16-21
/lib/modules
/lib/modules/2.2.16-21
/lib/modules/2.2.16-21/.rhkmvtag
/lib/modules/2.2.16-21/block
(rest of the listing deleted)
```

The following are several useful forms of rpm -q commands you can use to query information about a package. (To use any of these rpm -q commands, type the command followed by the package name.)

rpm -qa	Lists all installed RPMs.
rpm -qc	Lists all configuration files in a package.
rpm -qd	Lists all documentation files in a package. These are usually the online manual pages (also known as *man pages*).
rpm -qi	Displays detailed information about a package: version number, size, installation date, and a brief description.
rpm -ql	Lists all files in a package. For some packages, this can be a very long list.
rpm -qs	Lists the state of all files in a package.

Installing RPMs

To install an RPM, you have to use the rpm -i command. You must provide the name of the RPM file as the argument. A typical example is to install an RPM from this book's companion CD-ROM containing the Red Hat Linux RPMs. As usual, you have to mount the CD-ROM first and then change to the directory in which the RPMs are located. Then use the rpm -i command to install the RPM followed by the name of the RPM.

For example, to install the kernel-source RPM (which contains the source files for the Linux operating system) from my CD-ROM, I type the following commands:

```
mount /mnt/cdrom
cd /mnt/cdrom/RedHat/RPMS
rpm -i kernel-source*
```

You do not have to type the full RPM filename — you can use a few characters from the beginning of the name followed by an asterisk. Make sure you type enough of the name to identify the RPM file uniquely.

If you try to install an already installed RPM, the `rpm` command displays an error message. For example, here is what happens when I try to install the Emacs editor on my system by typing the `rpm -i emacs-20*` command:

```
package emacs-20.7-13 is already installed
```

To force the `rpm` command to install a package even if errors exist, just add `--force` to the `rpm -i` command as follows:

```
rpm -i --force emacs-20*
```

Removing RPMs

You can remove — uninstall — a package if you realize you don't really need the software. For example, if you install the X Window System development package but you are not interested in writing X applications, you can easily remove the package by using the `rpm -e` command.

You need the name of the package before you can remove it. One good way to find the name is to use `rpm -qa` in conjunction with `grep` to search for the appropriate RPM file. For example, you can type this command:

```
rpm -qa | grep XFree
```

to locate the X Window System development RPM.

```
XFree86-75dpi-fonts-4.0.1-0.43
XFree86-twm-4.0.1-0.43
XFree86-libs-4.0.1-0.43
XFree86-xfs-4.0.1-0.43
XFree86-4.0.1-0.43
XFree86-devel-4.0.1-0.43
XFree86-tools-4.0.1-0.43
XFree86-xdm-4.0.1-0.43
XFree86-SVGA-3.3.6-32
```

In this case, XFree86-devel is the package name you need. To remove the package, type:

```
rpm -e XFree86-devel
```

You do not need the full RPM filename. All you need is the package name — the first part of the filename up to the dash (-) before the version number.

The rpm -e command does not remove a package other packages need. For example, when I try to remove the kernel-headers package by typing rpm -e kernel-headers, I get the following error message:

```
error: removing these packages would break dependencies:
        kernel-headers   is needed by glibc-devel-2.1.92-5
        kernel-headers >= 2.2.1 is needed by glibc-devel-2.1.92-5
```

Upgrading RPMs

10 Min. To Go

When you use the rpm -U command to upgrade an RPM, you must provide the name of the RPM file that contains the new software. For example, suppose I have version 4.72 of Netscape Communicator installed on my system, but I want to upgrade to version 4.74. I download the RPM file netscape-communicator-4.74-0.6.2.i386.rpm from Red Hat's FTP server (ftp://ftp.redhat.com/pub/redhat/updates/ or from one of the mirror sites listed at http://www.redhat.com/mirrors.html). Then I use the following command:

```
rpm -U netscape-communicator-4.74-0.6.2.i386.rpm
```

The rpm command performs the upgrade by first removing the former version of the Netscape Communicator package and then installing the new RPM.

Whenever possible, you should upgrade (rather than remove) the former package and then install the new version. Upgrading automatically saves the former configuration files, which saves you the hassle of configuring the software after a fresh installation.

When you upgrade the kernel and the kernel module packages that contain a ready-to-run Linux kernel, do not use the rpm -U command. Instead, install it with the rpm -i command to ensure that you don't overwrite files the current kernel is using.

Verifying RPMs

You may not do this often, but if you suspect that a software package is not properly installed, use the `rpm -V` command to verify the package. For example, to verify the kernel package, type the following:

```
rpm -V kernel
```

This command causes `rpm` to compare size and other attributes of each file in the package against the original files. If everything verifies correctly, the `rpm -V` command does not print anything. If it detects any discrepancies, you see a report of the discrepancies. For example, I have modified the configuration files for the Apache Web server. Here is what I see when I verify the apache package by typing `rpm -V apache`:

```
S.5....T c /etc/httpd/conf/httpd.conf
```

In this case, the output from `rpm -V` shows that a configuration file has changed. Each line of this command's output consists of three parts:

- The line starts with eight characters; each character indicates the type of discrepancy found. For example, S means the size is different and T means the time of last modification is different. A period indicates that a specific attribute matches the original.

- For configuration files, a c appears next; otherwise, this field is blank, so you can tell whether a file is a configuration file. Typically, you don't have to worry if a configuration file has changed because you probably made the changes yourself.

- The last part of the line is the full pathname of the file. From this part, you can tell the exact location of the file.

Done!

REVIEW

This session introduced you to the Red Hat Package Manager (RPM) and its associated `rpm` commands. You learned to use the Gnome RPM graphical utility with which you can install and uninstall RPMs. You also learned the syntax of a number of `rpm` commands to query, install, upgrade, remove, and verify RPMs.

QUIZ YOURSELF

---

1. What is an RPM? (See "Using Gnome RPM to Install and Remove Packages.")

2. What can you do with Gnome RPM, and how do you run it? (See "Using Gnome RPM to Install and Remove Packages.")

3. What is the syntax of the `rpm` command you use to find all of the command-line options? (See "Using the rpm Command to Install and Remove Packages.")

4. Which `rpm` command do you use to view a list of all installed RPMs? (See "Querying RPMs.")

5. How do you install a new RPM from this book's companion CD-ROM containing the Red Hat Linux RPMs? (See "Installing RPMs.")

Building a New Kernel

Session Checklist

✔ Installing the source files and rebuilding the kernel

✔ Configuring the kernel

✔ Building and installing the kernel and modules

✔ Rebooting the system with a rebuilt kernel

**30 Min.
To Go**

Sometimes, you may have to rebuild the *kernel* — the core operating system —
from source files. For example, you may want to take advantage of some
experimental driver that the version of kernel shipped on the CD-ROMs does
not support. This session shows you how to install the source files for the kernel,
how to configure the kernel, and how to build and install the new kernel and modules. Finally, this session shows you how to reboot the system after you rebuild
and install the kernel.

Installing the Source Files and Rebuilding the Kernel

Rebuilding the kernel refers to creating a new binary file for the core Linux operating system. This binary file runs when Linux boots. You may have to build the kernel for various reasons:

- After you apply kernel patches that update the operating system's source files, you have to rebuild the kernel and reboot the system to use the new kernel.
- After you initially install Linux, you may want to create a new kernel that includes support for only the hardware installed on your system. In particular, if you have a SCSI adapter, you may want to create a kernel that links in the SCSI driver. The kernel in the companion CD-ROMs contains the SCSI driver as an external module you must load at startup.
- If you have a system with hardware for which only experimental support is available, you have to rebuild the kernel to include that support in the operating system.

Before you rebuild the kernel, make sure you have the emergency boot floppy (covered in Session 3) you prepare when installing Red Hat Linux. If you have installed a different distribution of Linux, be sure you have an appropriate boot disk. If the system does not boot after you rebuild the kernel, you can use that emergency boot floppy to start the system and to repeat the kernel's rebuild process.

Never rebuild and install a new kernel without making sure you have an emergency boot floppy. If you do not create the boot floppy during Linux installation, use the /sbin/mkbootdisk **command to create the boot floppy. Type** man mkbootdisk **to learn the syntax of that command.**

Rebuilding the kernel involves the following key phases:

- Installing kernel source files
- Configuring the kernel
- Building the kernel
- Building and installing the modules (if any)
- Installing the kernel and setting up LILO

Subsequent sections describe the phases of kernel building.

Installing kernel source files

To rebuild the Linux kernel, you need the kernel source files. In most cases, the kernel source files are not installed. If you have installed Linux from the companion CD-ROM supplied with this book, you can use the following steps to install the kernel source package on your system:

1. Log in as root, and insert the Red Hat Linux CD-ROM into the CD-ROM drive.

2. Use the mount command to mount the CD-ROM drive on a directory in the file system:

   ```
   mount /mnt/cdrom
   ```

3. Change the directory to the RedHat/RPMS directory on the CD-ROM, and use the following commands to install the kernel source files:

   ```
   cd /mnt/cdrom/RedHat/RPMS
   rpm -ivh kernel-source*
   ```

   The rpm command indicates progress by displaying a series of hash marks (#).

   ```
   kernel-source
   ########################################################
   ```

   After RPM finishes installing the kernel source package, the necessary source files appear in the /usr/src/linux directory.

Creating a monolithic versus a modular kernel

Before you start configuring the kernel, you need to understand your two options for the device drivers needed to support various hardware devices in Linux:

- *Link in support.* You can link the drivers for all hardware on your system into the kernel. As you can imagine, the size of the kernel grows as device driver code is incorporated into the kernel. A kernel that links all necessary support code is called a *monolithic kernel*.

- *Use modules.* You can create the necessary device drivers in the form of modules. A *module* is a block of code that the kernel can load after it starts running. You typically use modules to add support for a device without having to rebuild the kernel for each new device. Modules do not have to be device drivers; you can use them to add new functionality to the kernel. A kernel that uses modules is called a *modular kernel*.

You do not have to create a fully monolithic or fully modular kernel. In fact, linking some support directly into the kernel is common practice. Conversely, you can build infrequently used device drivers in the form of modules. All major distributions distribute a generic kernel along with a large number of modules to support many different types of hardware. Then, the installation program configures the system to load only those modules needed to support the hardware installed on a user's system.

When you create a custom kernel for your hardware configuration, you may link all required device drivers into the kernel. You can keep the size of such a monolithic kernel under control because you only link in device drivers for the hardware installed on your system.

Configuring the Kernel

The first phase in rebuilding a kernel is configuring the kernel. To configure the kernel, log in as `root`. Then change the directory to /usr/src/linux by using the `cd` command as follows:

```
cd /usr/src/linux
```

To configure the kernel, you have to indicate the features and device drivers (covered in the previous section) you want to include in your Linux system. In essence, you build a copy of Linux with the mix-and-match features you want.

Linux provides three ways for you to configure the kernel:

- Type `make menuconfig` to enter the kernel configuration parameters through a text-based interface, similar to the one the Red Hat installation program uses.

- Type `make xconfig` to use an X Window System-based configuration program to configure the kernel. You have to run X to use this configuration program with a graphical interface.

- Type `make config` to use a program that prompts you for each configuration option. You can use this configuration program from the Linux command prompt. When you use this option, you undergo a long question-and-answer process to specify configuration parameters.

As you configure the kernel, you have to select how to include support for specific devices. Typically, for each configuration option, you must type one of the following choices:

- y to link support into the kernel
- m to use a module
- n to skip the support for that specific device
- ? to get help on that kernel-configuration option

If a device does not have a modular device driver, you don't see the m option. For some configuration options, you may have to type a specific answer. For example, when responding to the processor type, you type Pentium to indicate that you have a Pentium PC.

The make menuconfig, make xconfig, and make config commands achieve the same result — each stores your choices in a text file named .config located in the /usr/src/linux directory. Because the filename starts with a period, you don't see it when you use the ls command alone to list the directory. Instead, type ls -a to see the .config file in the directory listing.

The kernel configuration step merely captures your choices in the .config **file. The kernel file does not change until you compile the kernel by using the** make **command. That means you can go through the kernel configuration option as many times as you want.**

As noted in the preceding section, you can use any of the configuration tools (make xconfig, make menuconfig, or make config) to perform the kernel configuration. The easiest way to perform the configuration is to type make xconfig. This builds an X Window System-based configuration tool and runs it. The initial window displays a set of buttons, each button representing a category of kernel configuration options (as shown in Figure 24-1).

Linux Kernel Configuration		
Code maturity level options	I2O device support	Console drivers
Processor type and features	Network device support	Sound
Loadable module support	Amateur Radio support	Kernel hacking
General setup	IrDA (infrared) support	
Plug and Play support	ISDN subsystem	
Block devices	Old CD-ROM drivers (not SCSI, not IDE)	Save and Exit
Networking options	Character devices	Quit Without Saving
Telephony Support	USB support	Load Configuration from File
SCSI support	Filesystems	Store Configuration to File

Figure 24-1
Buttons in xconfig showing categories of kernel configuration options

The four buttons, grouped together on the lower-right corner of the window, enable you to perform specific actions such as saving the configurations and exiting.

To change a configuration option, click a button. For example, if you click the button labeled Processor type and features in the upper-left corner, the configuration program displays another window with all the options you can set. From the new window, you can then set specific options. Next to each option in that window is a Help button. Whenever you have a question about an option, click the corresponding context-sensitive Help button to view help information for that option.

You can follow this approach — selecting a category button, locating the option, and clicking Help if you need help — to specify the options and to complete the configuration step. When you finish specifying the options, click the Save and Exit button in the main window (see Figure 24-1).

20 Min. To Go

Building and Installing the Kernel and Modules

This section describes the next three key phases of rebuilding a kernel: building the kernel, building and installing the modules, and setting up LILO to load the new kernel when you reboot the system.

Building the kernel

You should initiate the next three tasks with a single command line (by entering multiple semicolon-separated commands on the same line) so you can type the line, press Enter, and then take a break because building a kernel takes a while. Depending on your system, making a new kernel can take anywhere from a few minutes to over an hour.

Type the following on a single line to initiate the building process:

```
make dep; make clean; make zImage
```

The make dep command determines which files have changed and which need compiling again. The make clean command deletes old, unneeded files (such as old copies of the kernel). Finally, make zImage creates the new kernel in a compressed file and places it in a certain directory.

When configuring the kernel, do not link too many features into the kernel by answering Yes to configuration options. The kernel's file size may be too big to fit the 640KB of memory that a PC can use as it boots up. This 640KB limit exists because the Intel x86 processors start in what is known as real mode and can only access 1MB of memory (of which 640KB is available for programs). This limit is a leftover from the old MS-DOS days and applies only as the Linux kernel is initially loaded when the PC starts. If the kernel's file size is too big, the `make` command displays an error message such as the following:

```
System is too big. Try using bzImage or modules.
```

If you get a "System too big" error, type `make bzImage` to use a different type of compressed kernel that may fit within the memory limits. Otherwise, go through the `make config` step again, and eliminate unnecessary features by answering No to those configuration questions. For other features you really need or may want to try out, type `m` to create modules. Although the kernel's size is limited at startup, the kernel can load as many modules as it needs once the boot process is complete.

As the kernel is built, you see a lot of messages on the screen. When it's complete, a new kernel in the form of a compressed file named `zImage` appears in the `/usr/src/linux/arch/i386/boot` directory.

To use the new kernel, you have to copy the kernel to the `/boot` directory under a specific name and edit the `/etc/lilo.conf` file to set up LILO (the Linux Loader). You learn these steps in the "Installing the new kernel and other required files" section later in this session. Before you proceed with the kernel installation, however, you have to build and install the modules.

Building and installing the modules

If you select any modules during the kernel configuration, you have to build the modules and install them. Perform the following steps:

1. Type the following commands to build the modules:

```
cd /usr/src/linux
make modules
```

2. The current set of modules in a directory is named after the version of Linux kernel your system is running. For example, if your system runs kernel version 2.4.0, the modules reside in the following directory:

```
/lib/modules/2.4.0
```

Move the module directory to a new location, as follows:

```
mv /lib/modules/2.4.0 /lib/modules/2.4.0-old
```

3. Install the new modules by using the following command:

```
make modules_install
```

Now you can install the kernel and make it available for LILO to boot.

10 Min. To Go

Installing the new kernel and setting up LILO

Linux uses LILO to load the newly built Linux kernel from the disk. You must configure and install LILO to use the kernel. The configuration file /etc/lilo.conf lists the kernel binary that LILO runs. You can examine the contents of the LILO configuration file by typing the following command:

```
cat /etc/lilo.conf
```

Here is what I see when I try this command on one of my systems that contain a SCSI adapter:

```
boot=/dev/hda
map=/boot/map
install=/boot/boot.b
prompt
timeout=50
image=/boot/vmlinuz-2.4.0
        label=linux
        root=/dev/hda3
        initrd=/boot/initrd-2.4.0.img
        read-only
other=/dev/hda1
        label=dos
        table=/dev/hda
```

Note the following about the LILO configuration file:

- The last three lines are for booting from the DOS partition. (Microsoft Windows is installed in that partition.)

- The five lines starting with image=/boot/vmlinuz-2.4.0 define a specific kernel file LILO can boot. You can make LILO boot another kernel by adding a similar section to the configuration file.

- The image=/boot/vmlinuz-2.4.0 line identifies the kernel LILO loads. In this case, the kernel file is vmlinuz-2.4.0, which you can locate in the /boot directory.

- The label=linux line gives a name to the kernel. In this case, you can type linux at the boot: prompt to make LILO boot this particular kernel.

- The root=/dev/hda3 line specifies the disk partition where the root Linux file system is located. This may differ on your system.

- The initrd=/boot/initrd-2.4.0.img line specifies a file that contains an initial RAM disk image that serves as a file system before the disks are available. You see the initrd line only if your system has a SCSI adapter and the kernel uses a modular SCSI driver. In this case, the kernel uses the RAM disk — a block of memory used as a disk — to get started. Then it loads the SCSI driver module and begins using the SCSI hard disk. You do not need the initrd line if you create a kernel with the SCSI adapter support built into the kernel.

On systems that have an MS-DOS partition, the LILO configuration file can include another section with details for the operating system (perhaps Windows 95, 98, or 2000) on that partition.

To configure LILO to boot yet another kernel (the one you just built), follow these steps:

1. Copy the new kernel binary to the /boot directory. The newly compressed kernel file is in the /usr/src/linux/arch/i386/boot directory. I simply copy the new kernel binary file to the /boot directory that has the same name:

   ```
   cp /usr/src/linux/arch/i386/boot/zImage /boot
   ```

   If — when you build the kernel — you type the command make zImage, the kernel filename is zImage. If you build the kernel by using the make bzImage command because the kernel is too big, the filename is bzImage. You can use any other filename you want as long as you use the same filename when referring to the kernel in the /etc/lilo.conf file of step 3.

2. Save the former `System.map` file in the `/boot` directory, and copy the new map file. (I assume you rebuild kernel version 2.4.0 after changing some configuration options):

```
mv /boot/System.map-2.4.0 /boot/System.map-
2.4.0-old
cp /usr/src/linux/System.map /boot/System.map-2.4.0
cd /boot
ln -s System.map-2.4.0 System.map
```

3. Use your favorite text editor to edit the `/etc/lilo.conf` file, and add the following lines just after the `timeout` line in the file:

```
image=/boot/zImage
        label=new
        root=/dev/hda3
        read-only
```

On your system, you should make sure the `root` line is correct — instead of `/dev/hda3`, list the correct disk partition where the Linux root directory (/) is located. Also, use the correct filename for the kernel image file (for example, `/boot/bzImage` if the kernel file is so named).

 I don't show the `initrd` **line because I assume you are no longer using a modular SCSI driver even if your system has a SCSI adapter.**

4. Save the `lilo.conf` file, and exit the editor.
5. Install LILO again by using the following command:

```
/sbin/lilo
```

Now you are ready to reboot the system and to try out the new kernel.

Rebooting the System

After you finish configuring and installing LILO, you return to the Linux prompt. While you are still logged in as `root`, type the following command to reboot the system:

```
reboot
```

When you see the LILO `boot:` prompt, type the name you have assigned to the new kernel in the `/etc/lilo.conf` file. You do not have to type anything if you have added the new kernel description as the first entry in the LILO configuration file.

After the system reboots, you should see the familiar graphical login screen. To see proof that you are indeed running the new kernel, log in as a user, open a terminal window, and type `uname -srv`. This command shows you the kernel version as well as the date and time when this kernel was built. If you have upgraded the kernel source, you should see the version number for the new kernel. If you have rebuilt the kernel for the same old kernel version, the date and time should match the time when you rebuilt the kernel. That's your proof that the system is running the new kernel.

If the system *hangs* (nothing seems to happen — no output is on the screen and no disk activity), you may have skipped a step during the kernel rebuild. You can power the PC off and on to reboot. This time, enter `linux` **(the former working kernel's name) at the LILO** `boot:` **prompt.**

If you cannot boot the older version of Linux either, use the emergency boot disk (containing an earlier, but working, version of Linux) to start the system. Then you can repeat the kernel rebuild and installation process, making sure you follow all steps correctly.

Done!

Review

In this session, you learned to install the kernel source files and to configure the kernel by using the `make xconfig` command. Then you learned the command you use to build a new kernel and new driver modules. You also learned the procedure for installing the new kernel so that you can boot the system and start using the newly built kernel.

Quiz Yourself

1. What does "rebuilding the kernel" mean, and what are the key phases of rebuilding the kernel? (See "Installing the Source Files and Rebuilding the Kernel.")

2. What are the three ways you can configure the kernel? (See "Configuring the Kernel.")

3. What command line do you type to build the kernel? (See "Building and Installing the Kernel and Modules.")

4. How do you build and install the modules? (See "Building and Installing the Modules.")

5. How do you install the new kernel? (See "Installing the New Kernel and Setting Up LILO.")

Scheduling Jobs in Linux

Session Checklist

✔ Scheduling one time jobs

✔ Scheduling recurring jobs

*30 Min.
To Go*

A s a system administrator, you may need to run some programs automatically at regular intervals or to execute one or more commands at a specified time in the future. Your Linux system includes facilities that enable you to schedule jobs to run at any future date or time you want. You can set up the system to perform a task periodically or just once at any future date. Here are some typical tasks you can perform by scheduling jobs on your Linux system:

- Back up the files in the middle of the night.
- Download large files in the early morning when the system is not busy.
- Send yourself messages as a reminder of meetings.
- Analyze the system logs periodically and look for any abnormal activities.

You can perform these tasks on a one time basis by using the at command or on a recurring basis by using the crontab facility of Linux. This session introduces you to these job-scheduling features.

Scheduling One Time Jobs

You can use the at command to schedule the execution of one or more commands. The atd daemon — a program designed to process jobs submitted using at — executes the commands at the specified time and mails the output to you. The following configuration files control which users can use the at command to schedule tasks:

- /etc/at.allow contains the names of users who may use the at command to submit jobs.
- /etc/at.deny contains the names of users not allowed to use the at command to submit jobs.

If these files are not present or if there is an empty /etc/at.deny file, any user can submit jobs by using the at command. The default in Linux is an empty /etc/at.deny file, so anyone can use the at command. If you do not want some users to use at, simply list those user names in the /etc/at.deny file.

Submitting a one time job

To use at to schedule a one time job for execution, follow these steps:

1. Run the at command along with the date or time when you want your commands to execute. When you press Enter, the at> prompt appears as follows:

   ```
   at 21:30
   at>
   ```

   This is the simplest way to indicate the time you want to execute one or more commands — simply specify the time in a 24-hour format. In this case, you want to execute the commands at 9:30 p.m. tonight (or tomorrow, if it's already past 9:30 p.m.). You can, however, specify the execution time in many different ways (see Table 25-1 for examples).

2. At the at> prompt, type the commands you want to execute as you would type them at the shell prompt. After each command, press Enter, and continue with the next command. When you finish entering the commands you want to execute, press Ctrl+D to end this step. Here is an example showing a single command:

   ```
   at> ps
   at> <EOT>
   warning: commands will be executed using /bin/sh
   job 2 at 2000-05-15 21:30
   ```

After you press Ctrl+D, the at command responds with a job number and the date and time the job will execute.

Table 25-1
Specifying the Time of Execution with the at Command

Command	When the Job Runs
at now	Immediately
at now + 15 minutes	15 minutes from the current time
at now + 4 hours	4 hours from the current time
at now + 7 days	7 days from the current time
at noon	At noontime today (or tomorrow, if already past noon)
at now next hour	Exactly 60 minutes from now
at now next day	At the same time tomorrow
at 17:00 tomorrow	At 5:00 p.m. tomorrow
at 4:45pm	At 4:45 p.m. today (or tomorrow, if already past 4:45 p.m.)
at 3:00 Aug 16, 00	At 3:00 a.m. on August 16, 2000

Verifying scheduled one time jobs

After you enter one or more jobs, you can type the atq command to view the current list of scheduled jobs:

```
2       2000-05-15 21:30 a
3       2000-08-16 03:00 a
4       2000-05-16 21:57 a
5       2000-05-16 16:45 a
```

The first field on each line shows the job number — the same number the at command displays when you submit the job. The next field displays the year, month, day, and time of execution. The last field shows that the jobs are pending in the a queue.

Canceling one time jobs and receiving the output

If you want to cancel a job, use the `atrm` command to remove the job from the queue. When removing a job by using the `atrm` command, refer to the job by its number, as follows:

```
atrm 3
```

This deletes job number 3 scheduled for 3:00 a.m. August 16, 2000.

When a job executes, the output is mailed to you. Type `mail` to read your mail and to view the output from your jobs.

**20 Min.
To Go**

Scheduling Recurring Jobs

Although the `at` command is good for running commands at a specific time, it's not useful for running a program automatically at repeated intervals. You have to use `crontab` to schedule such recurring jobs. You need to do this, for example, if you want to back up your files to tape at midnight every day.

Schedule recurring jobs by placing job information in a file with a specific format and submitting this file with the `crontab` command. The cron daemon — `crond` — checks the job information every minute and executes the recurring jobs at the specified times. Because the cron daemon processes recurring jobs, such jobs are also referred to as *cron jobs*.

Any output from the job is mailed to the user who submits the job. (In the submitted job information file, you may specify a different recipient for the mailed output.)

As with the `at` command, two files control who can use `crontab` to schedule cron jobs:

- `/etc/cron.allow` contains the names of users who may use the `crontab` command to submit jobs.

- `/etc/cron.deny` contains names of users not allowed to use the `crontab` command to submit jobs.

If the `/etc/cron.allow` file exists, only users listed in this file can schedule cron jobs. If only the `/etc/cron.deny` file exists, users listed in this file cannot schedule cron jobs. If neither file exists, the default Linux setup enables any user to submit cron jobs.

Submitting a cron job

To submit a cron job, perform the following steps:

1. Prepare a shell script (or an executable program in any programming language) that can perform the recurring task you want to perform. You can skip this step if you want to execute an existing program periodically.

2. Prepare a text file with information about the times you want the shell script or program (from step 1) to execute. This is the file you submit by using `crontab`. You can submit several recurring jobs with a single file. Each line with timing information about a job has a standard format with at least six fields — the first five specify when the job runs, and the sixth and subsequent fields constitute the command to be run. For example, this line executes the `myjob` shell script in a user's home directory at 5 minutes past midnight each day:

   ```
   5 0 * * * $HOME/myjob
   ```

   Table 25-2 shows the meaning of the first five fields. Also, an entry in any of the first five fields can be a single number, a comma-separated list of numbers, a pair of numbers separated by a dash (indicating a range of numbers), or an asterisk. An asterisk (*) represents all possible values for that field.

3. Submit the information to `crontab` by using the following command:

   ```
   crontab jobinfo
   ```

   In this case, the text file `jobinfo` (in the current directory) contains the job information.

That's it! You're all set with the cron job. From now on, the cron job should run at regular intervals (as specified in the job information file), and you should receive mail messages that contain the output from the job.

Verifying the cron job is scheduled

To verify that the job is indeed scheduled, type the following command:

```
crontab -l
```

The output of the `crontab -l` command shows the cron jobs currently installed in your name.

```
# DO NOT EDIT THIS FILE - edit the master and reinstall.
# (jobinfo installed on Tue May 16 20:44:23 2000)
# (Cron version -- $Id: crontab.c,v 2.13 1994/01/17 03:20:37 vixie Exp $)
SHELL=/bin/sh
5 0 * * * $HOME/myjob
```

To remove your cron jobs, type `crontab -r`.

Table 25-2
Specifying the Time of Execution in crontab Files

Field Number	Meaning of Field	Acceptable Range of Values*
1	Minute	0-59
2	Hour of the day	0-23
3	Day of the month	0-31
4	Month	1-12 (1 means January, 2 means February, and so on) or the names of months using the first letters (Jan, Feb, Mar, Apr, May, Jun, Jul, Aug, Sep, Oct, Nov, Dec)
5	Day of the week	0-6 (0 means Sunday, 1 means Monday, and so on) or the three-letter abbreviations of the weekday (Sun, Mon, Tue, Wed, Thu, Fri, Sat)

* *An asterisk in a field represents all possible values for that field. For example, if an asterisk appears in the third field, the job executes every day.*

**10 Min.
To Go**

Setting up cron jobs for any user

If you log in as `root`, you can also set up, examine, and remove cron jobs for any user. To set up cron jobs for a user, use this command:

```
crontab -u username filename
```

Here, *username* is the user for whom you are installing the cron jobs, and *filename* is the file that contains information about the jobs.

Use the following `crontab` command to view a user's cron jobs:

```
crontab -u username -l
```

To remove a user's cron jobs, use the following command:

```
crontab -u username -r
```

The cron daemon also executes the cron jobs listed in the system-wide cron job file /etc/crontab. Here's the default /etc/crontab file in Linux (type cat /etc/crontab to view the file):

```
SHELL=/bin/bash
PATH=/sbin:/bin:/usr/sbin:/usr/bin
MAILTO=root
HOME=/

# run-parts
01 * * * * root run-parts /etc/cron.hourly
02 4 * * * root run-parts /etc/cron.daily
22 4 * * 0 root run-parts /etc/cron.weekly
42 4 1 * * root run-parts /etc/cron.monthly
```

The first four lines set up several environment variables for jobs listed in this file. The MAILTO environment variable specifies the user who receives the mail message that contains the output from cron jobs in this file.

The line that begins with a # is a comment line. The last four lines execute the run-parts shell script (located in the /usr/bin directory) at various times with the name of a specific directory as an argument. Each of the arguments that are part of run-parts — /etc/cron.hourly, /etc/cron.daily, /etc/cron.weekly, and /etc/cron.monthly — are directories. Essentially, run-parts executes all scripts located in the directory you provide as an argument. Here is what those directories contain:

Directory Name	Contents
/etc/cron.hourly	scripts executed every hour
/etc/cron.daily	scripts executed each day at 4:02 a.m.
/etc/cron.weekly	scripts executed weekly on Sunday at 4:22 a.m.
/etc/cron.monthly	scripts executed at 4:42 a.m. on the first day of each month
/etc/cron.allow	file containing names of users allowed to run cron jobs
/etc/cron.deny	file containing names of users not allowed to run cron jobs

You have to look at the scripts in these directories to learn what executes at periodic intervals. For example, the `/etc/cron.daily` contains the following scripts:

Script Name	Description
`logrotate`	Automatically rotates, compresses, and mails log files (based on configuration information in the `/etc/logrotate.conf` file)
`tmpwatch`	Removes old files from temporary directories such as `/tmp` and `/var/tmp`
`tetex.cron`	Removes old font files (script used by a typesetting program called TeX)
`updatedb.cron`	Updates the filename database that the `locate` command consults (for example, try typing `locate updatedb`. This shows you all files that contain `updatedb` in their names.)

Done!

REVIEW

This session showed you how to perform commands at a future time and to submit recurring jobs. You learned to use the `at` command to execute one or more commands on a one time basis in the future and to have the output mailed to you. Next, you used the `crontab` facility to set up periodic jobs — called cron jobs — that execute at recurring intervals and have the output mailed to you.

QUIZ YOURSELF

1. What are some of the tasks you can perform by scheduling jobs? (See the introduction to the session.)

2. What command do you use to schedule one time jobs? (See "Scheduling One Time Jobs.")

3. What feature of Linux do you use to set up recurring jobs? (See "Scheduling Recurring Jobs.")

4. How can you control which users are allowed to submit recurring jobs on your system? (See "Scheduling Recurring Jobs.")

5. How do you specify the time of execution for recurring jobs? (See "Scheduling Recurring Jobs.")

SESSION

Backing Up and Restoring Files

Session Checklist

✔ Selecting a backup strategy and storage media

✔ Using tar to backup and restore files

✔ Backing up on tapes

**30 Min.
To Go**

By now, you have learned a number of system-administration tasks, from configuring X to building a new kernel. This session introduces you to another important system administration task — backing up and restoring files from backup-storage media. In this session, you learn to back up and restore files by using the tape archiver (tar) program that comes with Linux. You also learn to perform incremental and automatic backups on tapes.

Selecting a Backup Strategy and Storage Media

Your Linux system's hard disk contains everything needed to keep the system running, as well as other files such as documents and databases you need to keep your business running. You need to back up these files so you can recover quickly and bring the system back to normal in case the hard disk crashes. Typically, you have to follow a strict regimen of regular backups because you can never tell when the hard disk might fail or when the file system might get corrupted. To implement such a regimen, you need to decide which files to back up, how often to back them up, and what backup storage media to use. This involves selecting a backup strategy and backup media.

Your choice of backup strategy and backup media depends on your assessment of the risk of business disruption due to hard disk failure. Depending on how you use your Linux system, a disk failure may or may not have much impact on you.

For example, if you use your Linux system as a learning tool (to learn about Linux or programming), all you may need are backup copies of some system files needed to configure Linux. In this case, your backup strategy may be to save important system-configuration files on one or more floppies every time you change any system configuration. You may also want to set up a script that runs at a scheduled time to send e-mail to yourself about the configuration changes. Session 25 explains setting up job scheduling.

On the other hand, if you use your Linux system as an office server that provides shared file storage for many users, the risk of business disruption due to disk failure is much higher. In this case, you have to back up all the files every week and back up any new or changed files every day. You should perform these backups in an automated manner (using the job-scheduling features you learned in Session 25). Also, you probably need a backup storage medium that can store large amounts (multiple gigabytes) of data on a single tape. In other words, for high-risk situations, your backup strategy is more elaborate and thus requires additional equipment such as a tape drive.

Your choice of backup media depends on the amount of data you have to back up. For a small amount of data, such as system-configuration files, you can use floppy disks as your backup media. If your PC has a Zip drive, you can use Zip disks as your backup media. (These are good for backing up a single-user directory.) To back up servers, you should use a tape drive — typically a 4mm or 8mm tape drive that connects to a SCSI controller. Such tape drives can store gigabytes of data per tape, and you can use them to back up an entire file system on a single tape.

When backing up files to these backup storage media, you have to refer to the backup device by name. Here are the device names for some common backup devices:

Backup Device	Linux Device Name
Floppy disk	/dev/fd0
IDE Zip drive	/dev/hdc4 or /dev/hdd4
SCSI Zip drive	/dev/sda (assuming it's the first SCSI drive); otherwise, the device name depends on the SCSI ID
SCSI tape drive	/dev/st0 or /dev/nst0 (the n prefix means that the tape does not rewind after files are copied to the tape)

Commercial Backup Utilities for Linux

Although you can manage backups with tar, a number of commercial backup utilities come with graphical user interfaces and other features to simplify backups. Here are some well-known backup utilities for Linux:

- **BRU** (A backup and restore utility from EST (see http://www.estinc.com/)
- **LONE-TAR** (A tape backup software package from Lone Star Software Corporation (see http://www.cactus.com/)
- **Arkeia** (Backup and recovery software for heterogeneous networks from Knox Software (see http://www.knox-software.com/)
- **CTAR** (Backup and recovery software for UNIX systems from UniTrends Software Corporation (see http://www.unitrends.com/)

Although this session focuses on backing up and restoring files by using the tape archiver (tar) program that comes with Linux, other commercially available utilities for Linux that perform backups are available. I highlight some well-known commercial utilities in the sidebar.

Using the Tape Archiver Program to Back Up and Restore Files

**20 Min.
To Go**

You can use the tape archiver program (tar command) to archive files to a device such as a floppy disk or tape. The tar program creates an archive file that can contain other directories and files and (optionally) can compress the archive for

*Part V—Sunday Morning
Session 26*

efficient storage. The archive is then written to a specified device or to another file. In fact, many software packages are distributed in the form of a compressed tar file. The command syntax of the tar program is as follows:

```
tar options destination source
```

A sequence of single letters usually specifies the *options*; each letter specifies what tar should do. The device name of the backup device is destination, and *source* is a list of file or directory names denoting the files to back up.

Backing up and restoring a single volume archive

Suppose you want to back up the contents of the /etc/X11 directory on a single floppy disk. Log in as root, place a disk in the floppy drive, and type the following command:

```
tar zcvf /dev/fd0 /etc/X11
```

The tar program displays a list of filenames as each file is copied to the compressed tar archive on the floppy disk. In this case, the options are zcvf, the destination is /dev/fd0 (the floppy disk), and the source is the /etc/X11 directory (which implies all its subdirectories and their contents). You can use a similar tar command to back up files to a tape. Simply replace /dev/fd0 with the tape device — such as /dev/st0 for a SCSI tape drive.

A few common tar options are defined here:

Option	Definition
Z	compresses the tar archive by using gzip
C	creates a new archive
V	displays verbose messages
X	extracts files from the archive
T	lists the contents of the archive
M	specifies a multivolume archive (see "Backing up and restoring a multivolume archive" later in this session)
F	specifies the name of the archive file or device

To view the contents of the tar archive you create on the floppy disk, type the following command:

```
tar zvtf /dev/fd0
```

You should see a list of the filenames (each filename begins with /etc/X11) indicating the contents of the backup. In this tar command, the t option lists the contents of the tar archive.

To learn how to extract the files from a tar backup, try the following steps while logged in as root:

1. Change the directory to /tmp by typing the command:

   cd /tmp

   That is where you extract the files from the tar backup.

2. Type the following command:

   tar zxvf /dev/fd0

   This tar command uses the x option to extract the files from the archive stored on /dev/fd0 (the floppy disk).

If you check the contents of the /tmp directory, you notice that the tar command creates an etc/X11 directory tree in /tmp and restores all files from the tar archive into that directory. The tar command strips off the leading / from the filenames in the archive and restores the files in the current directory. If you want to restore the /etc/X11 directory from the archive on the floppy, use the following command:

   tar zxvf /dev/fd0 /

The / at the end of the command denotes the directory where you want to restore the backup files.

As you can see, the tar command enables you to create, view, and restore an archive. You can store the archive in a file or in any device you specify with a device name.

Backing up and restoring a multivolume archive

Sometimes the capacity of a single storage medium is less than the total storage space needed to store the archive. In that case, you can use the M option for a multivolume archive — meaning the archive can span multiple tapes or floppies.

You cannot create a compressed, multivolume archive. That means you cannot use the z option.

To see how multivolume archives work, log in as root, place one disk in the floppy drive, and type the following tar command:

```
tar cvfM /dev/fd0 /usr/doc/ghostscript*
```

Note the M option in the option letters, which tells tar to create a multivolume archive. The tar command prompts you for a second floppy when the first fills to capacity. Take out the first floppy, and insert another floppy when you see the following prompt:

```
Prepare volume #2 for '/dev/fd0' and hit return:
```

When you press Enter, the tar program continues with the second floppy. In this example, you need only two floppies to store the archive. For larger archives, the tar program continues to prompt for floppies in case more floppies are needed.

To restore from this multivolume archive, type cd /tmp to change the directory to /tmp, and then type:

```
tar xvfM /dev/fd0
```

The tar program prompts you to feed the floppies as necessary.

Use the du -s **command to determine the amount of storage you need to archive a directory. For example, type** du -s /etc **to get the total size of the** /etc **directory in kilobytes:**

```
8040    /etc
```

The result shows that the /etc **directory requires at least 4,528K of storage space to back up. If you plan to back up on multiple high-density floppies, you need about 8,040/1,200 = 6 floppies.**

Backing up on Tapes

**10 Min.
To Go**

Although backing up on tapes is as simple as using the right device name in the tar command, you need to know some nuances of the tape device to use it well. When you use tar to back up to the device named /dev/st0 (the first SCSI tape drive), the tape device automatically rewinds the tape after the tar program finishes copying the archive to the tape. The /dev/st0 device is called a *rewinding tape device* because it rewinds tapes by default.

If your tape can hold several gigabytes of data, you may want to write several tar archives — one after another — to the same tape. (Otherwise, much of the tape may be empty.) To do this, you do not want the tape device to rewind the tape after the tar program finishes. To help you with this, some Linux tape devices are non-rewinding devices. The non-rewinding SCSI tape device is called /dev/nst0. Use this device name if you want to write one archive after another on a tape.

After each archive, the non-rewinding tape device writes an end-of-file (EOF) marker to separate one archive from the next. You can use the mt command to control the tape. Essentially, it moves from one marker to the next or rewinds the tape. For example, after you finish writing several archives to a tape by using the /dev/nst0 device name, you can use the following command to rewind the tape:

```
mt -f /dev/nst0 rewind
```

After rewinding the tape, you can use the following command to extract files from the first archive to the current disk directory:

```
tar xvf /dev/nst0
```

After that, you must move past the EOF marker to the next archive. To do this, use the following mt command:

```
mt -f /dev/nst0 fsf 1
```

This positions the tape at the beginning of the next archive. You can now use the tar xvf command again to read this archive.

If you save multiple archives on a tape, you have to keep track of the archives yourself.

Performing incremental backups

Suppose you backed up your system's hard disk on a tape by using the tar command. Because such a full backup can take quite some time, you do not want to repeat this task every night. Besides, only a small number of files may have changed during the day. You can use the find command to list those files that have changed in the past 24 hours, as follows:

```
find / -mtime -1 -type f -print
```

This command prints a list of files that have changed within the last day. The -mtime -1 option means you want the files that have been modified modified within the last day. You can now combine the find command with the tar command to back up only those files that have changed within the last day, as follows:

```
tar cvf /dev/st0 `find / -mtime -1 -type f -print`
```

When you place a command between single back quotes, the shell executes that command and places the output at that point in the command line. The net result is that the tar program saves only the changed files in the archive. Thus, you get an *incremental backup* that includes files that have changed since the previous day.

Performing automated full and incremental backups

In Session 25, you learned to use crontab to set up recurring jobs called cron jobs — tasks the Linux system performs at regular intervals. Backing up your system is a good use of the crontab facility. Suppose your backup strategy is as follows:

- Every Sunday morning at 1:15 a.m., you back up the entire disk on the tape.
- On the other days of the week (Monday through Saturday), you perform an incremental backup at 3:10 a.m. by saving only those files that have changed during the past 24 hours.

To set up this automated backup schedule, log in as root, and type the following lines in a file named backups. (This example assumes you are using a SCSI tape drive.)

```
15 1 * * 0 tar zcvf /dev/st0 /
10 3 * * 1-6 tar zcvf /dev/st0 `find / -mtime -1 -type f -print`
```

Next, submit this job schedule by using the following crontab command:

```
crontab backups
```

Done!

Now you should be set for an automated backup. You only need to place a new tape in the tape drive every day. You should also label each tape appropriately.

REVIEW

In this session, you learned the importance of backing up your files. This session highlighted the selection of a backup strategy and backup media based on your needs and your level of tolerance for the risk of business interruption from a hard disk failure. You also learned to use the tape archiver program — tar — to back up and restore files. Finally, the session showed you how to perform incremental tape backups and how to set up cron jobs for automated-full and incremental tape backups.

QUIZ YOURSELF

1. How do you decide what to back up and how often to back it up? (See "Selecting a Backup Strategy and Storage Media.")

2. What are some commercial backup utilities for Linux? (See the sidebar "Commercial Backup Utilities for Linux.")

3. How do you use the tar program to back up files if the total size of files exceeds the capacity of a single copy of the backup medium? (See "Backing up and restoring a multivolume archive.")

4. What commands do you use to back up only those files that have changed in the previous day? (See "Performing incremental backups.")

5. How do you automate the job of backing up files to a tape? (See "Performing automated-full and incremental backups.")

PART

V

Sunday Morning

1. What determines exactly which processes the `init` process starts at boot time?

2. By looking at the `/etc/inittab` file, how do you determine the default run level of your system?

3. What startup scripts does `init` run?

4. Why is it important to learn how to build software from source files?

5. What is the typical format in which the files for open software packages are distributed? How do you download and unpack such distributions?

6. Briefly outline the steps you follow to download, unpack, build, and install a typical open source software package on your Linux system.

7. What are RPMs? How do you figure out whether a specific RPM is installed on your system?

8. Name two ways you can install RPMs from this book's companion CD-ROMs. For command-line tools, show a sample command line.

9. Explain how you interpret the RPM filename for the RPMs on this book's companion CD-ROMs.

10. Why might you rebuild the Linux kernel?

11. How do you install the kernel sources so you can build the kernel?

12. Briefly describe the steps involved in rebuilding the kernel.

13. Give some examples of why you might want to run programs automatically at regular intervals or execute commands at a future time. What Linux facilities do you use to accomplish this goal?

14. Show an example of scheduling a one-time job.

15. Briefly describe how to set up a recurring job on your Linux system.

16. Explain how you ensure that only a number of authorized users can submit one-time or recurring jobs.

17. What are some of the backup media you can use to back up files on your system? What are the device names of these backup devices?

18. What utility can you use to back up files and directories on a backup device? Assume your system has a SCSI tape drive. Show the command line to backup the file system on a tape.

19. Suppose you want to back up several large files in the /home/share directory onto floppies, but they will not fit on a single floppy. Show a sample command line that backs up the files on multiple floppy disks.

20. Explain how to store multiple backup archives on a single tape. Show the commands to rewind the tape and skip over an archive.

PART

VI

*Sunday
Afternoon*

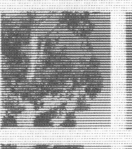

Performing Basic System-Administration Tasks

Session Checklist

✔ Understanding the Linux system and network administration

✔ Adding user accounts with Linuxconf

✔ Exploring other tasks performed by Linuxconf

**30 Min.
To Go**

This first Sunday afternoon session introduces you to Linux system and network administration. Then you learn to perform some system-administration tasks by using *Linuxconf*, a graphical system administration tool that comes with Red Hat Linux. Specifically, you learn to add user accounts, and you explore other tasks that Linuxconf enables you to perform. This overview of Linuxconf should help you execute other system-administration tasks as the need arises. Other distributions such as Caldera and SuSe also include graphical utilities you have seen in previous sessions. This session focuses on Red Hat because this is the distribution you have installed if you have used the CD-ROMs included with this book.

Understanding Linux System and Network Administration

System administration refers to tasks you must perform to keep a computer system up and running properly. Now that almost all computers are networked, another set of tasks is needed to keep the network up and running. These tasks are collectively called *network administration*. A site with many computers probably has a full-time *system administrator* who takes care of all system- and network-administration tasks. Really large sites may have separate system-administration and network-administration personnel. If you run Linux on a home PC or on a few systems in a small company, you probably perform the duties of both the system administrator and the network administrator.

As the following descriptions of system- and network-administration tasks demonstrate, you can perform these tasks by using the Linuxconf tool — an X Window application that enables you to perform most system and network-administration tasks without having to edit configuration files manually or to type cryptic commands. However, Linux does offer you the ability to edit the configuration files manually if you choose to learn to do so. After the overview of system and network administration, you learn to use Linuxconf.

System-administration tasks

As a system administrator, your typical tasks (which you can perform with Linuxconf) are the following:

- *Installing, configuring, and upgrading the operating system and various utilities.* You learned how to install Red Hat Linux in earlier sessions.

- *Adding and removing users.* Later in this session, you learn to use Red Hat's graphical Linuxconf tool to add a new user account. If a user forgets the password, you can also change the password by using Linuxconf.

- *Installing new software.* For the typical Linux software, which you get in source-code form, this task involves using tools such as `gunzip` (to uncompress the software), `tar` (to unpack the archive), and `make` (to build the executable programs). For software Red Hat distributes in Red Hat Package Manager (RPM) files, you have to use the `rpm` command to install the software.

 Session 23 shows you how to install RPM packages. In Session 22, you learn to use tools, such as ~~tar~~ and ~~make~~, to build software packages.

- *Making backups.* You can use the `tar` or `cpio` program to archive one or more directories and to copy the archive to a floppy disk (if the archive is small enough) or to a tape (if you have a tape drive).

In Session 26, you learn how to back up and restore files.

- *Mounting and unmounting file systems.* When you want to access the files on a CD-ROM, for example, you have to mount that CD-ROM's file system on one of the directories of the Linux file system. You have to use the mount command to accomplish this task. You can also use Linuxconf to mount a file system. (An example appears later in this session.)

Mounting is covered in Session 9.

- *Monitoring the system's performance.* You have to use a few utilities, such as top (to see where the processor spends most of its time) and free (to see the amount of free and used memory in the system).

You learn to use utilities to monitor system performance in Session 28.

- *Starting and shutting down the system.* Although starting the system typically involves nothing more than powering up the PC, you do have to take some care when you want to shut down your Linux system. You should use the shutdown command to stop all programs before turning off your PC's power switch. If your system is set up for a graphical login screen, you can perform the shutdown operation by selecting a menu item from the login screen.

Network-administration tasks

The following are typical network-administration tasks you can perform with Linuxconf:

- *Maintaining the network configuration files.* In Linux (as well as in other UNIX systems), the TCP/IP network is configured through several text files you may have to edit to make networking work. Linuxconf enables you to configure the network.

You learn about the TCP/IP configuration files in Session 14.

- *Setting up PPP and SLIP.* You can use Linuxconf to set up PPP and SLIP connections.

You learn about PPP and SLIP in Session 12.

- *Monitoring network status.* You have to use tools such as netstat (to view information about active network connections), /sbin/ifconfig (to check the status of various network interfaces), and ping (to make sure a connection is working).

Session 14 introduces you to the tools needed to monitor network status.

Using Linuxconf to Add User Accounts

**20 Min.
To Go**

When you install Red Hat Linux, one of the steps gives you the opportunity to set up user accounts other than root. If you have not added other user accounts during installation, you can do so now. You also must perform this step if you want to enable other users to access and use the system.

In addition to root, creating other user accounts is a good idea. Even if you are the only user of the system, logging in as a less-privileged user is good practice; that way, you cannot damage any important system files inadvertently. When necessary, you can log in as root and perform any system-administration tasks.

   To start Linuxconf from the GNOME Main Menu in Red Hat Linux, select Main Menu (Foot) ⇨ Programs ⇨ System ⇨ LinuxConf.
   The initial Linuxconf window shows three tabs — Config, Control, and Status (see Figure 27-1). Each tab includes buttons you can use to perform various tasks with Linuxconf. When you click a specific button in a tab, other windows appear that have more tabs and buttons that contain further options.

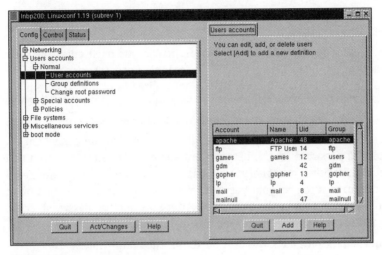

Figure 27-1
The initial Linuxconf window

To add myself as a new user, I follow these steps:

1. Click the User accounts button, and then click the User accounts button shown on the Normal tab. This causes Linuxconf to display the Users Accounts dialog box, as shown in Figure 27-2.

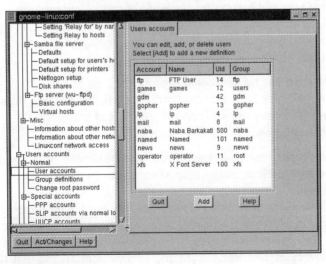

Figure 27-2
The Users Accounts dialog box in Linuxconf

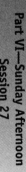

2. Click the Add button in the Users Accounts dialog box shown in Figure 27-2. This brings up the User account creation dialog box.

3. Fill in the requested information. In particular, you must enter the login name and the home directory. For my account, I use /home/naba as the home directory. You can use a similar home directory for your account. After I fill in all of the fields, I click the Accept button. If the /home/naba directory does not exist, Linuxconf creates the directory.

4. The Linuxconf tool displays the Changing password dialog box where I enter the password for the new account and click the Accept button. The tool then requires me to retype my password for confirmation. Notice that Linuxconf rejects your password if the password is a combination of words you can find in the dictionary. After entering the password, click the Quit button in the Users Accounts dialog box.

5. To quit Linuxconf, click the Quit button in the main window. The Linuxconf tool displays the Status of System dialog box that asks if you want to activate the changes. Click the Activate the Changes button to finish the task and to exit Linuxconf.

Exploring Other Tasks Performed by Linuxconf

Here, you explore the tabs and buttons for the kinds of tasks Linuxconf can perform. This session's coverage of Linuxconf, however, is far from complete. It would take many more pages to cover Linuxconf's features thoroughly and to explain each of the tasks it can perform.

Linuxconf has its own home page on the Web at http://www.solucorp.qc.ca/linuxconf/. **Visit the home page to learn the latest news about Linuxconf and to read online documentation.**

Linuxconf includes a Help button in the main Linuxconf window. This Help button provides an overview of Linuxconf. A Help window appears when you click the Help button.

Most Linuxconf windows also include Help buttons that provide *context-sensitive help* — information that relates to the task you are performing (see, for example, Figure 27-2). Press the nearest Help button to read relevant information about the task at hand. In a few cases, Linuxconf might display a message stating that the help file for that item is not written yet.

In the initial Linuxconf window (see Figure 27-1), note there are three tabs: Config, Control, and Status. The Config tab enables you to configure various system services, whereas the Control tab includes buttons for starting and stopping services and for controlling various features of Linuxconf. The Status tab includes buttons that enable you to view various message logs such as the messages the Linux kernel displays as your Red Hat Linux system boots.

**10 Min.
To Go**

To explore the Config, Control, and Status buttons, click each tab, and then click the buttons to see what happens. You should spend a few minutes exploring all three tabs in Linuxconf to get a feel for the types of system-administration and network- administration tasks you can perform with this tool.

Done!

REVIEW

This session began with an overview of Linux system-administration and network-administration tasks. Then you used Linuxconf to add one or more user accounts. Finally, you explored the tabs in Linuxconf to learn the types of system-administration and network-administration tasks you can perform by using Linuxconf.

QUIZ YOURSELF

1. What are some of the typical Linux system-administration tasks? (See "Understanding Linux System and Network Administration.")

2. In Linuxconf, which button do you click to add a new user account? (See "Using Linuxconf to Add User Accounts.")

3. Where can you get the latest information about Linuxconf? (See "Exploring Other Tasks Performed by Linuxconf.")

4. What are the three tabs in Linuxconf's main window? (See "Exploring Other Tasks Performed by Linuxconf.")

5. Can you view message logs from Linuxconf, and, if so, which tab enables you to perform this task? (See "Exploring Other Tasks Performed by Linuxconf.")

Monitoring System Performance

Session Checklist

✔ Using the top utility

✔ Using the GNOME System Monitor

✔ Using the vmstat utility

✔ Checking disk performance and usage by using the hdparm program and other commands

✔ Exploring the /proc file system

**30 Min.
To Go**

A key system-administration task is keeping track of how well your Linux system performs. You can monitor the overall performance of your Linux system by gathering information such as: central processing unit (CPU) usage, physical memory usage, virtual memory (swap space) usage, and hard disk usage. Linux comes with a number of utilities you can use to monitor one or more of these performance parameters. This session introduces you to a few of these utilities and shows you how to understand the information these utilities present.

Using the top Utility

To view the top CPU processes — those that use most of the CPU time — you can use the top program. To start that program, select Main Menu ⇨ Programs ⇨ Utilities ⇨ Top from the GNOME desktop, or type top in a terminal window (or text console). The top program then displays a text screen listing the current processes, arranged in descending order of CPU usage, along with other information such as memory and swap space usage. Figure 28-1 shows a typical output from the top program.

```
 naba@lnbp200: /home/naba                                            _ □ ×
 11:08am  up 1 day, 17:51,  3 users,   load average: 0.24, 0.15, 0.06
65 processes: 63 sleeping, 2 running, 0 zombie, 0 stopped
CPU states: 14.9% user,  2.7% system,  0.0% nice, 82.2% idle
Mem:    62900K av,   61276K used,    1624K free,   52524K shrd,     1568K buff
Swap:   72284K av,    7112K used,   65172K free                    20924K cached

  PID USER     PRI  NI  SIZE  RSS SHARE STAT %CPU %MEM   TIME COMMAND
 2867 naba      11   0 13392  12M  7060 R    11.8 20.4   0:11 netscape-commun
 2713 root       5   0 12372  11M  1156 S     3.5 18.7   0:20 X
 2958 naba       4   0  1028 1028   800 R     1.5  1.6   0:00 top
 1952 root       0   0   652  652   544 S     0.1  1.0   0:00 in.telnetd
 2759 naba       1   0  3432 3432  2072 S     0.1  5.4   0:04 sawfish
    1 root       0   0   120   80    52 S     0.0  0.1   0:05 init
    2 root       0   0     0    0     0 SW    0.0  0.0   0:00 kflushd
    3 root       0   0     0    0     0 SW    0.0  0.0   0:00 kupdate
    4 root       0   0     0    0     0 SW    0.0  0.0   0:00 kpiod
    5 root       0   0     0    0     0 SW    0.0  0.0   0:00 kswapd
    6 root     -20 -20     0    0     0 SW<   0.0  0.0   0:00 mdrecoveryd
   60 root       0   0     0    0     0 SW    0.0  0.0   0:00 khubd
  347 root       0   0   220  172   120 S     0.0  0.2   0:00 syslogd
  357 root       0   0   508  172   128 S     0.0  0.2   0:00 klogd
  372 rpc        0   0    88    0     0 SW    0.0  0.0   0:00 portmap
  388 root       0   0     0    0     0 SW    0.0  0.0   0:00 lockd
  389 root       0   0     0    0     0 SW    0.0  0.0   0:00 rpciod
```

Figure 28-1
Viewing top CPU processes

The top utility updates the display every five seconds. You can keep top running in a window so that you can continually monitor the status of your Linux system. Quit top by pressing Ctrl+C or by closing the terminal window.

The first five lines of the output screen provide summary information about the system. Here is what these five lines show:

1. The first line shows the current time, how long the system has been up, how many users are logged in, and three *load averages* (the average number of processes ready to run during the last 1, 5, and 15 minutes).

2. The second line lists the total number of processes and the status of these processes.

3. The third line shows CPU usage — what percentage of CPU time user processes employ, what percentage system (kernel) processes use, and what percentage of time the CPU is idle.

4. The fourth line shows how the physical memory is being used — the total amount of memory, how much is used, how much is free, how much is shared, and how much is allocated to buffers (for reading from disk, for instance).

5. The fifth line shows how the virtual memory (or swap space) is being used — the total amount of swap space, how much is used, how much is free, and how much is cached.

In top's output screen (Figure 28-1), the table below the summary information lists information about the current processes, arranged in decreasing order of CPU time usage. Type man top in a terminal window to learn the meanings of the column headings in the table top displays.

If the RSS field is drastically smaller than the SIZE field for a process, the process employs too little physical memory compared with what it needs. This results in a lot of swapping as the process runs. You can use the vmstat utility (which you try later in this session) to find out how much your system is swapping.

20 Min. To Go

Using the GNOME System Monitor

Like the text-mode top utility, the *GNOME System Monitor* tool also enables you to view the system load in terms of the number of processes currently running, their memory usage, and the free disk space on your system. To run the tool, select Main Menu ⇨ Programs ⇨ Systems ⇨ System Monitor. You can also start the tool by typing gtop in a terminal window. The tool starts and displays its output in the Processes tab of its main window, as shown in Figure 28-2.

This output resembles the output you see when you type top in a text-mode console or in a terminal window. In fact, the column headings in the table match what the top utility uses in its output. As with the text-mode top utility, the display keeps updating to reflect the current state of the system. You see the current processes in descending order of CPU usage.

The GNOME System Monitor window has two more tabs that display memory usage and free space on the file system. To view this information, click the appropriate tab. For example, to see how various processes are using memory, click the Memory Usage tab.

The bottom of the window shows the CPU usage summary, system up time (how long the system has been up and running), and load averages (the average number of processes ready to run in the last 1, 5, and 15 minutes).

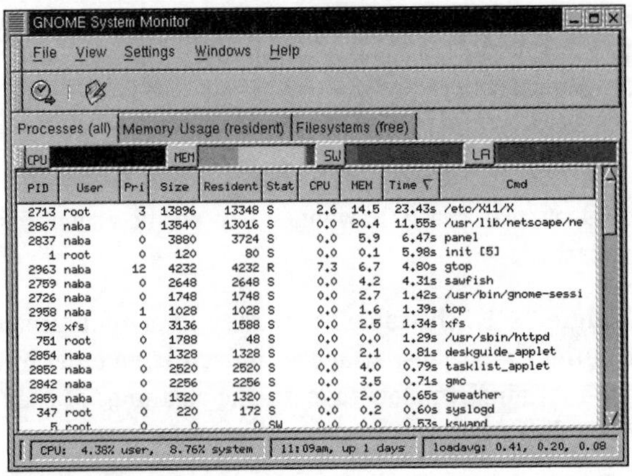

Figure 28-2
Viewing current processes in the GNOME System Monitor window

The load averages give you an indication of how busy the system is. In addition to the top and GNOME System Monitor programs, you can also get the load averages by using the uptime command, as follows:

```
11:40am  up 2 days, 57 min,  3 users,  load average: 0.13, 0.23, 0.27
```

The output shows the current time, how long the system has been up, the number of users, and the three load averages. Load averages greater than 1 imply that many processes are competing for CPU time simultaneously. You can then look at the top CPU processes and try to run these processes one after another (not all at the same time).

Using the vmstat Utility

You can get summary information about the overall system usage when you use the vmstat utility. To view system usage information averaged over 5-second intervals, type the following command (the second argument indicates the total number of lines of output vmstat should display):

```
vmstat 5 8
```

The tabular output is grouped into six categories of information, as the fields in the first line of output indicate. The second line shows categories for each of the six major fields.

```
     procs                      memory     swap        io     system        cpu
  r  b  w  swpd   free   buff  cache  si  so   bi    bo   in    cs   us  sy  id
  1  0  0  4724   1620   3420  18244   0   0    2     0  129   736   27   5  68
  3  0  0  4724   2068   3420  18244   0   0    0     2  124   179    3   8  89
  0  0  0  4724   2052   3420  18244   0   0    0     2  125   301   57  13  30
  0  0  0  4724   2124   3420  18232   0   0    0     3  134   213    6   8  86
  0  0  0  4724   1980   3416  18064   0   0    4     4  182   363   54  15  31
  2  0  0  4724   1960   3416  18064   0   0    0     4  142   126   13   7  80
  0  0  0  4724   1960   3416  18064   0   0    0     3  132   183    7   9  84
  0  0  0  4724   1948   3416  18076   0   0    0     1  112    90    7   8  86
```

You can use Table 28-1 to interpret the six fields and their categories.

Table 28-1
Output Categories for the vmstat Command

Field Name	Description
Procs	Number of processes and their types: r = processes waiting to run; b = processes in uninterruptible sleep; w = processes swapped out, but ready to run
Memory	Information about physical memory and swap space usage (all numbers in kilobytes): swpd = virtual memory used; free = free physical memory; buff = memory used as buffers; cache = cached virtual memory
Swap	Amount of swapping (all numbers in kilobytes per second): si = amount of memory swapped in from disk; so = amount of memory swapped to disk
Io	Information about input and output (all numbers in blocks per second in which the block size depends on the disk device): bi = rate of blocks sent to disk; bo = rate of blocks received from disk
System	Information about the system: in = number of interrupts per second (including clock interrupts); cs = number of context switches per second — the number of times the kernel changes the running process
cpu	Percentages of CPU time used: us = percentage of CPU time used by user processes; sy = percentage of CPU time used by system processes; id = percentage of time CPU is idle

The first line of output following the two header lines shows averages since the last reboot. After that, vmstat displays the 5-second average data seven times over the next 35 seconds. In the vmstat utility's output, high values in the si and so fields indicate too much swapping. High numbers in the bi and bo fields indicate too much disk activity.

Checking Disk Performance and Disk Usage

Linux comes with the /sbin/hdparm program you can use to check disk performance and usage. It controls IDE or ATAPI hard disks that are common on most PCs. One feature of the hdparm program is that the -t option enables you to determine the rate at which data can be read from the disk into a buffer in memory.

```
/sbin/hdparm -t /dev/hda
```

For example, here's the result of this command on my system:

```
/dev/hda:
 Timing buffered disk reads:  64 MB in 15.18 seconds =  4.22 MB/sec
```

As you can see, the command requires the IDE drive's device name (/dev/hda) as an argument. If you have an IDE hard disk, you can try this command to see how fast data can be read from your system's disk drive.

To display the space available in the currently mounted file systems, use the df command. If you want a more human-readable output from df, type df -h to see the following output:

```
Filesystem          Size  Used Avail Use% Mounted on
/dev/hda2           1.9G  1.1G  765M  59% /
/dev/hda1           2.0G  1.8G  256M  88% /dosc
```

As this example shows, the -h option causes the df command to show the sizes in gigabytes (G). If you want to see the output in megabytes (M), use the -m option.

To check the disk space a specific directory uses, employ the du command. You can specify the -h option to view the output in kilobytes (k) or the –m option to view the output in megabytes (M). Typing **du -h /var/log**, for example, provides the following example output:

```
12k     /var/log/httpd
4.0k    /var/log/news/OLD
8.0k    /var/log/news
```

```
4.0k    /var/log/vbox
20k     /var/log/samba
4.0k    /var/log/sa
576k    /var/log
```

The du command displays the disk space each directory uses, and the last line shows the total disk space a given directory uses. If you want to see only the total space a directory uses, type the command using the -s option. For example typing du -sh /home provides output similar to the following:

```
16M     /home
```

**10 Min.
To Go**

Exploring the /proc File System

You can learn a great deal about your Linux system by consulting the contents of a special file system known as the /proc (also called the *process file system*) file system. It can help you monitor a variety of information about your system. In fact, you can even change kernel parameters through the /proc file system and thereby modify the system's behavior.

The /proc file system is not a real directory on the disk, but a collection of data structures in memory (managed by the Linux kernel) that appears to the user as a set of directories and files.

You can access the /proc file system and navigate it just as you do any other directory, but you have to know the meaning of various files to interpret the information. Typically, you can use the cat or more command to view the contents of a file in /proc; the file's contents provide information about some aspect of the system.

As with any directory, you may want to start by looking at a detailed directory listing of /proc. To do so, type ls -l /proc. In the output, the first set of directories (indicated by the letter d at the beginning of the line) represents processes currently running on your system. Each directory that corresponds to a process has the process ID (a number) as its name.

You should also notice a very large file in the listing named /proc/kcore; that file represents the entire physical memory of your system. No physical file occupies that much space on your hard disk, so do not try to remove the file to reclaim disk space.

The `/proc/cpuinfo` file in /proc lists the key characteristics of your system, such as processor type and floating-point processor information. You can view the processor information by typing **cat /proc/cpuinfo**. For example, here is what I get when I type this command on my system:

```
processor       : 0
vendor_id       : GenuineIntel
cpu family      : 5
model           : 4
model name      : Pentium MMX
stepping        : 3
cpu MHz         : 199.616468
fdiv_bug        : no
hlt_bug         : no
sep_bug         : no
f00f_bug        : yes
fpu             : yes
fpu_exception   : yes
cpuid level     : 1
wp              : yes
flags           : fpu vme de pse tsc msr mce cx8 mmx
bogomips        : 398.13
```

This output is from a 200MHz Pentium MMX system. The listing shows many interesting characteristics of the processor. Notice the line that starts with `fdiv_bug`. Remember the infamous Pentium floating-point division bug? The bug is in an instruction called `fdiv` (for floating-point division). Thus, the `fdiv_bug` line indicates whether this particular Pentium has the bug (fortunately, my system's processor does not).

The last line in the `/proc/cpuinfo` file shows the BogoMips for the processor, as computed by the Linux kernel when it boots. BogoMips is something Linux uses internally to calibrate time-delay loops.

Table 28-2 summarizes some of the files in the /proc file system from which you can get information about your Linux system. You can view some of these files on your system to see what they contain.

Not all files shown in Table 28-2 are on your system. The contents of the /proc file system depends on the kernel configuration and the loaded driver modules (which, in turn, depend on your PC's hardware configuration).

Table 28-2
Some Files and Directories in /proc

Filename	Content
/proc/apm	Information about advanced power management (APM)
/proc/bus	Directory with bus-specific information for each bus type, such as PCI
/proc/cmdline	The command line used to start the Linux kernel (for example, auto BOOT_IMAGE=linux ro root=303)
/proc/cpuinfo	Information about the CPU (the microprocessor)
/proc/devices	Available block and character devices in your system
/proc/dma	Information about DMA (direct memory access) channels in use
/proc/filesystems	List of supported file systems
/proc/ide	Directory containing information about IDE devices
/proc/interrupts	Information about interrupt request (IRQ) numbers and how they are used
/proc/ioports	Information about input/output (I/O) port addresses and how they are used
/proc/kcore	Image of the physical memory
/proc/kmsg	Kernel messages
/proc/ksyms	Kernel symbol table
/proc/loadavg	Load average (average number of processes waiting to run in the last 1, 5, and 15 minutes)
/proc/locks	Current kernel locks (used to ensure that multiple processes do not write to a file at the same time)
/proc/meminfo	Information about physical memory and swap space usage
/proc/misc	Miscellaneous information
/proc/modules	List of loaded driver modules

Continued

Table 28-2 *Continued*

Filename	Content
/proc/mounts	List of mounted file systems
/proc/net	Directory with many subdirectories that contain information about networking
/proc/partitions	List of partitions known to the Linux kernel
/proc/pci	Information about PCI devices found on the system
/proc/rtc	Information about the PC's real-time clock (RTC)
/proc/scsi the system	Directory with information about SCSI devices found on
/proc/sound	Information about the sound driver module, if any
/proc/stat	Overall statistics about the system
/proc/swaps	Information about the swap space and how much is used
/proc/sys	Directory that contains information about the system (you can change kernel parameters by writing to files in this directory — this is one way to tune the system's performance, but one that requires expertise to do it properly)
/proc/uptime	Information about how long the system has been up
/proc/version	Kernel version number

Done!

REVIEW

This session showed you how to keep an eye on your Linux system's performance. You learned to use and interpret the displays produced by top, the GNOME System Monitor, vmstat, and the uptime command. You also learned some commands you can use to check available disk space as well as your hard disk's performance. Finally, you explored the /proc file system that contains extensive information about the system.

Quiz Yourself

1. What does the `top` utility do? (See "Using the top Utility.")

2. How do you start the GNOME System Monitor? (See "Using the GNOME System Monitor.")

3. What information does the `vmstat` utility provide? (See "Using the vmstat Utility.")

4. What program can you run to check the speed at which data can be read from your IDE hard disk? (See "Checking Disk Performance and Disk Usage.")

5. What command do you use to view information about interrupt requests (IRQs) from the `/proc` file system? (See "Exploring the /proc File System.")

Session Checklist

✔ Establishing a security policy

✔ Securing your system

✔ Monitoring system security

**30 Min.
To Go**

As a system administrator, you have to worry about your Linux system's security. For a standalone system or a system used in an isolated local area network (LAN), you must ensure that a user does not intentionally or inadvertently modify, delete, or destroy system files. If your Linux system is connected to the Internet, you must also secure the system from unwanted accesses. Intruders, also known as *crackers*, typically impersonate a user, steal or destroy information, and even deny you access to your own system (known as *denial of service*). This session only briefly covers some key aspects of securing your Linux system. As you'll see, Linux already has the tools you need to maintain system security.

To learn more about Linux security, consult the *Linux Security HOWTO* at http://metalab.unc.edu/pub/Linux/docs/HOWTO/ Security-HOWTO. **Another good resource is the *Linux Administrator's Security Guide*, which you can read online at** http://www.securityportal.com/lasg/.

Establishing a Security Policy

The first step in securing your Linux system is to set up a security policy. The security policy is your guide (or rules) to what you enable users (as well as visitors over the Internet) to do on the Linux system. The level of security depends on how you use the Linux system and how much is at risk if someone gains unauthorized access to your system.

If you are a system administrator for Linux systems at an organization of any sort, you probably want to involve management as well as users in setting up the security policy. Obviously, you cannot create an imposing policy that prevents users from working on the system. On the other hand, if the users are creating or using data that's valuable to the organization, you have to set up a policy that aims to protect the data from disclosure to outsiders. In other words, the security policy should strike a balance between users' needs and the need to protect the system.

For a standalone Linux system or a home system you occasionally connect to the Internet, the security policy can be just a listing of the Internet services you want to run on the system and the user accounts you plan to set up on the system. For any larger organization, you probably have one or more Linux systems on a LAN connected to the Internet — preferably through a *firewall* (a device that controls the flow of Internet Protocol (IP) packets between the LAN and the Internet). In such cases, the security policy typically addresses the following areas:

- *Authentication*: Who gets access to the system? What is the minimum length and complexity of passwords? How often must you change passwords? How long can a user be idle before that user is logged out automatically?

- *Authorization*: What can different classes of users do on the system? Who can have the root password?

- *Data Protection*: What data has to be protected? Who has access to data?

- *Internet Access*: What restrictions are on users (from the LAN) accessing the Internet? What Internet services (such as Web, Internet Relay Chat, and so on) can users access? Are incoming e-mails and attachments scanned for viruses? Is there a network firewall?

- *Internet Services*: What Internet services are allowed on each Linux system? Are there any file servers? Mail servers? Web servers? What services run on each type of server? What services, if any, run on Linux systems used as desktop workstations?

- *Security Audits*: Who tests whether security is adequate? How often is security tested? How are problems found during security testing handled?

- *Responsibilities*: Who is responsible for maintaining security? Who monitors log files and audit trails for signs of unauthorized access? If a security breach occurs, who must be informed?

The remainder of this session shows you some of the ways in which you can enhance and maintain the security of your Linux system.

Securing the System

Once you have defined a security policy, you can secure the system according to the policy. The exact steps depend on what you want to do with the system — whether it is a server or a workstation and how many users must access the system. The general steps for securing the system and maintaining security are as follows:

- When installing Linux, select only those package groups you need for your system. Do not install unnecessary software. For example, if your system is a workstation, you do not need to install most of the servers (Web server, news server, and so on).

- Create initial user accounts and make sure all passwords are strong ones that password-cracking programs can't "guess." As you'll learn soon, Linux contains the tools you need to enforce strong passwords.

- Enable only those Internet services you need on a system. In particular, do not enable services not properly configured. Later in this session, you learn about enabling and disabling Internet services.

- Periodically check various log files for signs of break-ins or attempted break-ins. These log files are in the /var/log directory of your system.

- Check security news by regularly visiting and installing updates from your distribution's Web site once a fix becomes available.

Securing passwords

Historically, UNIX passwords are stored in the /etc/passwd file, which any user can read. For example, a typical old-style /etc/passwd file entry for the root user looks like this:

```
root:t6Z7NWDK1K8sU:0:0:root:/root:/bin/bash
```

The fields are separated by colons (:), and the second field contains the password in encrypted form. To check if a password is valid, the login program encrypts the plain-text password the user enters and compares the password with the contents of the /etc/passwd file. If there is a match, the user is allowed to log in.

Password-cracking programs work just like the login program except that password-cracking programs pick one word at a time from a dictionary, encrypt the word, and compare the encrypted word with the encrypted passwords in the /etc/passwd file for a match. To crack the passwords, the intruder needs the /etc/passwd file. Often, crackers use weaknesses of various Internet servers (such as mail and FTP) to get a copy of the /etc/passwd file.

Recently, several improvements have been made to make UNIX passwords more secure. These include shadow passwords and pluggable authentication modules, which are described in the next two sections.

 Linux includes password security enhancements you can use by selecting them during installation. In Session 3, as you complete the Red Hat Linux installation, one step involves making selections on an Authentication Configuration screen. If you accept the default selections — Enable MD5 passwords **and** Enable shadow passwords — **you automatically enable more secure passwords in Red Hat Linux.**

20 Min.
To Go

Shadow Passwords

Instead of storing passwords in the /etc/passwd file, which any user can read, passwords are now stored in a shadow password file. In Linux, the shadow passwords are in the /etc/shadow file. Only the super user (root) can read this file. For example, here is the entry for root in the new-style /etc/passwd file:

```
root:x:0:0:root:/root:/bin/bash
```

As you can see, the second field contains an x instead of an encrypted password. The encrypted password is now stored in the /etc/shadow file where the entry for root is this:

```
root:$1$AAAni/yN$uESHbzUpy9Cgfoo1BfOtSO:11077:0:99999:7:-1:-1:134540356
```

The format of the /etc/shadow entries with colon-separated fields resembles the entries in the /etc/passwd file, but the meanings of many fields differ. The first field is still the user name, and the second field is the encrypted password.

The remaining fields in each /etc/shadow entry control when the password expires. You do not need to interpret or change these entries in the /etc/shadow file. Instead, you should use the chage command to change the password expiration information. For starters, you can check a user's password expiration information by using the chage command with the -l option as follows (in this case, you have to be logged in as root):

```
chage -l root
```

In this case, the following output shows various expiration information: you can change the root password any time (that's what zero minimum time means); it lasts for 99999 days; and the root user gets a warning seven days before the password expires.

```
Minimum:          0
Maximum:          99999
Warning:          7
Inactive:         -1
Last Change:              Apr 30, 2000
Password Expires:         Never
Password Inactive:        Never
Account Expires:          Never
```

If you want to ensure that the password changes every 90 days, you can use the -M option to set the maximum number of days the password stays valid. For example, to make sure that user naba is prompted to change the password in 90 days, I log in as root and type the following command:

```
chage -M 90 naba
```

You can do this for each user account to ensure that all passwords expire and that all users must pick new passwords.

Pluggable Authentication Modules

In addition to improving the password file's security by using the shadow passwords, Linux also improves the actual encryption of the passwords stored in the /etc/shadow file. Password encryption is now performed using the MD5 message-digest algorithm to convert the plain-text password into a 128-bit *fingerprint* or *digest*. The MD5 algorithm, described in RFC1321 (http://www.faqs.org/rfcs/rfc1321.html), compresses a large file in a secure manner so you can digitally sign it through encryption with a private key. It also works quite well for password encryption.

Another advantage of MD5 over the older-style password encryption is that the older passwords were limited to a maximum of eight characters in length; new passwords (encrypted with MD5) can be much longer. Longer passwords are harder to guess even if the /etc/shadow file falls into the wrong hands.

A clue to the use of MD5 encryption in the /etc/shadow file is the increased length of the encrypted password and the increased length of 1 prefix, as in the second field of the following sample entry:

```
root:$1$AAAni/yN$uESHbzUpy9Cgfoo1Bf0tS0:11077:0:99999:7:-1:-1:134540356
```

A Pluggable Authentication Module (PAM) performs the actual MD5 encryption. PAM provides a flexible method for authenticating users on Linux systems. Through settings in configuration files, you can change the authentication method on the fly without having to modify programs such as login and passwd that verify a user's identity.

Linux uses PAM extensively, and the configuration files are in the /etc/pam.d directory of your system. Check out the contents of this directory on your system.

Securing Internet services

For an Internet-connected Linux system (or even one on a TCP/IP LAN), a significant threat is the possibility that someone will use one of many Internet services to gain access to your system. Each service — such as mail, Web, or FTP — requires running a server program that responds to client requests arriving over the TCP/IP network. Some of these server programs have weaknesses that can allow an outsider to log into your system — maybe with root privileges. Luckily, Linux comes with facilities you can use to make Internet services more secure.

Potential intruders can employ a *port-scanning tool* — a program that attempts to establish a TCP/IP connection at a port and to look for a response — to check which Internet servers are running on your system. Then the intruder can potentially exploit any known weaknesses of one or more services to gain access to your system.

Linuxconf, COAS, YaST2

To avoid opening unnecessary entry points to your system, make sure you run only those Internet services you need. You can enable and disable services by using Linuxconf for Red Hat, COAS for Caldera, and YaST2 for SuSe, all graphical system administration utilities. If you have installed Red Hat from the companion CD-ROMs, you can follow the next steps to use Linxconf. Log in as root and select Main Menu ➪ Programs ➪ System ➪ LinuxConf from the GNOME desktop. Then click the Control Panel button on the Control tab. In the next dialog box, click the button labeled `Control service activity`. This shows you a list that contains the status of the current services. To control services by using COAS or YaST2, choose the services options after opening the configuration utilities.

To control a service, click the service's name. For example, to control the Web server, click `httpd`. This causes Linuxconf to display the Service httpd dialog box through which you can control the Web server.

If you do not want the Web server to start automatically at boot time, click the Automatic button to turn it off. To immediately stop the Web server, click the Stop button.

**10 Min.
To Go**

xinetd Server

In addition to the standalone servers such as Web server (`httpd`), mail (`sendmail`), and domain name server (`named`), you have to configure another server separately. The other server, `xinetd` (the Internet super server), starts a host of other Internet services such as FTP, TELNET, and so on. Here, you briefly look at security aspects of the `xinetd` server.

The `xinetd` server reads a configuration file named `/etc/xinetd.conf` at startup. This file, in turn, refers to configuration files stored in the `/etc/xinetd.d` directory. The configuration files in `/etc/xinetd.d` tell `xinetd` which ports to listen to and which server to start for each port. You can browse the files in the `/etc/xinetd.d` directory on your system to find the kinds of services `xinetd` is set up to start. Some of these services provide information intruders may use to break into your system. You should turn off these services by placing a `diasble = yes` line in that service's configuration file. To learn more about the `xinetd` configuration files, type `man xinetd.conf` at the shell prompt in a terminal window.

Depending on what you need on your system, you may want to disable everything but the `ftp` and `telnet` services. After making changes to the `xinetd` configuration files, you must restart the `xinetd` server by typing the following command:

```
/etc/rc.d/init.d/xinetd restart
```

This command displays the following messages:

```
Stopping xinetd: [  OK  ]
Starting xinetd: [  OK  ]
```

Another security feature of `xinetd` is its use of the TCP wrapper facility to start various services. The TCP wrapper provides an access-control facility for Internet services. The TCP wrapper can start other services such as FTP and TELNET; but before starting the service, it consults the /etc/hosts.allow file to see if the host requesting service is allowed that service. If nothing appears in /etc/ hosts.allow about the host, TCP wrapper checks the /etc/hosts.deny file to see if it should deny the service. If both files are empty, TCP wrapper allows the host to access the requested service.

You can place the line ALL:ALL in the /etc/hosts.deny file to deny all hosts access to any Internet services on your system. Then you can add to /etc/ hosts.allow the names of those hosts that can access services on your system. For example, to allow only hosts from the 192.168.1.0 network to access services on your system, place the following line in the /etc/hosts.allow file:

```
ALL: 192.168.1.0/255.255.255.0
```

If you want to permit a specific remote host access to a specific Internet service, you can do so using the following syntax for a line:

```
server_program_name: hosts
```

Here, *server_program_name* is the name of the server program (for example, in.telnetd for TELNET and in.ftpd for FTP), and *hosts* is a comma-separated list of hosts allowed to access the service. The *hosts* argument can also take the form of a network address or an entire domain name such as .mycompany.com. For example, here's how you can allow TELNET access to all systems in the mycompany.com domain:

```
in.telnetd: .mycompany.com
```

Monitoring System Security

After you set up your system securely, you have to monitor the log files periodically for any signs of intrusion. You should also check security news periodically to learn about recently discovered weaknesses in any of your system components (such as mail server or Web server). If your distribution provides an upgrade to fix a security problem, download the new RPM files, and install them on your system.

Follow the steps covered in Session 23 to download the new RPM files and to install them.

Log files

Many Linux system applications, including some servers, write log information by using the logging capabilities of syslogd. On Linux systems, the log files written by syslogd reside in the /var/log directory. Make sure only the root user can read and write these files.

You should routinely monitor the following log files:

- /var/log/messages contains a variety of logging messages from user logins to messages from services the TCP wrapper starts.
- /var/log/secure contains reports from services such as in.telnetd and in.ftpd the TCP wrapper starts.
- /var/log/maillog contains reports from sendmail.
- /var/log/xferlog contains a log of all FTP file transfers.

Unfortunately, there is no easy-to-use tool for viewing these log files. The best approach is to browse them routinely. You can open the log file in the vi editor in read-only mode by typing a command such as **vi -R /var/log/messages**, which prevents you from accidentally overwriting the log file. In the editor, you can search for a date of interest and begin browsing from that point.

Because many potential intruders use port-scanning tools that attempt to establish TCP/IP connections to well-known ports on your system, you should look for messages that indicate attempted connections from unknown hosts (indicated by names or IP addresses). For such attempted network accesses, you should browse the /var/log/secure file. For example, here's what a line in the /var/log/secure file shows when I connect to my Linux system from one of the PCs on the LAN:

```
Aug 16 20:18:19 lnbp200 xinetd[511]: START: ftp pid=23824 from=192.168.1.40
```

Notice the text pid=23824 that appears next to the word ftp. That's the process ID of the FTP server program xinetd starts. You can use this number to look at corresponding messages in the /var/log/messages file to see whether this attempt did or did not succeed. Here is a sample of how I check this:

```
grep "\[23824\]" messages
```

The output that follows tells me the user naba successfully logged in and sometime later closed the FTP session.

```
Aug 16 20:30:01 lnbp200 ftpd[23824]: FTP LOGIN FROM lnbp400 [192.168.1.40], naba
Aug 16 20:30:22 lnbp200 ftpd[23824]: FTP session closed
```

In a similar manner, you should analyze any suspicious messages you find in these log files. You may be surprised by the number of attempts curious outsiders make to gain access to your system.

Security news and updates

To keep up with the latest security alerts, you may want to visit one or more of the following sites on a daily basis:

- CERT Coordination Center at `http://www.cert.org/`
- Computer Incident Advisory Capability (CIAC) at `http://www.ciac.org/`
- National Infrastructure Protection Center at `http://www.nipc.gov/`

If you have access to Internet newsgroups, you can periodically browse the following newsgroups:

- `comp.security.announce`: a moderated newsgroup that includes announcements from CERT about security
- `comp.security.unix`: a newsgroup that includes discussions of UNIX security issues, including items related to Linux

If you prefer to receive regular security updates through e-mail, you can also sign up on, or subscribe to, various mailing lists.

- FOCUS-LINUX: Fill out the form in `http://www.securityfocus.com/focus/linux/list/subscribe.html` to subscribe to this mailing list focused on Linux security issues.
- Cert Advisory mailing list: Send an e-mail message to `cert-advisory-request@cert.org` with SUBSCRIBE *myname@myisp.com* in the Subject line. (Replace *myname@myisp.com* with your e-mail address.)

Done!

Finally, you should check the Web site for your distribution for updates that may fix any known security problems.

REVIEW

This session introduced you to security for your Linux system. You learned the importance of establishing a security policy for a medium to large organization. Next, the session showed you how to secure two key elements — the passwords and the network services — on your Linux system. Finally, I closed with a discussion of how to review log files for signs of intrusion attempts and how to keep up with any late-breaking security news. Because this session could not cover many security topics, I provided you with some additional online resources from which you can learn more about securing your Linux system.

QUIZ YOURSELF

1. Why should you set up a security policy? (See "Establishing a Security Policy.")
2. What are shadow passwords? (See "Shadow Passwords.")
3. What does MD5 refer to? (See "Pluggable Authentication Modules.")
4. Why should you secure Internet services? (See "Securing Internet services.")
5. Which log files should you review periodically for signs of intrusion attempts? (See "Monitoring System Security.")

Getting Help from Available Resources

Session Checklist

✔ Using the help viewers

✔ Using the commands

✔ Looking up online HOWTO files

✔ Accessing other Linux resources

**30 Min.
To Go**

By now, you have learned a lot about Linux, but there is much more that this book cannot cover because of its time constraint. To make sure you can find help when you need it, this weekend's final session introduces you to a variety of Linux resources that provide more information if you are experiencing a problem with a particular topic. Some of the help is available right on your system, but you can find many more resources on the Internet.

Using the Help Viewers

Both GNOME and KDE desktops come with help viewers — the Gnome Help Browser and KDE Help — to view online help information. You try these two help viewers in this session.

The GNOME Help Browser

From the GNOME desktop, select Main Menu ⇨ Programs ⇨ Help system, or click the question mark icon on the GNOME Panel to launch the Gnome Help Browser. The *Gnome Help Browser* provides a Web browser-like graphical interface through which you can access various forms of documentation available on your Linux system and on the Internet. The initial screen of the Gnome Help Browser organizes the help information into several categories:

- *GNOME User's Guide* is a hyperlink to information on how to use the GNOME desktop.
- *GNOME Documents* is a link that provides access to documentation on some GNOME applications and games.
- *Man Pages link* refers to online manual pages (called *man pages* for short).
- *Info Pages link* refers to online documentation for the GNU utilities (mostly software-development tools).

Typically, you look for help in the man pages. To view a table of contents of the available man pages, click the *Man Pages* link. The table of contents is organized by categories and by alphabet within each category. You can jump to a category by clicking a link in the category list at the beginning of the page. For example, clicking Administration takes you to the system-administration commands. You can then scroll down in that category and click a command for which you want more help. You should explore the table of contents of the man pages and view other man pages that interest you.

You can also access your distribution's Web site by clicking the distribution's icon on the GNOME desktop. The icon is labeled with the name of the distribution. That probably gives you a clue that this is a link to the distribution's Web site. Clicking that icon causes Netscape Communicator to start and go to the distribution's URL.

KDE Help

From the KDE desktop, you can start KDE Help by selecting K ⇨ KDE Help or by clicking the icon that shows a light bulb on a book. The KDE Help application has a Web browser-like user interface through which you can view online help information. When it starts, KDE Help shows a number of links organized into a number of categories. There are links to learn about KDE and obtain information about the KDE Project. Another set of links provides information that teaches how to use and get the most out of KDE. A third set of links provides access to the man pages and GNU info pages, just as the Gnome Help Browser does. One of the links in the third set enables you to search for online help by using one or more keywords.

To look for a man page, click the link labeled System man page contents. This brings up the online man pages' table of contents, organized by sections such as User Commands, File Formats, and System Administration. Click a section head to view the list of items in that section. You can then click a specific item to read the man page for that item. For example, to learn more about the xinetd configuration files, select the section labeled File Formats. Then click the link labeled xinetd.conf. KDE Help then displays the man page that contains information about the xinetd configuration file.

You can also access your distribution's Web site directly from the KDE desktop by clicking the distribution's icon. Depending on the distribution, there may be more than one icon.

Using the Linux Commands to Get Help

**20 Min.
To Go**

Although it's convenient to browse help information through graphical help browsers, you often need help while typing Linux commands in a terminal window.

Another trick you should know is that most Linux commands have a help option. Typically, if you invoke the command by using the --help option, the command prints some help information. At minimum, this information includes the command-line options the command accepts. Often, the help information can span more than one screen, so you should pipe the output through more, **as shown in the following example:**

```
ls --help | more
```

man command

Suppose you vaguely recall a command's name but cannot remember the exact syntax you are supposed to type. This is a situation in which the man command can come to your rescue. With the man command, you can view the man page on a Linux command and then use that command correctly.

You do have to remember *that* command to look up online help. For example, to view the man page for the modprobe command, type the following command in a terminal window:

```
man modprobe
```

The man command then displays the help information page by page. Press the Spacebar to move to the next page. Press **b** to move backward by a page. To look for a specific word in the man page, press the forward slash, type the word, and press Enter. For example, to search for the word "debug," type /debug and press Enter. When you finish reading the man page, press **q** to return to the Linux command prompt.

whatis command

If you do not want to read the full man page, you can use whatis to read a one-line summary of a command. For example, here's how you use whatis to see a brief description of the modprobe command:

```
whatis modprobe
```

In the following output, the number (8) indicates the man page section where the modprobe command is listed.

```
modprobe           (8)  - high level handling of loadable module
```

You should try the whatis command to view one-line descriptions of a few other commands.

You can use the shell's wildcard feature and the whatis command to explore the files in various system directories such as /bin, /sbin, /usr/sbin, /usr/bin, and so on. Simply change the directory to one of interest, and type whatis * to view one-line descriptions of the programs in that directory. (whatis displays information for programs for which such information is available.) For example, you can explore the /sbin directory by typing the following command:

```
cd /sbin; whatis * | more
```

As you can see, the following output is an alphabetical list of all programs in the current directory, along with the one-line descriptions where available.

```
arp                (7)  - Linux ARP kernel module
arp                (8)  - manipulate the system ARP cache
askrunlevel: nothing appropriate
badblocks          (8)  - search a device for bad blocks
cardctl            (8)  - PCMCIA card control utility
cardmgr            (8)  - PCMCIA device manager
... rest of the output not shown ...
```

The whatis command displays a message stating nothing appropriate if there is no information available for a program.

apropos command

The man and whatis commands are useful when you know the name of a command. If you do not know the exact name of a command, you can use the apropos command to search for a command by keyword (even part of a word). For example, if you remember the command contains the word probe, type the following apropos command to search:

```
apropos probe
```

In this case, the following search result shows three candidate commands, each with a brief description. You can then select the command that does what you want to do.

```
modprobe          (8)   - high level handling of loadable modules
pnpprobe          (8)   - scan ISA bus for PnP sound cards
SuperProbe        (1x)  - probe for and identify installed video hardware
```

If apropos **displays a long list of commands that scroll by too fast for you to read, you can type** apropos *keyword* | more **to view the output one screen at a time.**

Looking Up Online HOWTO Files

Another form of online documentation you can refer to is the HOWTO file listing you access by opening the URL http://www.redhat.com/mirrors/LDP/ in Netscape Communicator. The *LDP* in that URL refers to the *Linux Documentation Project,* and on that Web page you can find links to Frequently Asked Questions (FAQs) and HOWTOs. You can click the HOWTOs link and download (or read) HOWTO documents in several formats, including text and HTML format. For example, if you click to view text-format HOWTOs, the Web browser shows a list of over 170 HOWTO files (see Figure 30-1).

Each HOWTO file contains information about some area of Linux, such as how to configure hardware in Linux or how to create a boot disk. To view any of these HOWTO files, click the name, and the Web browser loads the full text file. For example, Figure 30-2 shows the result of clicking the CD-Writing HOWTO, which explains how to record a CD using a CD-ROM recordable (CD-R) device installed in a Linux system.

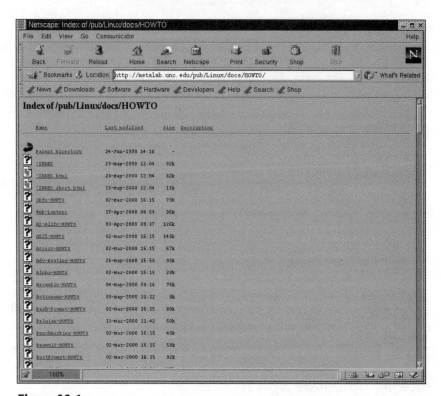

Figure 30-1
A partial list of HOWTO files accessible through the GNOME desktop's LDP icon

You should browse the list of HOWTO files (see Figure 30-1) and view one or more that interest you.

At the end of the list of HOWTO files, you see a folder named mini. Click that link to view the list of mini-HOWTOs, which cover many more narrowly focused topics.

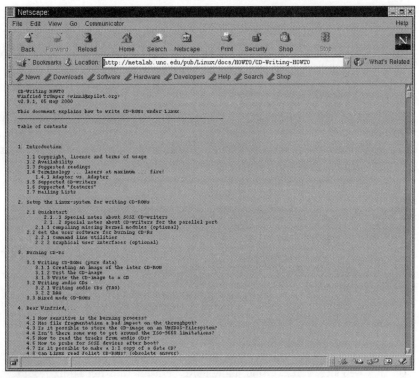

Figure 30-2
Browsing the plain-text version of the CD-Writing HOWTO file

**10 Min.
To Go**

Accessing Other Linux Resources

In addition to the online help I have just described, several other resources can provide more information on specific topics. Most of the resources are on the Internet because that's where you can get the latest information on Linux. The rest of this session introduces you to some of these Linux resources. Instead of providing a long list of URLs, I show a few key Web sites you can use as a starting point for your search.

Part VI—Sunday Afternoon
Session 30

Web pages

If you browse the Internet, you may notice quite a few Web pages with Linux-related information. A good starting point is the following Linux page:

```
http://www.linux.org/
```

This page provides a starting point for locating information about Linux. You can click the buttons to access more information on the topic the button's label identifies. On this page, you also find an organized collection of links to Linux-related Web sites.

To browse recent news about Linux, visit the Linux Resources page at:

```
http://www.linuxresources.com/
```

Specialized Systems Consultants (SSC), Inc., the publisher of the *Linux Journal*, maintains this page. You can scan the articles in the latest issue of *Linux Journal* and find other information such as the latest version of the kernel and links to other Linux resources.

Another popular and definitive source of Linux information is the home page of the Linux Documentation Project (LDP) at the following URL:

```
http://www.linuxdoc.org/
```

On this Web site, you can find many more pointers to other Linux resources on the Internet. In particular, you can browse and download the latest HOWTO documents from `http://metalab.unc.edu/pub/Linux/docs/HOWTO/`.

For Red Hat Linux-specific questions, you can visit Red Hat's Support Web site at:

```
http://www.redhat.com/apps/support/
```

For Caldera Open Linux-specific questions, you can visit Caldera'a Web site at:

```
http://www.calderasystems.com/support/
```

For SuSe Linux-specific questions, you can visit SuSe at:

```
http://www.suse.com/us/support/
```

These Web sites provide links such as Product Updates and Errata, Hardware Compatibility Lists, and Installation Guides and Manuals.

Internet newsgroups

To keep up with Linux developments, you really need access to the Internet and especially to the newsgroups. You can find discussions on specific Linux-related topics in the newsgroups listed in Table 30-1.

Table 30-1
Linux Newsgroups on the Internet

Newsgroup	Provides the Following
`comp.os.linux.admin`	Information about Linux system administration
`comp.os.linux.advocacy`	Discussions about promoting Linux
`comp.os.linux.announce`	Important announcements about Linux (This is a moderated newsgroup, which means you must mail the article to the moderator who then posts it to the newsgroup.)
`comp.os.linux.answers`	Questions and answers about Linux (All the Linux HOWTOs are posted in this moderated newsgoup.)
`comp.os.linux.development`	Current Linux development work
`comp.os.linux.development.apps`	Linux application development
`comp.os.linux.development.system`	Linux operating system development
`comp.os.linux.hardware`	Discussions about Linux and various hardware
`comp.os.linux.help`	Help with various aspects of Linux
`comp.os.linux.misc`	Miscellaneous topics about Linux
`comp.os.linux.networking`	Networking under Linux
`comp.os.linux.setup`	Linux setup and installation
`comp.os.linux.x`	Discussions about setting up and running the X Window System under Linux

You can use Netscape Communicator to read the newsgroups. For a newsgroup, use a URL of the form news://*newsserver*/*newsgroup* in which *newsserver* is the fully qualified domain name of your news server (your Internet Service Provider should give you this name) and *newsgroup* is the name of the newsgroup you want to read. For example, assuming your news server is *news.myisp.net*, you can browse the comp.os.linux.setup newsgroup by typing the following URL in the Location field of the Netscape Web browser:

news://news.myisp.net/comp.os.linux.setup

You can also use the Deja.com Power Search page at http://www.dejanews.com/home_ps.shtml **to search for specific items in the** comp.os.linux **newsgroups.**

FTP archive sites

You can download Linux distributions from one of several FTP sites around the world. In addition to the Linux distribution itself, these sites also contain many other software packages that run under Linux.

For the latest list of Linux FTP sites worldwide, visit the following Web site:

http://www.linux.org/dist

This page has links to information about Linux. These links take you to language-specific versions of Linux, books about Linux, and sites where you can download Linux for free.

Magazines

Linux Journal is a monthly magazine devoted entirely to Linux. On the Web, the magazine home page is at http://www.linuxjournal.com/. There you can find information on how to subscribe to this magazine.

Linux Magazine is another monthly magazine that covers everything Linux. Visit the magazine's home page at http://www.linux-mag.com/ to learn more about Linux Magazine and to subscribe.

Done!

REVIEW

This session showed you how to get help on various aspects of Linux. You learned to use the Gnome Help Browser and the xman man page viewer. You also learned to use several helpful commands such as man, whatis, and apropos. Finally, you familiarized yourself with a number of Internet-based Linux resources such as Web pages, FTP archives, and two popular Linux magazines.

QUIZ YOURSELF

1. What types of help information can you view with the Gnome Help Browser? (See "Using the Help Viewers.")

2. What is xman, and what can you do with it? (See "Using the Help Viewers.")

3. How can you view a brief description of a command? (See "Using the Linux Commands to Get Help.")

4. How do you access the HOWTO files? (See "Looking Up Online HOWTO Files.")

5. What are some of the Linux newsgroups? (See "Internet newsgroups.")

PART

VI

Sunday Afternoon

1. What is Linuxconf, and how do you start it from the GNOME desktop? Mention some tasks you can perform with Linuxconf.

2. What information do you have to provide when you add a new user account using Linuxconf?

3. Does Linuxconf check the password for words that are easily guessed?

4. What information do you observe to monitor your Linux system's performance?

5. What are some of the tools available in Linux to monitor system performance?

6. What is the purpose of the top tool?

7. What is the "load average?"

8. Show the vmstat command line that displays 10-second averages and prints a total of 5 lines of output. What does the first line of output from vmstat show?

9. What is the /proc file system? What is its purpose?

10. What purpose does a security policy serve?

11. What are some of the areas addressed in a security policy?

12. What are the general steps for securing the system and maintaining security?

13. What are the two ways to make passwords more secure in Linux?

14. Show the command you type as root to make sure the user mary is prompted to change the password in 30 days.

15. Explain how the TCP wrapper program provides an access-control facility for Internet services `xinetd` starts.

16. Name two help viewers you can access from the graphical desktops in Linux. What can you view with these help-viewer programs?

17. Show the command you use to read a one-line description of the `tr` command. What command do you type to view the manual page for the `tr` command?

18. What command can you use to search for other commands by using a keyword?

19. What are HOWTO files? How can you access them from the GNOME desktop, assuming your system is connected to the Internet?

20. What are some of the online and print resources you can use to find specific information about Linux?

APPENDIX

A

Answers to Part Reviews

This appendix contains the answers to the part review questions that appear at the end of each Part in this Weekend Crash Course. Think of these reviews as mini-tests designed to help you prepare for the final — the Skills Assessment Test on the CD.

Friday Evening Review Answers

1. I can find information about a PC's hardware from any manuals I may have received from the manufacturer. If the PC is currently running Windows 95/98, I can gather some of this information by double-clicking the System icon in the Control Panel and then clicking the Device Manager tab in the System Properties window. From there I can view information about specific devices installed in the PC.

2. The Red Hat boot disk allows me to start an initial version of Linux under which the Red Hat Linux installation program runs. To create the boot disk, I place a floppy in the A drive, open an MS-DOS window, and run the `rawrite.exe` program from the `\dosutils` directory of the CD-ROM. When prompted for the name of a boot image, I specify the `\images\boot.img` file and press Enter.

3. Usually, a new PC's hard disk has a single partition that Windows 95/98 uses. If I decide to keep Windows on my PC, I have to repartition the hard disk to create room for the Linux file system. I can repartition the hard disk in two ways: by backing up everything and destructively

repartitioning my disk by using the FDISK command or by using the FIPS program to non-destructively create room for a new partition. I use the FIPS program because that's easier than destructive repartitioning. I can also use tools such as PartitionMagic to non-destructively create a new partition for Linux.

4. The Red Hat Linux installation program provides four installation types: Server, GNOME Workstation, KDE Workstation, and Custom. If I select Server class installation, the installation program deletes all existing disk partitions, including any existing Windows partitions. Then it creates a fixed-size swap partition, a small /boot partition for the kernel, a larger root partition, two even larger partitions for the /usr and /home file system, and another partition for the /var file system. All in all, the Server-class installation requires approximately 1.6GB of disk space.

5. The IDE disk devices are /dev/hda, /dev/hdb, /dev/hdc, and /dev/hdd. The SCSI disk devices are /dev/sda, /dev/sdb, and so on. The partition names for the /dev/hda disk are /dev/hda1, /dev/hda2, /dev/hda3, and so on.

6. Linux uses the swap space as virtual memory where disk storage is used as an extension of physical memory (RAM). When the Linux kernel runs out of physical memory to run a program, it can move (or swap out) the contents of currently unneeded parts of RAM to make room for a program that needs more memory. As soon as the time comes to access anything in the swapped-out data, the Linux kernel has to find something else to swap out; then it swaps in the required data from disk into physical memory. I should set aside at least 32MB or the amount of RAM in my PC, whichever is more.

7. In Disk Druid, I must specify / as the mount point for this disk partition.

8. To mount a DOS partition during installation, I assign a Linux directory name for the location where the DOS partition should appear.

9. On the LILO Configuration screen, I select the DOS partition from the list and click the Default boot image button.

10. I can add one or more normal users during Red Hat Linux installation. To add a user account, I enter user information on the Account Configuration screen and click the Add button to add the user.

11. Package groups are collections of several Red Hat packages. I can select individual packages from a package group by selecting the item labeled Select individual packages, which appears below the list of package groups on the Package Group Selection screen.

12. On the Network Configuration screen, I click the `Configure Using DHCP` button.

13. I can either click my geographic location in the map that appears on the Location tab or select the time offset from UTC from the UTC Offset tab. On the UTC Offset tab, I can enable Daylight Saving Time.

14. To start text mode installation, I type `text` at the `boot:` prompt after I start the PC from the Red Hat Linux boot floppy. I might use text mode installation if the X Window System fails to start and the graphical user installation screens do not appear.

15. I have to use expert mode installation if the Red Hat installation program does not detect the SCSI controller or network card installed in my PC. I can start expert mode by typing `expert` at the `boot:` prompt in the initial text screen that appears after booting from the Red Hat boot disk.

16. Typical parameters for a SCSI adapter or network card that I may have to specify are the Interrupt Request (IRQ) number and the I/O port address. I may also have to specify the SCSI ID of the SCSI adapter. For example, for an Adaptec AHA-152x card, I might specify the options like this: `aha152x=0x340,11,7`.

17. I log in at the text console and run the `Xconfigurator` utility to create a new X configuration file; then I reboot the system.

18. The horizontal synchronization frequency is the number of times per second the monitor can display a horizontal raster line, usually expressed in kilohertz (kHz). The vertical refresh rate specifies how many times a second the monitor can display the entire screen. I can find the value of these parameters in my monitor's manual.

19. I type `dmesg | grep par` and look for any indication of parallel port information in the output.

20. With the Red Hat Linux Print System Manager, I can set up five types of printers: local, remote Unix, SMB/Windows 95/NT, Netware, or direct TCP/IP. To configure my Linux system to print to a Windows printer, I select the SMB/Windows 95/NT printer type.

Saturday Morning Review Answers

1. The *X server* is a process (computer program) running on a computer that has a bitmapped display, a keyboard, and a mouse. X clients are applications that need to display graphical output, and they do so by communicating with the X server. The X server controls the monitor, the keyboard, and the mouse. The X server responds to commands X clients send that open windows and draw in those windows.

2. The X configuration file is `/etc/X11/XF86Config`. I use the `xf86config` program to create a new X configuration file.

3. If the X graphical screen is partially working, I press Ctrl+Shift+F1 to switch to the text console and log in as root at the text login prompt. Then I run `xf86config` to create a new X configuration file. After that, I press Ctrl+Alt+F7 to switch back to the graphical login screen and press Ctrl+Alt+Backspace to kill the X server to force it to restart with the new configuration file.

4. Data is first sent to a print queue, an area that holds print jobs before they are sent to the printer. When the print job is sent to the printer, it passes through a filter program to convert it to a language the printer understands. Common printer languages are ASCII, Postscript, PCL3, PCL 4, and PCL 5.

5. Stair-stepping is a printer-output problem characterized by lines of text being broken across the page and on separate lines, resembling a staircase. To correct this, choose the correct stair-stepping option in the Printconf program.

6. The Linux file system provides a unified model of all storage in the system. The file system has a single root directory, indicated by a forward slash (/). Then there is a hierarchy of files and directories. Parts of the file system can reside in different hard drives or different partitions of a hard disk.

7. I type `cd` and press Enter to change to my home directory. Then I type `ls -la` to view detailed information about all files.

8. I type `find /usr/doc -name "README*"` to locate all files that begin with README in the `/usr/doc` directory tree.

9. I separate the commands by semicolons (for example, `cd /usr/doc; ls -la`). To continue a command on multiple lines, I type a backslash (\) and then press Enter after each line.

10. The command `ls -l /usr/doc | more` provides an example of using the output of one command as the input of another.

11. The I/O redirection feature of the shell allows me to redirect the standard output to a file or to redirect the standard input to come from a file.

12. An alias is an alternative name for a command. To view a list of current aliases, I type **alias**. I define `docdir` alias by using the command `alias docdir='cd /home/httpd/html'` and undefine it by using the command `unalias docdir`.

13. To set the date and time to December 31, 2001, I type `date -s 123122302001` for the command line.

14. To find all processes with `gnome` in their name, I type `ps ax | grep gnome` for the command line.

15. I type `ps ax | grep gpm` to find the process ID of the `gpm` process. Then I type `kill -9` *N* where *N* is that process ID.

16. I first type

    ```
    split -b 1024k filename part.
    ```

    This creates four files named `part.aa`, `part.ab`, `part.ac`, and `part.ad`. I copy these on four floppy disks, one per floppy. Later, I recombine the files by using the following command:

    ```
    cat part.?? > filename
    ```

17. It's important to learn to edit text files in Linux because many system-configuration files happen to be text files. I use the `vi` text editor from a text console.

18. I type:

    ```
    ed -p: /etc/inittab
    ```

    To enter a text in front of line 16, I first type 16 and press Enter. Then I type `i` and press Enter. I then type the line of text and type `wq` to save the file and exit.

19. I type `vi /etc/inittab` to begin editing the file. Then I type `:16` to go to line 16. I then press `i` and begin typing the line. After I press Enter at the end of the line, I type `:wq` to save the file and exit.

20. To cut a line, I type `dd`. To paste that line, I type `p`.

Saturday Afternoon Review Answers

1. The Linux device name for COM1 is `/dev/ttyS0`, and the device name for COM2 is `/dev/ttyS1`. COM1 uses IRQ 4 and I/O port 0x3f8, whereas COM2 uses IRQ 3 and I/O port 0x2f8.

2. I type `minicom` in a terminal window to start the Minicom program. Then I type the modem dialing command ATDT followed by the phone number to dial out by using Minicom. To be able to run Minicom as an ordinary user, I have to log in as root and, assuming the modem is on COM1, type `chmod o+rw /dev/ttyS0` to give everyone write permission for that device.

3. I type `dmesg | grep ttyS*` or `grep ttyS /var/log/messages` and look for the serial device names `ttyS0` or `ttyS1` in the output of the commands.

4. Ethernet is a standard way to move packets of data between two or more computers connected to a single cable. You need an Ethernet card and a cable to connect a PC to an Ethernet LAN. The term 10Base2 refers to Ethernet that uses thin, flexible coaxial cables as the data transmission media. 10BaseT is Ethernet over unshielded twisted-pair cable that looks like ordinary phone wires. To check if my Linux system has loaded the Ethernet driver, I type `dmesg | grep eth0` and look for messages about the Ethernet card in my PC.

5. The common TCP/IP diagnostic commands are `/sbin/ifconfig`, `/sbin/route`, `ping`, and `netstat`. I use the `/sbin/ifconfig` command to see if the network interfaces are running. I use `ping` to check if my Linux system has a network path to another host.

6. Some TCP/IP configuration files are `/etc/hosts`, `/etc/host.conf`, `/etc/resolv.conf`, `/etc/hosts.allow`, and `/etc/hosts.deny`. The `/etc/resolv.conf` file contains the IP addresses of the name servers.

7. A typical home office or small office connects to the Internet by using a dialup PPP connection. DSL or cable modem offers an always-on connection that has much higher data transfer rates than dial-up networking. As the name implies, dial-up networking requires me to dial out through a modem when I want to connect to my Internet Service Provider.

8. Dial-up networking puts my PC on the Internet, and any applications on the PC (including Web browsers and e-mail programs) can communicate over the dial-up connection. A serial communication program such as Minicom exclusively uses dial-up connection. For example, I cannot run another copy of Minicom and use the same modem connection.

9. PPP stands for Point-to-Point Protocol, which is a protocol for establishing a TCP/IP connection over any point-to-point link, including dial-up serial links. To set up a PPP connection, I need from the ISP a phone

number, a user name and password, and the IP addresses for the Domain Name Server (DNS). On my Linux system, I run `pppd` and `chat` to set up the PPP connection.

10. I can use the IP masquerading feature of Linux to share a single Internet connection with other systems on the LAN. I use the IPCHAINS software (`/sbin/ipchains`) to set up IP masquerading.

11. TELNET, FTP, e-mail, and the World Wide Web are some of the common Internet services. A port is a number between 1 and 65,535 that uniquely identifies each end point of a TCP/IP communication link between two processes. The `/etc/services` file contains information about Internet services and the services' corresponding port numbers.

12. To provide e-mail service, I need a mail transport agent and a mail user agent. Simple Mail Transfer Protocol (SMTP) is the TCP/IP protocol for transporting e-mail among systems.

13. The Apache Web server configuration files are located in the `/etc/httpd/conf` directory. The `/var/log/httpd` directory is where the Apache Web server's log files (access logs and error logs) are located. The `/etc/rc.d/init.d/httpd` script starts the `httpd` process as the Red Hat Linux system boots.

14. When I use FTP to transfer files to or from a remote system, I have to log in to the remote system before I can use FTP. With anonymous FTP, I log in using the user name `anonymous`, which anyone can use with FTP to transfer files from a system. On my system, I place in the `/home/ftp/pub` directory any files I want other users to download by using anonymous FTP.

15. To set up a Network File System (NFS) file server, I first export one or more directories by listing them in the `/etc/exports` file. Then I start the NFS server by using Linuxconf. On each client system, I mount the directories the server exports by using the `mount` command.

16. I have to configure the Samba software to make my Linux system work as a Windows server. To check if Samba is installed, I type the command `rpm -q samba` and look for the output to show a line that contains the Samba software's version. The Samba configuration file is `/etc/smb.conf`. To restart the Samba software, I type:

    `/etc/rc.d/init.d/smb restart`

17. On my Linux system, I use the `smbclient` program to access shared directories and printers on Windows systems on the LAN.

18. The following command mounts the /dev/hda2 file system at the mount point /mnt/dos:

    ```
    mount -t vfat /dev/hda2 /mnt/dos
    ```

    To make sure Linux automatically mounts /dev/hda2 whenever the system boots, I add the following line to the /etc/fstab file:

    ```
    /dev/hda2   /mnt/dos  vfat    defaults   0 0
    ```

19. With the mtools package, I can use common DOS commands to access DOS floppies and DOS file systems. I type rpm -q mtools to check if mtools is installed on my system. The mtools configuration file is /etc/mtools.conf.

20. Here are a mtools commands: mdir, mcd, mcopy, mformat, and mdel. The commands are patterned after MS-DOS commands. The following command copies all files that have the .doc extension from a DOS floppy to the current directory on the hard disk:

    ```
    mcopy "a:\*.doc".
    ```

Saturday Evening Review Answers

1. Like Windows 95/98/NT, the GNOME desktop has a status bar at the bottom of the window and a Main Menu button like the Windows Start button. Also, I can place files and icons on the desktop just as I do in Windows 95/98/NT.

2. I can customize the look and feel of the GNOME desktop by using the GNOME Control Center. I can customize the background, the window manager, or select a theme for the user interface.

3. Sawfish is a window manager. It's the default window manager in GNOME. To configure Sawfsh, I select Desktop ⇨ Window Manager from the GNOME Control Center menu.

4. To change the default desktop from GNOME to KDE, I select the Main menu ⇨ System ⇨ Desktop Switching Tool and then select KDE as the desktop. From KDE, I can also use the same Desktop Switching Tool to change the default desktop back to GNOME.

5. I use the KDE Control Center to customize various aspects of KDE desktop.

6. To select and try out a screen saver from the GNOME desktop, I start the GNOME Control Center by clicking the toolbox icon on the GNOME Panel, and I select Desktop ⇨ Screensaver from the tree menu in the Control Center.

7. To "lock the screen" means the screen saver does not turn off until the user's password is entered. When configuring the screen saver in GNOME, I click the Require Password checkbox and enable it. Then the screen saver locks the screen.

8. I select K ⇨ KDE Control Center. Then I select Desktop ⇨ Screensaver from the tree menu in the KDE Control Center. From there I can select and configure a screen saver.

9. AisleRiot, Gnome-Stones, and GNOME Mahjongg are games in GNOME. AisleRiot is a card-playing program that can play 30 different card games, including well-known ones such as Freecell and Klondike.

10. Minesweeper, Patience, and Shisen-Sho are games in KDE.

11. I switch to a text-mode console by pressing Ctrl+Alt+F1. Then I log in as root and type /usr/sbin/sndconfig to start the sound configuration program. I then follow the program's prompts to configure the sound card.

12. To play audio CDs in Red Hat Linux, I can use xplaycd or the CD players in GNOME or KDE. To allow a normal user to play audio CDs, I log in as root and type chmod o+r /dev/cdrom.

13. The GNOME CD player gets the song titles from CDDB — a CD database on the Internet. Assuming there is an active Internet connection, the GNOME CD Player downloads song information from the CD database.

14. The GIMP and Xpaint are two image-manipulation programs that come with Red Hat Linux. The GIMP is a program for viewing images and performing tasks such as photo retouching, image composition, and image creation. Xpaint is a bitmap painting program patterned after MacPaint.

15. I use Ghostview to view the PostScript document.

16. Spreadsheet, spell checker, calendars, and calculators are some of the office utilities on this book's Red Hat Linux CD-ROM. The CD-ROM does not include any complete office productivity suites.

17. The name of the spreadsheet application is Gnumeric. Gnumeric's default file format is XML (eXtensible Markup Language). Gnumeric can exchange files with Microsoft Excel.

18. `ispell report.txt`

19. WordPerfect Office 2000 for Linux, Applixware Office for Linux, and StarOffice are commercial office-application suites for Linux. I can learn more about these commercial applications by visiting their Web sites.

20. StarOffice is a cross-platform solution. It includes StarOffice Writer for word processing, StarOffice Calc for spreadsheets, StarOffice Impress for presentations, ands StarOffice Base for database.

Sunday Morning Review Answers

1. The processes the `init` process starts at boot time depend on the run level, the contents of the `/etc/inittab` file, and a number of shell scripts (located in the `/etc/rc.d` directory and its subdirectories).

2. I look for the line that contains the keyword initdefault in the third field (the fields are separated by colons). The second field of this line specifies the default run level for my system.

3. The `init` process runs the `/etc/rc.d/rc.sysinit` script. This script, in turn, runs many other scripts from the subdirectories in the `/etc/rc.d` directory.

4. Many open source software packages are distributed in source code without any executable binaries. Before I can use such software, I have to build the executable binary files. That's why it's important to learn to build software from source files.

5. Open source software is typically distributed in compressed tar archives, also known as compressed tarballs. I can download the file by using anonymous FTP or through the Web browser. To unpack, I can use a command of the form `tar zxvf tarball_name` where `tarball_name` is the name of the file I have downloaded.

6. After downloading and unpacking the source files, I look for files with the name README or INSTALL for instructions on how to build and install the software.

7. RPM refers to the Red Hat Package Manager, which is a system for packaging all necessary files for a software product in a single file (referred to as an RPM file, or simply an RPM). Red Hat Linux and the bundled applications are distributed in the form of a large number of RPMs. To check if a

specific RPM is installed on my system, I type the command *rpm -q package_name* where *package_name* is the name of the RPM. For example, to check if the samba RPM is installed, I type rpm -q samba.

8. I can install RPMs by using the Gnome RPM graphical program or the rpm command-line tool. To install an RPM by using the command-line tool, I change directory to the CD-ROM's RPM directory (usually, /mnt/cdrom/RedHat/RPMS) and type rpm -i *filename* where *filename* is the name of the RPM file.

9. A typical RPM file has the form XFree86-3.3.6-20.i386.rpm. Everything up to the first dash is the RPM name (XFree86); the numbers between the two dashes form the version number (3.3.6); the next number is Red Hat's release number (20); the next extension (i386) is the architecture; and the final extension is rpm to denote that this is an RPM file.

10. I might rebuild the Linux kernel after I patch the kernel sources, to add SCSI support directly into the kernel, or to add support for some experimental hardware.

11. I log in as root and mount the CD-ROM by using the command mount /mnt/cdrom. Then I type the following commands:

```
cd /mnt/cdrom/RedHat/RPMS
rpm -ivh kernel-source*
```

12. To rebuild the kernel, I have to configure the kernel, make the kernel, make the modules, and install the kernel and a few other files.

13. I might want to back up files late at night, download large files at night, or send myself e-mail reminders at a future time. I can use the at command to submit commands to be executed. I can use the crontab facility to run programs automatically at regular intervals.

14. For an example of scheduling a one-time job, suppose I want to execute the /usr/local/bin/ppp-off script at 11:35 P.M.; I log in as root and type the following commands:

```
at 23:35
at> /usr/local/bin/ppp-off
at> (Press Ctrl+D)
```

15. I first create a shell script containing the commands that I want to execute periodically. I then prepare a text file with information about the times when I want the shell script executed. Then I submit this file by using the crontab command.

16. I create the /etc/at.allow file containing the names of users who are allowed to submit one-time jobs. For recurring jobs, I create the /etc/cron.allow file containing the names of the users who are allowed to submit recurring jobs with the crontab command.

17. Floppy disk, SCSI Zip disk, and SCSI tape are some of the backup media on which I can back up files. The device name for floppy drive is /dev/fd0, SCSI Zip drive is /dev/sda (assuming it's the first drive), and SCSI tape drive is /dev/st0.

18. I can use the tar utility to back up files and directories. To back up the entire file system on a SCSI tape drive, I type:

    ```
    tar cvf /dev/st0 /
    ```

19. To back up several large files in the /home/share directory onto multiple floppies, I type the following command:

    ```
    tar cvfM /dev/fd0 /home/share
    ```

20. To store multiple backup archives on a single tape, I use a non-rewinding tape device with a command such as tar cvf /dev/nst0 /home and use similar tar commands to create one archive after another. I can rewind the tape by using the following command:

    ```
    mt -f /dev/nst0 rewind
    ```

    I can skip over an archive with the following command:

    ```
    mt -f /dev/nst0 fsf 1
    ```

Sunday Afternoon Review Answers

1. Linuxconf is an X Windows application I can use to perform many system-administration tasks such as adding user accounts, mounting a CD-ROM drive, and configuring a dialup PPP connection. To start Linuxconf, I select Main Menu ⇨ System ⇨ LinuxConf from the GNOME desktop.

2. I enter the login name, the user's home directory, and a password.

3. Linuxconf checks the password for words that can be easily guessed.

4. I look for information such as CPU usage, physical memory usage and swap space usage, and hard disk usage to monitor the system's performance.

5. Linux includes tools such as the GNOME System Monitor, top, and vmstat to monitor system performance.

6. The top tool is used to see a graphical representation of system performance.

7. The "load average" is the average number of processes that have been ready to run for the past few minutes. Typically, system monitors compute load average over the past 1, 5, and 15 minutes.

8. The vmstat 10 5 command-line displays 10-second averages and prints a total of 5 lines of output. The first line of output from vmstat shows the averages since the last reboot.

9. The /proc file system is not a real directory on the disk but a collection of data structures in memory. The Linux kernel manages these data structures, and they appear to the user as a set of directories and files. The purpose of /proc is to allow users to access information about the Linux kernel and the processes currently running on the system.

10. The security policy provides rules I can apply to secure the system.

11. The security policy should address areas such as the following: how users are authenticated; what various users can do; what data must be protected; which Internet services are allowed to run; and who is responsible for maintaining and auditing security.

12. The general steps are to install only those packages I need, create user accounts with strong passwords, enable only the necessary Internet services, and periodically check log files for signs of break-in attempts. I should also keep up with security news and install upgrades from Red Hat.

13. Shadow passwords and the use of MD5 encryption are two ways in which passwords are made more secure in Linux.

14. To make sure user mary is prompted to change the password in 30 days, I type chage -M 30 mary when logged in as root.

15. The xinetd server starts Internet services by using the TCP wrapper program. As specified in the /etc/inetd.conf file, the /usr/sbin/tcpd program starts other services such as FTP and TELNET; before starting a service, the TCP wrapper consults the /etc/hosts.allow file to see if the host requesting service is allowed that service. If nothing is in /etc/hosts.allow about that host, the TCP wrapper checks the /etc/hosts.deny file to see if the service should be denied. If both files are empty, the TCP wrapper allows the host access to the requested service. In this way, the TCP wrapper program provides an access-control facility for Internet services xinetd starts.

16. GNOME Help Browser and KDE Help are two help viewers I can use to view online help information from the graphical desktops in Linux.

17. I type `whatis tr` to read a one-line description of the `tr` command. To view the manual page for the `tr` command, I type `man tr`.

18. I can use the `apropos` command to search for other commands by using a keyword.

19. Each HOWTO file contains information about some area of Linux, such as how to configure hardware in Linux or how to create a boot disk. If my system is connected to the Internet, I can access the HOWTO files by clicking the LDP icon on the GNOME desktop and then clicking the link to HOWTO documents.

20. I can visit Linux Web sites such as `http://www.linux.org/`. I can access Linux newsgroups such as `comp.os.linux.answers` at the Deja.com Web site. I can subscribe to magazines such as *Linux Journal* and *Linux Magazine* to keep up with Linux news.

What's on the CD-ROMs?

The CD-ROMs that accompany this book contain Red Hat Linux 7.1. They also contain the Linux Weekend Crash Course Assessment Test. The following sections briefly explain both.

Red Hat Linux 7.1

The CD-ROMs contain all Red Hat Linux 7.1 binary files with the Linux 2.4.0 kernel, which is the latest version of the Linux kernel available as of this writing (Winter 2001). In addition to the Linux kernel, Red Hat Linux includes a large selection of Linux applications. Here are some significant software packages on the Red Hat Linux 7.1 CD-ROMs:

- Linux kernel 2.4.0 with driver modules for all major PC hardware configurations, including IDE/EIDE and SCSI drives, PCMCIA devices, some USB devices, and CD-ROM drives
- Complete set of installation and configuration tools for setting up devices (such as keyboard and mouse) and services
- Graphical user interface based on the XFree86 package with GNOME and KDE desktops
- Full TCP/IP networking for Internet, LANs, and intranets
- Tools for connecting your PC to your Internet Service Provider by using PPP or dialup serial communications programs

- Complete suite of Internet applications, including electronic mail (`sendmail`, `elm`, `pine`, `mailx`), news (`inn`, `tin`, `trn`), Internet Relay Chat (`ircii`), TELNET, FTP, and NFS

- Apache Web server 1.3.12 (to turn your PC into a Web server) and Netscape Communicator 4.74 (to surf the Net)

- Samba 2.0.7 LAN Manager software for Microsoft Windows connectivity

- Several text editors (GNU Emacs 20.7, `vim`)

- Graphics and image manipulation software, such as The GIMP, XPaint, Ghostscript, Ghostview, and ImageMagick

- Programming languages (GNU C and C++ 2.96, Perl 5.6.0, Tcl/Tk 8.3.1, Python 1.5.2, GNU AWK 3.0.5) and software development tools (GNU Debugger 5.0, CVS 1.10.8, RCS 5.7, GNU Bison 1.28, flex 2.5.4a, TIFF, and JPEG libraries)

- Complete suite of standard UNIX utilities

- Tools to access and use DOS files and applications (`mtools` 3.9.7)

- Games such as GNU Chess, Mahjongg, Reversi, Minesweeper, FreeCell, Gnobots, and AisleRiot

Linux Weekend Crash Course Assessment Test

The CD-ROMs contain 60 multiple-choice questions with answers. The assessment test is provided in a Linux-compatible format. You can use them to assess how much you already know about Linux and thereby determine what sessions you can skip. You can also go through the questions after reading individual sessions of this book to assess how much you have learned. The questions are organized by session; therefore, they follow the order of topics discussed in this book. The session each question corresponds with is noted next to each question.

Index

Continued

Continued

Get Up to Speed
in a Weekend!

red**hat**®

www.redhat.com

HUNGRY MINDS, INC.
END-USER LICENSE AGREEMENT

READ THIS. You should carefully read these terms and conditions before opening the software packet(s) included with this book ("Book"). This is a license agreement ("Agreement") between you and Hungry Minds, Inc. ("HMI"). By opening the accompanying software packet(s), you acknowledge that you have read and accept the following terms and conditions. If you do not agree and do not want to be bound by such terms and conditions, promptly return the Book and the unopened software packet(s) to the place you obtained them for a full refund.

1. **License Grant.** HMI grants to you (either an individual or entity) a nonexclusive license to use one copy of the enclosed software program(s) (collectively, the "Software") solely for your own personal or business purposes on a single computer (whether a standard computer or a workstation component of a multi-user network). The Software is in use on a computer when it is loaded into temporary memory (RAM) or installed into permanent memory (hard disk, CD-ROM, or other storage device). HMI reserves all rights not expressly granted herein.

2. **Ownership.** HMI is the owner of all right, title, and interest, including copyright, in and to the compilation of the Software recorded on the disk(s) or CD-ROM ("Software Media"). Copyright to the individual programs recorded on the Software Media is owned by the author or other authorized copyright owner of each program. Ownership of the Software and all proprietary rights relating thereto remain with HMI and its licensers.

3. **Restrictions On Use and Transfer.**

   (a) You may only (i) make one copy of the Software for backup or archival purposes, or (ii) transfer the Software to a single hard disk, provided that you keep the original for backup or archival purposes. You may not (i) rent or lease the Software, (ii) copy or reproduce the Software through a LAN or other network system or through any computer subscriber system or bulletin-board system, or (iii) modify, adapt, or create derivative works based on the Software.

   (b) You may not reverse engineer, decompile, or disassemble the Software. You may transfer the Software and user documentation on a permanent basis, provided that the transferee agrees to accept the terms and conditions of this Agreement and you retain no copies. If the Software is an update or has been updated, any transfer must include the most recent update and all prior versions.

4. **Restrictions on Use of Individual Programs.** You must follow the individual requirements and restrictions detailed for each individual program in Appendix B of this Book. These limitations are also contained in the individual license agreements recorded on the Software Media. These limitations may include a requirement that after using the program for a specified period of time, the user must pay a registration fee or discontinue use. By opening the Software packet(s), you will be agreeing to abide by the licenses and restrictions for these individual programs that are detailed in Appendix B and on the Software Media. None of the material on this Software Media or listed in this Book may ever be redistributed, in original or modified form, for commercial purposes.

5. Limited Warranty.

(a) HMI warrants that the Software and Software Media are free from defects in materials and workmanship under normal use for a period of sixty (60) days from the date of purchase of this Book. If HMI receives notification within the warranty period of defects in materials or workmanship, HMI will replace the defective Software Media.

(b) **HMI AND THE AUTHOR OF THE BOOK DISCLAIM ALL OTHER WARRANTIES, EXPRESS OR IMPLIED, INCLUDING WITHOUT LIMITATION IMPLIED WARRANTIES OF MERCHANTABILITY AND FITNESS FOR A PARTICULAR PURPOSE, WITH RESPECT TO THE SOFTWARE, THE PROGRAMS, THE SOURCE CODE CONTAINED THEREIN, AND/OR THE TECHNIQUES DESCRIBED IN THIS BOOK. HMI DOES NOT WARRANT THAT THE FUNCTIONS CONTAINED IN THE SOFTWARE WILL MEET YOUR REQUIREMENTS OR THAT THE OPERATION OF THE SOFTWARE WILL BE ERROR FREE.**

(c) This limited warranty gives you specific legal rights, and you may have other rights that vary from jurisdiction to jurisdiction.

6. Remedies.

(a) HMI's entire liability and your exclusive remedy for defects in materials and workmanship shall be limited to replacement of the Software Media, which may be returned to HMI with a copy of your receipt at the following address: Software Media Fulfillment Department, Attn.: *Linux® Weekend Crash Course™*, Hungry Minds, Inc., 10475 Crosspoint Blvd., Indianapolis, IN 46256, or call 1-800-762-2974. Please allow four to six weeks for delivery. This Limited Warranty is void if failure of the Software Media has resulted from accident, abuse, or misapplication. Any replacement Software Media will be warranted for the remainder of the original warranty period or thirty (30) days, whichever is longer.

(b) In no event shall HMI or the author be liable for any damages whatsoever (including without limitation damages for loss of business profits, business interruption, loss of business information, or any other pecuniary loss) arising from the use of or inability to use the Book or the Software, even if HMI has been advised of the possibility of such damages.

(c) Because some jurisdictions do not allow the exclusion or limitation of liability for consequential or incidental damages, the above limitation or exclusion may not apply to you.

7. U.S. Government Restricted Rights. Use, duplication, or disclosure of the Software for or on behalf of the United States of America, its agencies and/or instrumentalities (the "U.S. Government") is subject to restrictions as stated in paragraph (c)(1)(ii) of the Rights in Technical Data and Computer Software clause of DFARS 252.227-7013, or subparagraphs (c) (1) and (2) of the Commercial Computer Software - Restricted Rights clause at FAR 52.227-19, and in similar clauses in the NASA FAR supplement, as applicable.

8. General. This Agreement constitutes the entire understanding of the parties and revokes and supersedes all prior agreements, oral or written, between them and may not be modified or amended except in a writing signed by both parties hereto that specifically refers to this Agreement. This Agreement shall take precedence over any other documents that may be in conflict herewith. If any one or more provisions contained in this Agreement are held by any court or tribunal to be invalid, illegal, or otherwise unenforceable, each and every other provision shall remain in full force and effect.

GNU General Public License

Version 2, June 1991
Copyright © 1989, 1991 Free Software Foundation, Inc.
59 Temple Place, Suite 330, Boston, MA 02111-1307, USA
Everyone is permitted to copy and distribute verbatim copies of this license document, but changing it is not allowed.

Preamble

The licenses for most software are designed to take away your freedom to share and change it. By contrast, the GNU General Public License is intended to guarantee your freedom to share and change free software — to make sure the software is free for all its users. This General Public License applies to most of the Free Software Foundation's software and to any other program whose authors commit to using it. (Some other Free Software Foundation software is covered by the GNU Library General Public License instead.) You can apply it to your programs, too.

When we speak of free software, we are referring to freedom, not price. Our General Public Licenses are designed to make sure that you have the freedom to distribute copies of free software (and charge for this service if you wish), that you receive source code or can get it if you want it, that you can change the software or use pieces of it in new free programs; and that you know you can do these things.

To protect your rights, we need to make restrictions that forbid anyone to deny you these rights or to ask you to surrender the rights. These restrictions translate to certain responsibilities for you if you distribute copies of the software, or if you modify it.

For example, if you distribute copies of such a program, whether gratis or for a fee, you must give the recipients all the rights that you have. You must make sure that they, too, receive or can get the source code. And you must show them these terms so they know their rights.

We protect your rights with two steps: (1) copyright the software, and (2) offer you this license which gives you legal permission to copy, distribute and/or modify the software.

Also, for each author's protection and ours, we want to make certain that everyone understands that there is no warranty for this free software. If the software is modified by someone else and passed on, we want its recipients to know that what they have is not the original, so that any problems introduced by others will not reflect on the original authors' reputations.

Finally, any free program is threatened constantly by software patents. We wish to avoid the danger that redistributors of a free program will individually obtain patent licenses, in effect making the program proprietary. To prevent this, we have made it clear that any patent must be licensed for everyone's free use or not licensed at all.

The precise terms and conditions for copying, distribution and modification follow.

Terms and Conditions for Copying, Distribution, and Modification

0. This License applies to any program or other work which contains a notice placed by the copyright holder saying it may be distributed under the terms of this General Public License. The "Program", below, refers to any such program or work, and a "work based on the Program" means either the Program or any derivative work under copyright law: that is to say, a work containing the Program or a portion of it, either verbatim or with modifications and/or translated into another language. (Hereinafter, translation is included without limitation in the term "modification".) Each licensee is addressed as "you".

    Activities other than copying, distribution and modification are not covered by this License; they are outside its scope. The act of running the Program is not restricted, and the output from the Program is covered only if its contents constitute a work based on the Program (independent of having been made by running the Program). Whether that is true depends on what the Program does.

1. You may copy and distribute verbatim copies of the Program's source code as you receive it, in any medium, provided that you conspicuously and appropriately publish on each copy an appropriate copyright notice and disclaimer of warranty; keep intact all the notices that refer to this License and to the absence of any warranty; and give any other recipients of the Program a copy of this License along with the Program.

    You may charge a fee for the physical act of transferring a copy, and you may at your option offer warranty protection in exchange for a fee.

2. You may modify your copy or copies of the Program or any portion of it, thus forming a work based on the Program, and copy and distribute such modifications or work under the terms of Section 1 above, provided that you also meet all of these conditions:

    a) You must cause the modified files to carry prominent notices stating that you changed the files and the date of any change.

    b) You must cause any work that you distribute or publish, that in whole or in part contains or is derived from the Program or any part thereof, to be licensed as a whole at no charge to all third parties under the terms of this License.

    c) If the modified program normally reads commands interactively when run, you must cause it, when started running for such interactive use in the most ordinary way, to print or display an announcement including an appropriate copyright notice and a notice that there is no warranty (or else, saying that you provide a warranty) and that users may redistribute the program under these conditions, and telling the user how to view a copy of this License. (Exception: if the Program itself is interactive but does not normally print such an announcement, your work based on the Program is not required to print an announcement.)

These requirements apply to the modified work as a whole. If identifiable sections of that work are not derived from the Program, and can be reasonably considered independent and separate works in themselves, then this License, and its terms, do not apply to those sections when you distribute them as separate works. But when you distribute the same sections as part of a whole which is a work based on the Program, the distribution of the whole must be on the terms of this License, whose permissions for other licensees extend to the entire whole, and thus to each and every part regardless of who wrote it.

Thus, it is not the intent of this section to claim rights or contest your rights to work written entirely by you; rather, the intent is to exercise the right to control the distribution of derivative or collective works based on the Program.

In addition, mere aggregation of another work not based on the Program with the Program (or with a work based on the Program) on a volume of a storage or distribution medium does not bring the other work under the scope of this License.

3. You may copy and distribute the Program (or a work based on it, under Section 2) in object code or executable form under the terms of Sections 1 and 2 above provided that you also do one of the following:

   a) Accompany it with the complete corresponding machine-readable source code, which must be distributed under the terms of Sections 1 and 2 above on a medium customarily used for software interchange; or,

   b) Accompany it with a written offer, valid for at least three years, to give any third party, for a charge no more than your cost of physically performing source distribution, a complete machine-readable copy of the corresponding source code, to be distributed under the terms of Sections 1 and 2 above on a medium customarily used for software interchange; or,

   c) Accompany it with the information you received as to the offer to distribute corresponding source code. (This alternative is allowed only for noncommercial distribution and only if you received the program in object code or executable form with such an offer, in accord with Subsection b above.)

The source code for a work means the preferred form of the work for making modifications to it. For an executable work, complete source code means all the source code for all modules it contains, plus any associated interface definition files, plus the scripts used to control compilation and installation of the executable. However, as a special exception, the source code distributed need not include anything that is normally distributed (in either source or binary form) with the major components (compiler, kernel, and so on) of the operating system on which the executable runs, unless that component itself accompanies the executable.

If distribution of executable or object code is made by offering access to copy from a designated place, then offering equivalent access to copy the source code from the same place counts as distribution of the source code, even though third parties are not compelled to copy the source along with the object code.

4. You may not copy, modify, sublicense, or distribute the Program except as expressly provided under this License. Any attempt otherwise to copy, modify, sublicense or distribute the Program is void, and will automatically terminate your rights under this License. However, parties who have received copies, or rights, from you under this License will not have their licenses terminated so long as such parties remain in full compliance.

5. You are not required to accept this License, since you have not signed it. However, nothing else grants you permission to modify or distribute the Program or its derivative works. These actions are prohibited by law if you do not accept this License. Therefore, by modifying or distributing the Program (or any work based on the Program), you indicate your acceptance of this License to do so, and all its terms and conditions for copying, distributing or modifying the Program or works based on it.

6. Each time you redistribute the Program (or any work based on the Program), the recipient automatically receives a license from the original licensor to copy, distribute or modify the Program subject to these terms and conditions. You may not impose any further restrictions on the recipients' exercise of the rights granted herein. You are not responsible for enforcing compliance by third parties to this License.

7. If, as a consequence of a court judgment or allegation of patent infringement or for any other reason (not limited to patent issues), conditions are imposed on you (whether by court order, agreement or otherwise) that contradict the conditions of this License, they do not excuse you from the conditions of this License. If you cannot distribute so as to satisfy simultaneously your obligations under this License and any other pertinent obligations, then as a consequence you may not distribute the Program at all. For example, if a patent license would not permit royalty-free redistribution of the Program by all those who receive copies directly or indirectly through you, then the only way you could satisfy both it and this License would be to refrain entirely from distribution of the Program.

If any portion of this section is held invalid or unenforceable under any particular circumstance, the balance of the section is intended to apply and the section as a whole is intended to apply in other circumstances.

It is not the purpose of this section to induce you to infringe any patents or other property right claims or to contest validity of any such claims; this section has the sole purpose of protecting the integrity of the free software distribution system, which is implemented by public license practices. Many people have made generous contributions to the wide range of software distributed through that system in reliance on consistent application of that system; it is up to the author/donor to decide if he or she is willing to distribute software through any other system and a licensee cannot impose that choice.

This section is intended to make thoroughly clear what is believed to be a consequence of the rest of this License.

8. If the distribution and/or use of the Program is restricted in certain countries either by patents or by copyrighted interfaces, the original copyright holder who places the Program under this License may add an explicit geographical distribution limitation excluding those countries, so that distribution is permitted only in or among countries not thus excluded. In such case, this License incorporates the limitation as if written in the body of this License.

9. The Free Software Foundation may publish revised and/or new versions of the General Public License from time to time. Such new versions will be similar in spirit to the present version, but may differ in detail to address new problems or concerns.

    Each version is given a distinguishing version number. If the Program specifies a version number of this License which applies to it and "any later version", you have the option of following the terms and conditions either of that version or of any later version published by the Free Software Foundation. If the Program does not specify a version number of this License, you may choose any version ever published by the Free Software Foundation.

10. If you wish to incorporate parts of the Program into other free programs whose distribution conditions are different, write to the author to ask for permission. For software which is copyrighted by the Free Software Foundation, write to the Free Software Foundation; we sometimes make exceptions for this. Our decision will be guided by the two goals of preserving the free status of all derivatives of our free software and of promoting the sharing and reuse of software generally.

No Warranty

11. BECAUSE THE PROGRAM IS LICENSED FREE OF CHARGE, THERE IS NO WARRANTY FOR THE PROGRAM, TO THE EXTENT PERMITTED BY APPLICABLE LAW. EXCEPT WHEN OTHERWISE STATED IN WRITING THE COPYRIGHT HOLDERS AND/OR OTHER PARTIES PROVIDE THE PROGRAM "AS IS" WITHOUT WARRANTY OF ANY KIND, EITHER EXPRESSED OR IMPLIED, INCLUDING, BUT NOT LIMITED TO, THE IMPLIED WARRANTIES OF MERCHANTABILITY AND FITNESS FOR A PARTICULAR PURPOSE. THE ENTIRE RISK AS TO THE QUALITY AND PERFORMANCE OF THE PROGRAM IS WITH YOU. SHOULD THE PROGRAM PROVE DEFECTIVE, YOU ASSUME THE COST OF ALL NECESSARY SERVICING, REPAIR OR CORRECTION.

12. IN NO EVENT UNLESS REQUIRED BY APPLICABLE LAW OR AGREED TO IN WRITING WILL ANY COPYRIGHT HOLDER, OR ANY OTHER PARTY WHO MAY MODIFY AND/OR REDISTRIBUTE THE PROGRAM AS PERMITTED ABOVE, BE LIABLE TO YOU FOR DAMAGES, INCLUDING ANY GENERAL, SPECIAL, INCIDENTAL OR CONSEQUENTIAL DAMAGES ARISING OUT OF THE USE OR INABILITY TO USE THE PROGRAM (INCLUDING BUT NOT LIMITED TO LOSS OF DATA OR DATA BEING RENDERED INACCURATE OR LOSSES SUSTAINED BY YOU OR THIRD PARTIES OR A FAILURE OF THE PROGRAM TO OPERATE WITH ANY OTHER PROGRAMS), EVEN IF SUCH HOLDER OR OTHER PARTY HAS BEEN ADVISED OF THE POSSIBILITY OF SUCH DAMAGES.

End Of Terms And Conditions

CD-ROM Installation Instructions

This book's companion CD-ROMs contain Red Hat Linux 7.1. These CD-ROMs include all Red Hat Linux 7.1 binary files with the Linux 2.4.0 kernel. Installing Red Hat Linux is a big job — too big to adequately describe in the space available here. For complete instructions, see Sessions 1, 2, and 3.

This book's companion CD-ROMs contain Red Hat Linux 7.1. These CD-ROMs include all Red Hat Linux 7.1 binary files with the Linux 2.4.0 kernel. Installing Red Hat Linux is a big job — too big to adequately describe in the space available here. For complete instructions, see Sessions 1, 2, and 3.

The book includes a copy of the Publisher's Edition of Red Hat Linux from Red Hat, Inc., which you may use in accordance with the license agreements accompanying the software. The Official Red Hat Linux, which you may purchase from Red Hat, includes the complete Official Red Hat Linux distribution, Red Hat's documentation, and may include technical support for Official Red Hat Linux. You also may purchase technical support from Red Hat. You may purchase Official Red Hat Linux and technical support from Red Hat through the company's web site (www.redhat.com) or its toll-free number 1.888.REDHAT1.